OPEN

OPEN

*The Progressive Case for
Free Trade, Immigration,
and Global Capital*

KIMBERLY CLAUSING

Harvard University Press

Cambridge, Massachusetts

London, England

2019

First Printing

Library of Congress Cataloging-in-Publication Data

Names: Clausing, Kimberly A., author.
Title: Open : the progressive case for free trade, immigration, and global capital /
    Kimberly Clausing.
Description: Cambridge, Massachusetts : Harvard University Press, 2019. |
    Includes bibliographical references and index.
Identifiers: LCCN 2018033462 | ISBN 9780674919334 (alk. paper)
Subjects: LCSH: Free trade—United States. | Globalization—Economic aspects—
    United States. | Employees—United States. | United States—Commerce.
Classification: LCC HF1713 .C59 2019 | DDC 330.973—dc23 LC record available
at https://lccn.loc.gov/2018033462

For Arthur, Willa, Ursula, and Holden

Contents

OPEN

I

Introduction

One

Making the Global Economy Work for Everyone

In January 2017, Donald J. Trump was sworn in as president of the United States. His election reflected a tide of populist dissatisfaction with economic stagnation, and the perceived threats of globalization and immigration, although of course there were other factors at work in his victory.

In his inaugural address, Trump acknowledged popular discontent with globalization explicitly and repeatedly. One excerpt:

> From this day forward, it's going to be only America first. America first. Every decision on trade, on taxes, on immigration, on foreign affairs will be made to benefit American workers and American families. We must protect our borders from the ravages of other countries making our products, stealing our companies and destroying our jobs. Protection will lead to great prosperity and strength.

Despite his harsh rhetoric, Trump's diagnosis and policy solutions are attractive to many Americans, including some on the left. And these nationalist sentiments are not a uniquely American phenomenon; backlashes against globalization have intensified in many other countries, from both the right and left ends of the political spectrum.

This book defends global economic integration, arguing from a perspective that consistently prioritizes the needs of American workers. The substantial challenges of middle-class economic stagnation and increasing income inequality require bold, serious policy responses. But they don't require a retreat from globalization.

The plight of the American worker is very real. For decades, economic inequality has increased, and the vast majority of income growth in our economy has ended up in very few hands. Median wages have grown very slowly and, for the first time in generations, American children can no longer reasonably expect standards of living higher than those of their parents.[1]

At the same time, the importance of capital and corporate profits in the economy has surged; since 2000, corporate profits are 50 percent higher as a share of national income than they were in previous decades, and the share of national income accruing to workers as wages has fallen steadily.[2]

These changes have been systematic, they have happened over decades, and they are large. Indeed, these are the most pressing economic problems of modern-day America. However, knee-jerk solutions to these problems risk making matters worse, harming the very people they claim to help, hurting the future potential of the economy, and weakening our international relations and our capacity to respond to policy challenges.

Blaming foreigners (whether trading partners or immigrants) implies quick and easy solutions to our economic problems. With more restrictive immigration laws, tighter borders, tariff barriers, tough negotiating with our trading partners, and tough talks with our own companies, we are promised a return to the halcyon days of yore: a time when the American dream was alive and well, economic growth benefited all, and children grew up to earn more than their parents.

As politically palatable as these quick-and-easy solutions may be, they are dangerous and wrongheaded, more likely to hurt the very people who voted for them than to return us all to easier times. For example, tariffs on foreign products will make the foreign goods we buy at the store more expensive, harming our purchasing power as consumers. While tariffs advantage domestic companies over foreign ones, any resources that move into producing goods that would otherwise have been imported have to come from somewhere. Other sectors of the economy will contract. This will subject the labor market to more "shocks," as industries that produce the formerly imported goods expand, while other industries contract.

While there will be more demand for labor at companies that make the goods that were previously imported, tariffs will not remove the incentive to innovate and mechanize to make production more efficient. Indeed, technological progress is a larger threat to American workers than foreign trade is. Almost every study comparing the two forces argues that technological change has had the more dominant influence on US labor markets.

So should we instead rally against our computers? Perhaps so. If we simply discarded our computers, dumping them into the harbor like so much imperial tea, that would generate a great deal of demand for labor throughout the US economy. We would need labor to do all those things computers used to do more efficiently: computations, filing, data entry, and consumer interactions of all sorts, from booking travel to selling clothes to trading financial assets. Of course, giving up computers would put us at a tremendous disadvantage relative to workers and consumers in other countries who had access to these technologies. Forsaking technology would also generate huge shocks to the economy, as those industries that relied on computers for their production processes would be harmed, and those workers who used computers to be more productive would see their productivity decline. Further, people really enjoy all the modern conveniences that computers provide; they would not easily give up their smartphones, movie streaming, computer games, and online shopping—or even their less frivolous work efficiency.

Yet turning to trade protectionism, and reducing immigration, generates shocks that are quite analogous to the shocks associated with giving up technological progress. Thirty percent tariffs would make almost every item at Gap or Walmart 30 percent more expensive. Steel tariffs harm workers in industries using steel as an input, such as construction. Retaliation from trading partners hurts workers making US exports. Restrictive immigration policies harm the technological leads of our companies, and fewer immigrants mean fewer entrepreneurs in Silicon Valley and beyond. Withdrawing from trade agreements and negotiating "tougher" terms with our partners gives us fewer friends and weaker allies, making battles against terrorism and climate change more difficult.[3] Reducing the mutual economic interests that link China and the United States makes it more likely that small disagreements transform into broader conflict.

In short, blaming foreigners is easy, but acting on that blame with policies is dangerous and shortsighted. There are a lot of truly wonderful things about international trade, international capital mobility, international business, and international migration that we risk when we threaten globalization. There is a good reason why almost every economist on the planet values international economic integration. The case for global markets is strong indeed.

Yet economists peddling international integration have not always explained clearly and persuasively what is at stake. Equally important, they have not spent enough time reckoning with those harmed by the forces of globalization. While plenty of economists study the economic inequality, job loss, and disruption that are caused by the forces of globalization and technical change, they often shy away from the difficult questions of how to address these problems in a politically feasible way. It is a quite common affliction of the economist to smugly pronounce what an optimal policy would look like, acknowledge that such a policy may prove politically contentious or impossible, and then pass off the resulting problem as one of "politics," a field too dirty for clean hands.

Something more is required today. It is not enough to simply show that free international trade and unfettered technological progress are optimal for society. It is not enough to explain that these forces create enough gains for society so that "winners" can compensate "losers," and then walk away, dusting off one's hands, job done. We need to engage with the "art of the possible." At times, settling for rough justice and second-best (or third-best) policies is better than insisting on the ideal outcome as seen from thirty thousand feet, disengaged from the political mess on the ground.

For the arguments for trade, immigration, and technological progress to be persuasive, the losers from these policies must be reckoned with. The winners actually need to compensate the losers. Economic growth has to be broad enough to benefit all, or at least the vast majority of, Americans. Along these lines, there are many easily identified policies that would help American workers, such as a more progressive tax system, more society-wide investments in education and infrastructure, and a more robust safety net to catch workers who are left behind.

Yet, while we have made some incremental progress here and there, policy-makers have too often been more interested in conflict than compromise. At present, there is a large political problem. The very political polarization that has resulted from economic inequality has made it much harder to come up with an effective policy response to the inequality.[4]

Solving this problem is not easy, but it begins with a battle of ideas. This book argues that economic inequality is indeed the dominant economic problem of our time, but that the policy solutions to this problem should involve both an embrace of globalization, trade agreements, immigration, and international business, and a much more thorough policy framework to make sure that the benefits from these economic forces accrue to all Americans. The opposite approach—of erecting walls and trade barriers while dismantling safety nets (by, for example, making health insurance more expensive for the poor) and providing tax cuts for those at the top of the income distribution—is dangerous and misguided. It will leave the United States a poorer nation with fewer friends, and it will hurt the very workers it claims to help.

The Road Ahead

The remainder of this introduction takes you through the main arguments of the book ahead, organized by chapter.

Chapter 2 documents the large, vexing problems of middle-class wage stagnation and rising income inequality. While the period from 1946 to 1980 generated broadly shared economic prosperity, the period since 1980 is another story. Incomes at the top of the income distribution have surged, whereas the incomes of the bottom half of the population have been entirely stagnant. These trends have left a large part of the population disappointed. Households are indebted, economic insecurity is widespread, and discontent is expressed through votes for politically polarized candidates. Chapter 2 explores the causes of these trends. Foremost is technological change, which has transformed our lives in the years since 1980. Trade and global competition have also contributed to making work-places more competitive, hurting some workers. But other factors also play crucial roles, including the phenomenon of "superstars" driving huge pay packages at the top, the rise in business profits resulting from market power and innovation, changes in social norms and bargaining power across groups, and large changes in tax policy.

Chapters 3 to 5 consider international trade. Chapter 3 makes the case for international trade, beginning with intuitive arguments. Just as it is nearly impossible for individuals to produce all the things they wish to consume, it would be foolish for one country to make everything its people desire. The United States *could* produce its own T-shirts, shoes, and bananas, and we could also forsake foreign varieties of cars, appliances, and wine, but these choices would come at a large cost. The resources we devoted to making goods previously imported would have to be pulled from other parts of the economy, shrinking those sectors. Making everything ourselves would mean fewer economies of scale and fewer choices for consumers. In the end, the country would be far poorer without the benefits of international trade.

In fact, the international community punishes wayward countries by withholding trade; economic sanctions are used as weapons precisely because they impose great costs by removing the gains from trade. Chapter 3 explains that international trade has been a powerful force for good in the world economy, raising living standards both at home and abroad. This chapter also explains how high-wage countries like the United States, Denmark, and Japan still manage to "compete" in the world economy with countries like India, China, and Mexico, where workers are paid less.

Chapter 4 tackles the important distributional consequences of trade, showing that international trade generates both winners and losers. Without strong accompanying policies, we have no way to be sure that large segments of society are not harmed by trade. In the United States, international trade is more likely to reward capitalists and high-income, high-skill workers, while reducing wages and opportunities for low-income, low-skill workers. Chapter 4 also tackles other sources of workers' woes, and most importantly, the effects of rapid technological change, including automation and the rapid spread of computers and the Internet. These technological forces have been more important than international trade in terms of harmful effects on low- and middle-income workers. Mechanization and computerization have replaced labor in many jobs, and the same technological changes have created outsized profits for those at the top of society. Beyond these two big trends, monopoly profits and luck also play important roles in generating the large pay packages of those at the top. It was recently reported that *eight people* have a combined wealth that is similar to that of the bottom half of the *world's* people.[5] This type of wealth is typically the result of luck and market power. And this concentration of income has important effects on social norms, the bargaining position of workers, and the concentration of political power.

Chapter 5 considers both trade politics and trade policies. People have two big economic roles in their lives: everyone is both a producer and a consumer. Trade can make life uncomfortable for us in our producer roles, by heightening competition. (If a professor in India or Sweden teaches a better economics course online, will there be no more demand for my services?) But in our consumer roles, our lives are made more comfortable by trade. Low prices, broad availability, and a staggering variety of goods all benefit consumers, and these benefits are particularly large for lower- and middle-income households.

How can the United States keep the benefits of trade while reducing the collateral damage? Ending trade agreements is not the answer. Rather, new and better trade agreements will help solve these problems. International agreements help countries coordinate, avoiding harmful policy competition. Other important steps we can take on our own. The best way to help workers is to focus on workers. Investments in education, training, and infrastructure will increase the productivity and wages of American workers. Changes in the tax system will help economic growth translate into increased well-being for most Americans. Wage insurance can help workers who have lost high-paying jobs.

Chapters 6 to 8 discuss the international mobility of capital and labor. Chapter 6 considers international capital markets. Consider the United States and China. The Chinese save a lot—more than they invest in plant and equipment. In comparison, US savings are low, and our desired investments exceed our savings. Therefore, the United States (as a whole) borrows from China; this borrowing is the flip side of our trade deficit with China. We receive more goods from China than we send to China, and China accumulates US assets (like US government bonds) in response, effectively loaning us money. This benefits both countries. US companies (and the government) can borrow at lower interest rates, and US consumers receive more goods to consume. Chinese savers get safe returns on their assets, and China benefits from export-driven growth.

Politicians and journalists too often treat these imbalances as a marker in some struggle for global supremacy, the score of a zero-sum game. The US trade deficit is not a moral failure that places us at a disadvantage on the global chess board. Trade balances have little to do with the competitiveness of a country's companies or workers. At current levels, reducing the trade deficit should not be a policy priority.

Chapter 7 discusses international business. Multinational corporations are becoming larger and more important. Among publicly-traded companies, those with more than a billion dollars of annual sales are responsible for the vast majority of revenues and stock market value. International business comes with important benefits, but it also raises essential concerns. Workers have far less bargaining power than companies do, and this imbalance is heightened by the mobility of multinational companies. National governments fear that tax or regulatory policies might discourage economic activity at home. When governments attempt to tax the profits of mobile multinational companies, teams of corporate lawyers and accountants swiftly move the profits to tax havens. Indeed, tax avoidance now costs non-haven countries over $300 billion in tax revenues each year!

This does not mean that governments are powerless. Chapter 7 explains how economic policy should be modernized to suit the global economy. Countries may benefit from strengthening international cooperation. Even without international agreements, however, there are many policy options for the United States. We can protect our corporate tax base through simple, commonsense measures, while focusing on building the fundamental strengths of the US economy.

Chapter 8 describes how immigrants are a source of tremendous strength for the US economy. Immigrants are often innovators and entrepreneurs; they are more likely to found businesses and to win Nobel prizes. Both high-skilled and low-skilled immigrants provide the economy with abilities that complement those of native workers. Immigrants boost economic growth and reduce the demographic pressures of an aging population. In turn, immigrants receive tremendous economic benefits from moving to the United States.

With so many advantages, what accounts for the backlash against immigrants? Backlash stems from cultural concerns and economic fears among middle-class workers. Yet, evidence shows that immigrants do not generate large negative wage effects for workers; on the contrary, most workers benefit from immigrants. Even when small groups of workers are hurt, the large gains from immigration are sufficient to offset those harms. With these lessons in mind, Chapter 8 suggests immigration policy reforms.

Chapters 9 to 11 provide a roadmap to keep the gains from the global economy that are described in Chapters 3 to 8, while responding in a serious, bold way to the problems described in Chapter 2. Foremost, we should not shoot ourselves in the foot with counterproductive policies. Beyond that, there are smart, substantial ways to combat middle-class stagnation and income inequality. Policy ideas fit into three big areas.

Chapter 9 describes better policies to equip workers for a global economy: modern trade agreements, better tools to help workers, improved support for communities, and strong investments in fundamentals.

Chapter 10 describes the benefits of a grand bargain on tax reform: greater after-tax incomes for those left behind in prior decades; a simpler tax system to reduce distortions, avoidance, and complexity; and lower tax rates and a cleaner planet due to reliance on a carbon tax. These reforms satisfy goals of both those on the left (who want a more progressive tax system and a cleaner environment) and those on the right (who want lower tax rates and fewer distortions).

Chapter 11 describes a better partnership between society and the business community. The goals of the business community can be met, but a good partnership also requires more tax payments from some businesses, more business transparency on both tax and labor issues, and robust antitrust laws to counter undue market power.

Finally, we must counter political polarization to respond to these big challenges. In Chapter 12, I conclude with some guiding principles and constructive solutions.

We are at an important moment in our national history; crucial decisions lie ahead. Do we rise to meet the challenges of the world economy, modernizing our policies so that all Americans benefit from a more equitable globalization? Or do we turn inward, attempting to shelter workers from one aspect of a storm that comes from many directions? Do we work with friends and allies to make more stable international institutions and a more prosperous world? Or do we alienate our friends by shortsightedly (and erroneously) putting America first, and thereby making future conflicts and problems more difficult to solve? These questions are essential to our future. Let's get the answers right.

Two

Middle-Class Stagnation and Economic Inequality

In recent decades, middle-class incomes have stagnated, fueling economic insecurity. Economic growth did not benefit American households as long expected; although growth continued, inequality surged, and prosperity failed to reach the middle class. These trends began around 1980 and they continue today. This chapter takes a close look at this serious problem. What is happening to the American middle class? And what has caused these discouraging trends?

Does a Rising Tide Lift All Boats?

Economic growth is supposed to benefit everyone. If national income (GDP, for gross domestic product) grows year after year, beyond the growth in population, we expect that economic growth should raise living standards of typical workers. Yet, when we compare growth in GDP per person to growth in median household income, we see that something is clearly amiss.

In the past thirty years, GDP per capita has increased by about $20,000, an increase of over 60 percent. But the typical household has seen its income grow by only 16 percent in the same time period (fig. 2.1).

These figures explain why typical American households are not content with the pace of economic progress. The standard

Figure 2.1: Growth in US Median Household Incomes Lags Behind GDP Per Capita

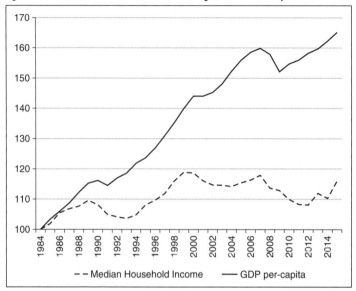

Notes: Both series are indexed so that 1984 = 100. The median shows the typical household in the middle of the economy's distribution of income. Unlike averages, medians are not affected by large incomes at the top of the distribution. Data source: Federal Reserve Economic Data.

expectation that every generation would be better off than the one before it has been disappointed. Nearly 90 percent of children born in the 1940s outearned their parents, but that share has fallen steadily. For children born in 1970, only 60 percent outearn their parents. For those born in the 1980s, only half do.[1]

How does so much GDP growth occur without benefiting the typical worker? In short, the growth has been accompanied by increasing inequality. This was not always the case. Pretax income growth over the period 1946 to 1980 exceeded 100 percent for the bottom 90 percent of the population, and the percentage growth in incomes was actually *lower* for the richest members of the population.

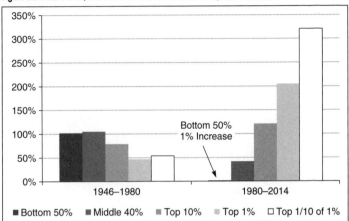

Figure 2.2: Before 1980, Growth Lifted All Boats. Since Then, Not So Much.

Data source: Thomas Piketty, Emmanuel Saez, and Gabriel Zucman, "Distributional National Accounts: Methods and Estimates for the United States." Working Paper 22945. NBER Working Papers. National Bureau of Economic Research, 2016.

That pattern has since reversed. Between 1980 and 2014, the income growth of the bottom 50 percent of the population is literally invisible in the chart, at 1 percent. Growth in incomes for the middle 40 percent is 42 percent, and it accelerates from there, with the growth of the top 1 percent exceeding 200 percent.

As a result, there has been an increasing concentration of national income at the top of the income distribution. The top 1 percent now command a fifth of national income, 50 percent more income than is earned by the bottom *half* of the income distribution. The bottom 90 percent share has shrunk from 68 percent of all income in 1980 to only half of all income in 2015. These trends are a dramatic reversal from the experience of the post–World War II years, when income inequality fell between 1946 and 1970, and was relatively unchanged in the 1970s.

Figure 2.3: The Top 1 Percent and Bottom 50 Percent Trade Places

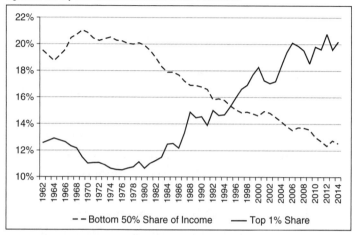

Data source: World Top Incomes Database. Accessed March 14, 2017.

Figure 2.4: In 2015, the Bottom 90 Percent Earn What the Top 10 Percent Earn

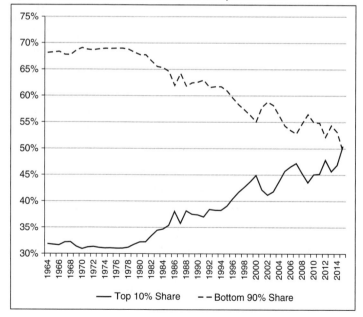

Data source: World Top Incomes Database. Accessed March 14, 2017.

Labor and Capital in the Global Economy

Middle-class income stagnation, economic insecurity, and patterns of increasing economic inequality have been accompanied by ongoing changes in the role of labor in the economy.[2] Workers are getting a smaller share of the pie than they did in prior decades. For a long time in the United States, workers' share of national income held steady at roughly two-thirds.[3] But in recent decades, both in the United States and elsewhere, the labor share of income has been falling. Since employment in good jobs is the key engine for raising middle-class standards of living, the falling share of labor is of enormous concern.

If capital income (the income people receive from their investments, such as interest, dividends, and capital gains) were distributed across households in the same way that labor income is, there might be less concern, since declining work opportunities might be offset by increased income in the form of interest or dividends. Capital income, however, is far more concentrated at the upper end of the income distribution than labor income. For example, the top 5 percent of taxpayers report 37 percent of all income (both labor and capital) in 2012, but 68 percent of dividend income and 87 percent of long-term capital gains.[4] Thus, the reduced role of labor has made an important contribution to income inequality.

The declining labor share of income has been confirmed by many studies. Economists focusing on the corporate sector have found that the US labor share declined by 8 percentage points over the period 1980–2012, from 65 percent to 57 percent, and other sources suggest similar declines.[5] Labor shares have also declined in other large economies, although the steepness of the decline varies.[6] [7]

Figure 2.5: For Most Countries, the Role of Labor Has Declined in Recent Decades

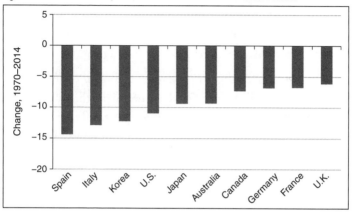

Panel A: Advanced Economies

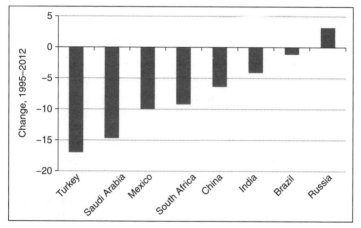

Panel B: Emerging Economies

Notes: Figures show the change in the labor share of income. These data were also depicted in ILO and OECD, "The Labour Share in G20 Economies" Report, International Labour Organization and Organisation for Economic Co-operation and Development, 2015. Figures refer to the change from 1970 to 2014 for advanced economies and from 1995 to 2012 for emerging economies. Exceptions are the Republic of Korea 1991–2014; Saudi Arabia 2002–09; Turkey and Mexico 1995–2014; South Africa 1995–2013; and Brazil 1995–2009. Note that prior to 1991, "Germany" refers to West Germany. Data source: International Labour Organization.

The labor share of income and income inequality are not the same thing, since income inequality can also arise from an increased dispersion of labor incomes, if workers at the top experience higher wage increases than workers at the bottom.[8]

Notably, income inequality has also increased in many (but not all) other countries, despite a wide variety of economic policies and circumstances. Still, income inequality has increased more rapidly in the United States than in most other countries (fig. 2.6).

Are Things Really So Bad?

The data reported above come from work that uses the broadest definition of income, including capital income from investments.[9] Using other sources of data would somewhat moderate the increase in income inequality, though all sources of data agree that income inequality in the United States has increased substantially in recent decades.

Inequality need not be associated with wage stagnation, but it is particularly troubling when it is.[10] Some argue that the wage stagnation of the US middle class is not measured accurately, since there have been huge gains in standards of living due to new products. The numbers shown here are adjusted for inflation, and since inflation does a poor job of measuring the benefits of new goods and services, it is possible that living standards have increased more than these data indicate.[11] As an example, thirty years ago, there was no Internet and we spoke on dumb phones that were tethered to the wall, whereas today a wealth of information and entertainment awaits anyone with Internet access, and most people use smart phones that

Figure 2.6: In Many Countries, the Share of the Top 10 Percent Rises

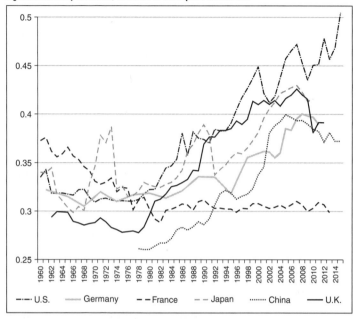

Data source: World Top Incomes Database. Accessed March 14, 2017.

are more powerful than advanced computers were thirty years ago. Do the inflation numbers accurately account for gains in consumer happiness from these inventions?

There are also larger philosophical questions. Do people care only about their absolute living standards, or are there other important economic desires? Is meaningful work itself a source of happiness? Do people determine their well-being by comparisons to broader society, and if so, how large is their circle of comparison? Are they considering the neighborhood, the city or state, the country, or the world?

Regardless of the answers to these larger questions, a few basic facts stand out. First, the United States has recently experienced several decades of large increases in income inequality. Second, middle-class incomes have not grown as rapidly as GDP. Third, recent generations have not realized the same degree of economic progress that past generations experienced.

Finally, economic discontent and insecurity are a prevalent and recurrent theme in our political discourse, so it is not unreasonable to think this discontent is rooted in reality. For example, in a recent Pew survey, 57 percent of Americans said they were not financially prepared for unexpected events, and a third of Americans had no savings. A majority of Americans spend as much as, and often more than, they earn each month.[12] Economic insecurity is more than just inequality. When growth in household incomes does not keep pace with expectations, the economic status of many households becomes less secure.

One general marker of financial strain on households is rising household debt (fig. 2.7). While some categories of debt have not increased, the overall trend of increasing household debt is particularly notable given the very low interest rates since 2009.

Why Are These Trends Important?

In addition to the clear economic consequences for the middle class, these troubling trends have grave consequences for society. Stagnant incomes are harmful during recessions, since income gains that are concentrated at the top are less likely to fuel consumption and, in turn, greater production of goods

Figure 2.7: Debt in US Households is Still Rising Steadily

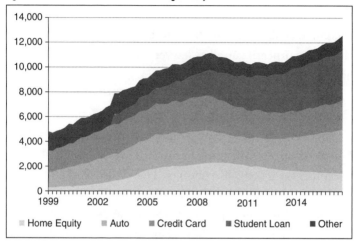

Notes: This is total household debt per capita in US dollars. Student loan debt was not included until 2003. Data sources: New York Federal Reserve Bank and World Bank.

and services. Increased inequality amidst wage stagnation also creates social tension and dissatisfaction. When workers' wages fall short of expectations, people often express their discontent by turning to populist solutions.[13]

The rise of populists like Bernie Sanders and Donald Trump speaks to the depth of public dissatisfaction. Political polarization extends beyond the 2016 election in both time and space. The US Congress is nearly synonymous with dysfunction, in large part due to ever-increasing polarization. In Europe, both far-left and far-right parties are ascendant.[14] The shrinking importance of moderate political groups likely generates several costs: more policy variability, more policy uncertainty, more difficulty enacting policy, and more extreme policies.

Concentration of incomes also creates disproportionate political power for those who are affluent. Those at the top of the income distribution can afford to hire lobbyists to influence the policy process as well as lawyers and accountants to work around existing policies.[15] Affluence also brings greater access to policy-makers, since the wealthy are more likely to frequent the same elite institutions and social circles.

There are also important implications for the tax system. Since recent gains in national income have accrued to those at the top of the income distribution, a progressive tax system becomes more important. Meanwhile, when the share of labor income shrinks, the tax base also falls—since most of the federal tax burden falls on labor income via income and payroll taxes—and this makes capital taxation more important. These policy implications are fully addressed in the final section of the book.

Why Has This Happened?

Six major factors have contributed to these troubling trends, each of which is discussed below. While this list is not exhaustive, it captures the crucial mechanisms at work. There are clear causal forces behind each of these six factors, and there are also important interdependencies among them.

Technological Change

The technology of today bears little resemblance to that of 1980. In 1980, there were a few computers, but they were the size of a desk and about as user-friendly as a block of wood.

The Sears catalog still arrived in most American homes, and if you wanted to place an order, you dialed a large, landline phone. Your orders arrived slowly. Gasoline was paid for by interacting with people, most people waited in line at banks instead of using the relatively new and scarce ATMs, and secretaries did the vast majority of professional typing and phone answering. Long-distance phone calls were very costly; international phone calls were still more costly, and rare. Manufacturing processes were mechanized, but rarely computerized.

Since 1980, a computing and Internet revolution has occurred, and this has changed every facet of American life. Computers are everywhere: in our phones, in our gas pumps, on our desktops, at the grocery store, in our cars, and embedded in most aspects of our manufacturing processes. Professionals do their own typing, and voicemail takes what phone messages remain, though most have been replaced by email and texts. The Internet has changed the way we shop, the way we gather information, the amount of information we have access to, and the ease and speed of communicating both within countries and across borders.

These changes have been pervasive, and they have had profound effects on workers and their incomes. The effects have been mixed, given that technology acts as a competitor for some workers, reducing demand for their labor, while it serves as an assistant to other workers, increasing their productivity. Secretaries, gas station attendants, bank tellers, and manufacturing workers all experience less demand for their work, as much of their work can be done by computers. Meanwhile, investment bankers, software developers, engineers, scientists, and managers all use computers to become more productive.

Technological change helps explain the diminished role of labor in the economy. The price of investment goods for firms (like computers, machinery, and so forth) has been falling even as the capabilities of these machines improve. This has caused an increased demand for machinery relative to workers.

These technological shifts in the role of labor also help explain the increasing income inequality of the past few decades. There is a strong pattern of increasing rewards to education in the data. Earnings are rising only for those with a lot of education—workers whom technological change makes more productive rather than redundant (figs. 2.8 and 2.9).

For American workers to benefit from technological change, their skill set must keep pace with changes in the economy. Unfortunately, progress in US educational attainment has fallen short of progress in technological innovation. In earlier decades, US educational attainment increased steadily, at a rate of 0.8 years of education per decade between 1890 and 1970. While less than 10 percent of Americans graduated from high school in 1890, by 1970 that portion had risen to 80 percent.[16] Since then, American educational attainment has increased more slowly; the most recent statistics show high school graduation rates only slightly above their 1970 levels, at 83 percent in 2015. (That was after five consecutive record-setting years; the rate a few years earlier was unchanged from its 1970 level.)[17]

US students lag behind those in other countries in terms of both high school graduation rates (ranking twelfth among a group of rich countries) and college graduation rates (ranking eleventh).[18] In the 2015 international PISA tests, US students were ranked thirty-seventh in math, twenty-fifth in science, and twenty-third in reading.[19] This inability of US educational attainment to keep pace with technological progress has likely

Figure 2.8: Earnings Rise with Education (Men)

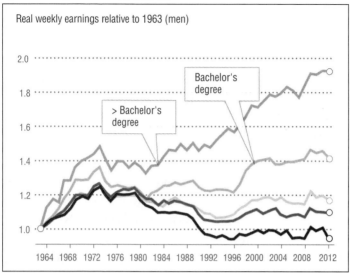

Source: David Autor, "Skills, Education, and the Rise of Earnings Inequality among the 'Other' 99 Percent," *Science* 344:6186 (2014): 843–851. Reprinted with permission from the American Association for the Advancement of Science.

Figure 2.9: Earnings Rise with Education (Women)

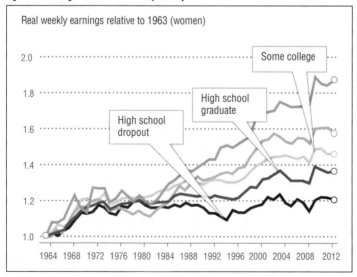

Source: David Autor, "Skills, Education, and the Rise of Earnings Inequality among the 'Other' 99 Percent," *Science* 344:6186 (2014): 843–851. Reprinted with permission from the American Association for the Advancement of Science.

been a large contributing factor in the woes of middle-class workers. For a subset of workers, technological change makes them more productive. But for another subset of workers, technological change is a threat, as machinery and robots displace the demand for workers. This problem will be further described in Chapter 4.

Trade and Global Competition

In recent decades, there have been large increases in global trade and investment flows. Political decisions made by foreign countries were the key driving force in these trends. Countries that had been more closed to international trade joined the world trading system, increasing trade flows. The number of World Trade Organization (WTO) members, for example, increased dramatically. (The WTO is an organization that facilitates international trade treaties, working to liberalize trade.) Membership expanded from 18 members at inception, to 84 members in 1980, to 164 members today (fig. 2.10).[20]

Also helping to fuel increasing trade have been falling communication and transportation costs. The greater access to information afforded by computerization and the Internet makes it far easier to do business across borders. Technological changes have also enabled global production processes, by solving the complicated logistical puzzles of global supply chains. Finally, economic growth abroad has also increased international trade flows, which tend to increase with the size of the economy.

For the United States and more broadly the world, the importance of trade in the overall economy has grown by about 50 percent relative to its level in 1980. Both then and now, the rest of the world is about twice as globalized as the United

Figure 2.10: More and More Countries Join the World Trade System

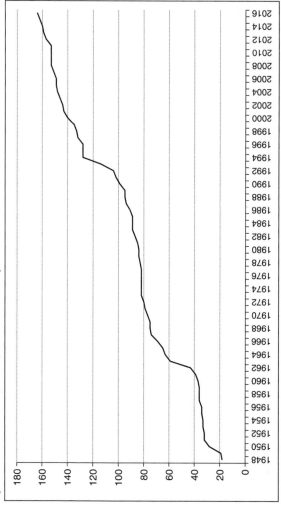

Data source: World Trade Organization.

Figure 2.11: Trade is Increasing, But the United States Trades Less Than the World

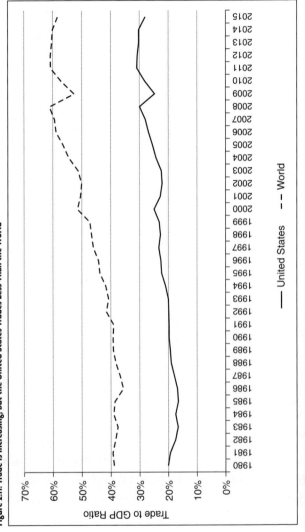

Data source: World Development Indicators, World Bank.

States (fig. 2.11). Foreign countries rely on international trade to a greater extent due to their smaller domestic economies.[21]

International investment flows have also increased, both in terms of *portfolio* investments (people and institutions purchasing foreign stocks, bonds, and other assets) and *foreign direct* investments (companies purchasing other companies or undertaking new investments abroad). Here, the United States is as globalized as the world as a whole.

Of course, foreign investment goes in both directions, and the United States receives amounts of *inward* foreign direct investment (by foreign companies investing here) similar to what it sends in *outward* foreign direct investment (when US firms invest abroad). Both types of foreign direct investment are increasing over time (fig. 2.12).

In general, these flows of foreign direct investment understate the role of multinational firms in the world economy, since they capture only changes in investments from year to year, not the size or importance of global firms. By most indicators (sales, profits, assets, or market capitalization), multinational firms have become steadily more important in recent decades.[22]

Net migration flows have been steadier for the United States. That said, the share of the population that is foreign-born has been climbing in recent decades, and now stands only a bit lower than it was during a previous peak era of immigration, around the beginning of the twentieth century (fig. 2.13).

International trade, international capital mobility, and international migration are all chief suspects in the search for a culprit to blame for poor US labor market outcomes. For example, since trade with developing countries has increased

Figure 2.1.2: Foreign Direct Investment Flows Are About Three Times Their 1980 Levels

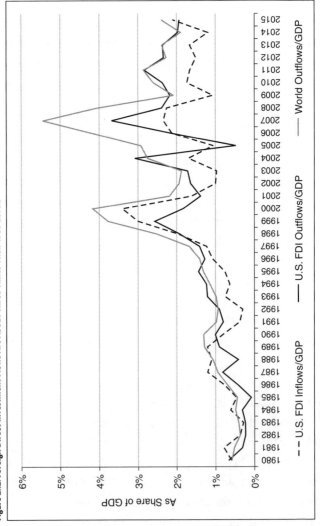

Data source: World Development Indicators, World Bank.

particularly rapidly, and these countries have large, low-wage labor forces, this may increase competition facing US workers, lowering wages. Competition from low-wage countries may also encourage US firms to innovate in order to economize on labor, accelerating the adoption of technology that replaces labor with machinery.

Both foreign direct investment and immigration could also bear some responsibility for the woes of US workers. If immigrants are more likely to compete with workers at the bottom of the income distribution, that could reduce wage growth for those workers, exacerbating income inequality (though there are also many ways in which immigration helps workers, as discussed in Chapter 8). The international business operations of global corporations likely reduce the bargaining power of labor and labor unions, as companies may use the threat of

Figure 2.13: Immigrants are Increasingly Important, But Still Less So than in Early 1900s

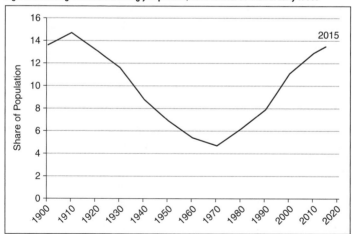

Data source: Migration Policy Institute.

moving abroad to restrain wage growth at home. And if some types of operations are systematically moved abroad, that reduces demand for those types of workers at home.

Still, puzzles remain. First, in poorer countries, income inequality is also increasing alongside reductions in the labor share of income.[23] That is counter to expectation, since integration with the world economy should be *increasing* demand for workers in poorer countries. It could be that technological change is the dominant force throughout the world, increasing demand for machinery and higher-skilled workers relative to less-skilled labor. Indeed, computers, the Internet, and broader technological change have affected the entire world economy.[24]

Another puzzle concerns how much income has been concentrated at the very top of the income distribution, among the top 5 percent, the top 1 percent, and even the top tenth of 1 percent. Neither trade nor technological change does a good job explaining the huge gains in income at the very top of society. Trade should increase demand for the products of our export industries, while reducing demand for import-competing industries; while such demand shifts should move income across broad groups of people, they should not concentrate it at the very top. Similarly, technological change should harm those whose labor is replaced by technology, while helping those whose productivity is boosted by technology. Again, as these changes affect broad groups of people, there is no reason to think the gains should be concentrated at the very top of society. The next four items do a better job explaining what is happening at the top end of the income distribution.

The Role of Superstars

The superstars at the top of the income distribution reap outsized rewards. Top investment bankers, information technology entrepreneurs, corporate CEOs, hedge fund managers, and corporate lawyers occupy plum spots in the top 1 percent, as do household names in entertainment and sports like Beyoncé and LeBron James. These labor markets have characteristics of "superstar" or "winner-take-all" compensation patterns; those at the top receive salaries that are many multiples of those a bit lower in the distribution.

As an example, consider America's favorite pastime, baseball. In 1970, the average major league baseball player earned $184,000 in 2017 dollars. Now, the typical major league baseball player earns over *twenty times* as much, $4.5 million dollars. Salaries have climbed especially steeply since the 1980s (fig. 2.14).

Yet, while being in the major league pays well, being slightly less talented pays terribly. Minor league baseball players typically earn $1,200–$3,000 per month for a five-month season, with no pay for spring training. If they only played baseball for a living, they would live under the federal poverty line!

Similar trends hold in music, with greater shares of revenues captured by the most popular artists. The top 1 percent of artists took in 26 percent of all concert revenue in 1982, and by 2003 commanded 56 percent.[25]

Both globalization and technical change buttress the superstar effect, turbocharging the relative earnings of the stars. The combination of larger world markets and the ease of digitizing and distributing information creates big paychecks for the most productive (or lucky) talents in society. The best entertainers and athletes earn premium returns, since their

Figure 2.14: Average US Major League Baseball Salary, Twenty-Three Times Higher in 2017 than in 1970

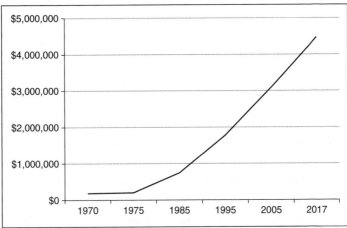

Data sources: US Bureau of Labor Statistics; Paul D. Staudohar, "Baseball's Changing Salary Structure," *Compensation and Working Conditions*, Fall 1997; http://hosted.ap.org/specials/interactives/_sports/baseball08/documents/bbo_average_salary2009.pdf.

talents are now accessible to their fans throughout the world, who can watch videos and sporting events remotely. This increases the size of the entertainment sector.

Slightly lesser talents (or less lucky ones) often earn *far* less, however, than those at the top. Less renowned singers and ballplayers (and businesspeople) face increased competition from other talented people across the world. They also face the increased costs associated with paying the superstars. The princely pay packages of superstars squeeze pay for the less talented. Some superstar returns also accrue to capital, as the investors and producers that control the ownership of talent are amply rewarded.

Similar mechanisms are at work in terms of entrepreneurial or corporate returns. The makers of the best search engines, phones, and social networking sites can sell their products all over the world, benefiting from the scale allowed by the world economy. The best hedge fund managers command ever larger pots of investment capital, and earning "2 plus 20" becomes an enormous sum. (Hedge fund managers often charge 2 percent of asset value as a management fee and also receive 20 percent of earned profits.)

Since someone must pay for these outsized rewards, that leaves less national income for the less successful versions of these entertainers, athletes, managers, or entrepreneurs. Being a 90th percentile talent in these fields can pay orders of magnitude less than being a top talent. And increased competition means that very few become superstars.

The Rise of Profits

A closely related issue has to do with the excess (above normal) profits that arise from entrepreneurial and corporate success. The world economy provides large rewards to the most successful and innovative entrepreneurs and businesses; these profits play an important role in labor market trends.

It is tempting to label these profits as the just desserts of ingenuity and innovation, or the economic "carrot" that offers incentives for risk-taking. To be sure, the creators of Apple Computer, Microsoft, Google, and Facebook have changed the way we use computers and the Internet, benefiting billions of people. Yet for every Bill Gates and Mark Zuckerberg, there are tens of thousands of technology talents that have contributed to this industry, and despite very similar levels of ingenuity and hard work, have not become even a thousandth as rich.

Alongside entrepreneurial profits, there is substantial evidence of increased market power for many large corporations.

In parallel with declining labor shares of income, there have been large and pervasive increases in corporate profits and retained earnings of corporations.[26] In the United States, corporate profits since 2000 are about 50 percent higher as a share of GDP than they were in the previous twenty years, and corporations are responsible for more and more of the total savings of our society.[27]

As compared to 1980, corporate savings have come to constitute a much larger share of total savings. Globally, since that year, corporations' share of total savings has increased by about thirty percentage points (fig. 2.15).[28] This staggering increase is mirrored by a declining share of global savings in the hands of households. Why are corporations doing more of the saving? Simply put, they are earning more of national income, as the capital share of income is rising relative to the labor share of income in most countries.

These trends are related to the troubling issue of secular stagnation: rising corporate profits and changes in the distribution of income have increased savings, but investment opportunities are declining—which reduces economic growth. In the meantime, corporations are awash in cash.[29]

While we expect all businesses to earn some "normal" level of profit to justify their efforts, excess profits (above the normal rate) are now the norm in the US corporate sector. In the United States, the share of corporate earnings that represent excess profits is over 75 percent.[30] This is not just an American phenomenon. Worldwide, the corporate sector is getting more concentrated, and large companies are dominating in terms of profits, sales, and scale. The top 10 percent of the world's public companies earn 80 percent of the profits, and companies with

Figure 2.15: Globally, Corporate Savings Are Now About Two-Thirds of All Savings

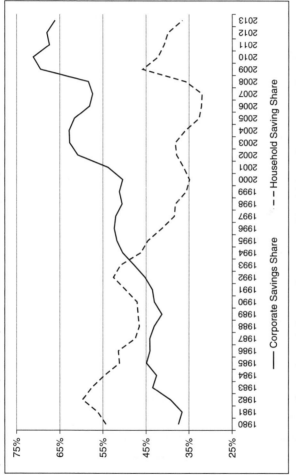

Data source: Peter Chen, Loukas Karabarbounis, and Brent Neiman, "The Global Rise of Corporate Saving." NBER Working Paper 23133 (2017).

more than $1 billion in revenues account for the vast majority of all global revenues and market capitalization.[31] And because these superstar companies use less labor than typical companies, so as the dominant companies account for more of all economic activity, the labor share of income falls.[32]

Bargaining, Power, and Norms

At the same time that corporate profits and power have become more important, the role of labor unions has shrunk, and worker bargaining power is steadily weakening. In the United States, the unionization rate has fallen from 31 percent in 1960 to 11 percent today. Focusing particularly on private-sector unionization rates, the fall is even greater; now, only 7 percent of private sector employees are unionized. Abroad, the average unionization rate for workers in peer countries was 35 percent in 1960, and fell to 17 percent by 2014.[33] These falls in unionization have important effects on labor markets; unions have historically played an important role in narrowing income inequality.[34]

The sources of declining unions are various. Right-to-work laws, which make it more difficult to have effective unions, have spread to twenty-eight US states, up from nineteen US states that had right-to-work laws in 1980.[35] The decline of the manufacturing sector plays a role, too, since manufacturing jobs are more often unionized. Meanwhile, the dual threats of global competition and technological innovation do their part to weaken labor bargaining power.

Other factors also affect labor. The real value of the federal minimum wage has hovered near its current level in recent decades, but it was higher (in inflation-adjusted terms) in the

1960s and 1970s. Shifts in social norms have reduced the bargaining power of labor relative to management. As one example, American Airlines recently tried to give its workers raises to match pay offered at other airlines, but its stock price was punished as a result.[36] Investor pressures make it more difficult for labor to succeed in wage negotiations.

While both globalization and technological change have contributed to the erosion of labor bargaining power, they are clearly not the only factors at work. Industries like trucking have experienced similar pressures, yet they are largely immune from foreign competition and from labor-replacing technological innovation (so far). For example, the real wages of truckers and warehousing workers have fallen by a third since the early 1970s; the Bureau of Labor Statistics estimates that drivers were paid 6 percent less, on average, in 2013 than they were in 2003. Plummeting salaries are the product of dramatic changes in union membership, from a 38 percent rate of driver unionization in 1983 to a 13 percent rate in 2016.

At the same time, the levels of compensation considered acceptable for those at the top have never been higher. CEO pay is now three hundred times that of typical company workers, a ratio that has increased *tenfold* since 1980, when CEOs earned "only" thirty times the salary of typical company workers (fig. 2.16). CEO salaries have increased over 900 percent since the late 1970s, while worker wages have risen 10 percent.[37] To precisely what degree these salaries reflect productivity is a matter for legitimate arguments, but it is unlikely that CEOs are ten times more productive than they were in 1980 relative to their workers. Likely, social norms, market power, and tax policy all contribute to these large ratios.

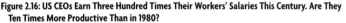

Figure 2.16: US CEOs Earn Three Hundred Times Their Workers' Salaries This Century. Are They Ten Times More Productive Than in 1980?

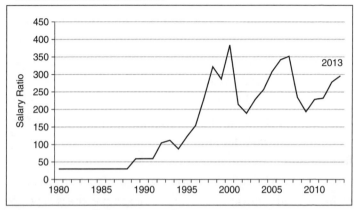

Note: See Lawrence Mishel and Alyssa Davis, "Top CEOs Make 300 Times More than Typical Workers," Issue Brief 399, Economic Policy Institute, June 2015. Data sources: Economic Policy Institute calculations from Compustat's ExecuComp database, Current Employment Statistics program, and the Bureau of Economic Analysis NIPA tables.

Tax Policy

Tax policy plays a role in driving income inequality, the incomes at the very top of the income distribution, and the declining share of income that ends up in the hands of workers. Since 1900, the top 1 percent share of the income distribution has followed a u-shaped pattern in the United States.[38] Between 1929 and the 1970s, the top 1 percent share fell steadily. Since the 1980s, it has increased (fig. 2.17).

Tax rates have moved in the opposite direction. Top marginal income tax rates increased in the first half of the twentieth century, and they have declined steeply since 1980.

This negative correlation between the share of the top 1 percent and the top marginal tax rates is striking.[39] Tax avoidance provides one explanation for this pattern, since top incomes are more likely to be hidden when tax rates are

Figure 2.17: US Tax Rates and Income Shares for the Top 1 Percent

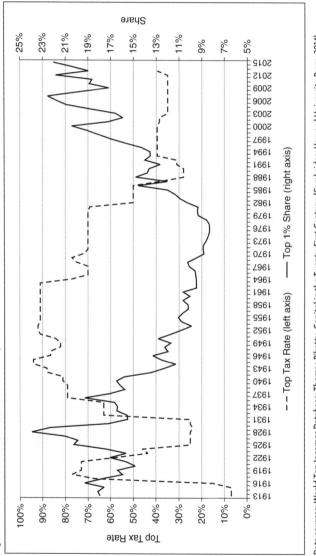

Data sources: World Top Incomes Database; Thomas Piketty, *Capital in the Twenty-First Century*, (Cambridge: Harvard University Press, 2014).

high. But many argue that the bargaining process between workers and their managers is affected by tax rates. If tax rates at the top of the distribution decline, this provides more incentive for those at the top to aggressively increase their compensation.

The era of increasing income inequality has also corresponded to lower tax rates on capital income, a source of income that is far more concentrated in the hands of high-income households. Capital gains tax rates were over 30 percent for most of the 1970s, fell to between 20 percent and 29 percent during the 1980s and the 1990s, and then fell to about 15 percent for most of this century, before increasing to 25 percent in 2013.[40] Dividends were taxed as ordinary income until 2003, but have since been taxed at far lower rates, with a top rate of 15 percent before 2013, and a top rate of 20 percent since then.[41]

Indeed, high tax rates serve as a brake, or speed limit, on earnings by high-income earners. Yet the restraint of higher tax rates was eased dramatically over recent decades, just as other forces were ramping up the pay packages for those at the top. The global economy and technological change have increased demand for capital and the most highly skilled workers and superstars. As top earners are also more aggressive in seeking higher pay, compensation at the top surges, and wages further down stagnate.[42]

What to Do

Beyond these six important forces, there are likely other factors at work, complicating matters further. Also, among these explanations, there is no clear way to unpack the precise contribution of each to the problems at hand. The six factors are deeply intertwined.

International trade is spurred by changes in communications and technology, while new technologies are adopted in part due to the pressures of international competition. Lower tax rates reward individuals and companies that increase their compensation and profits, and higher profits and incomes at the top of the income distribution beget political power, which leads to tax and regulatory policies that are more favorable to high-income groups. Superstars earn more due to global markets and the easy distribution of their products—distribution facilitated by technological change. The success of superstars fuels changes in social norms about what level of compensation is "justified" by the marketplace.

Still, different societies mediate these same economic forces in different ways. While many countries have experienced aspects of the trends described here (increased income inequality, surges in top 1 percent shares, reduced labor income shares), the United States' experience of increasing income inequality, accompanied by middle-income economic stagnation, has been particularly dramatic and sustained. Common economic forces like trade and technological change create different consequences in different places, due to different institutions, social norms, and economic policies.[43]

The remainder of this book will argue that global forces (namely, international trade, international capital mobility, international business, and immigration) are not the chief culprits behind the woes of the American middle class—and that, while these global forces certainly contribute to the economic insecurity facing American workers, clamping down on globalization would harm American workers more than it would help them.

This is not to imply that the problems of American workers are not real. On the contrary, increasing income inequality combined with middle-class wage stagnation is the single largest economic problem of our era.[44] The response to this challenge needs to be swift and bold.

Chapters 9 through 11 will outline an agenda for moving toward a more equitable globalization. This agenda involves three key components, all of which directly target the problem at hand, avoiding the large collateral damage that results from erecting walls and raising trade barriers.

First, we need better policies to equip workers for a modern, global economy: updated trade agreements, improved support for struggling workers and communities, and strong investments in fundamentals such as education, research and development, and infrastructure.

Second, a grand bargain on tax reform would generate benefits along three lines: greater after-tax incomes for those left behind in prior decades; a simpler tax system to reduce distortions, avoidance, and complexity; and lower tax rates and a cleaner planet due to reliance on a carbon tax. Such reforms would satisfy goals of both those on the left (a more progressive tax system, a cleaner environment) and those on the right (lower tax rates, fewer distortions).

Third, we need a better partnership between society and the business community. The goals of the business community can be met, but a mutually beneficial partnership would also entail more tax payments from some businesses, more business transparency on both tax and labor issues, and robust antitrust laws to counter undue market power.

To make these important policy changes, we will also need a better politics—a vexing problem that is addressed in the concluding chapter. By boldly addressing the challenges of the modern economy, we can create a more equitable globalization that benefits all Americans—and we can retain the benefits of the world economy, fostering longstanding peace and prosperity.

II

International Trade

The next three chapters discuss the role of international trade in the American economy. Chapter 3 explains why so many economists find international trade to be a compelling and even necessary ingredient to a country's economic success. The US economy would be far less prosperous without the benefits of international trade.

Chapter 4 discusses why international trade also poses vexing concerns for society. Evidence indicates that international trade has likely lowered wage growth for many US workers, aggravating income inequality. Because rising income inequality and middle-class wage stagnation are such large problems in the United States, these concerns are serious. Still, Chapter 4 argues that trade is not the dominant source of workers' troubles. Technological change, market power, and other factors are more important.

Chapter 5 turns to the policy implications of Chapters 3 and 4. International trade is not easily reversible without doing lasting damage to the economy and American workers. An ideal policy response to international trade likely involves more, not fewer, trade agreements. Even more important, we need to give workers the tools they need to succeed in today's economy; we need stronger support for struggling workers and communities; and we must modernize economic policy to suit our global, technologically sophisticated economy.

Three

The Case for International Trade

It is difficult to find a good economist who does not recognize the merits, and even the magic, of international trade for raising living standards and contributing to the felicity of humankind. At root, the case for international trade is not much different from the case for markets; the presence of international borders does not change the basic logic.

Consider a person who, in an extreme show of self-sufficiency, tried to produce everything they planned to consume: food, clothes, tools, medicine, and all the rest. It is hard to imagine a quicker path to poverty. Even in the earliest, most basic societies, people swiftly began to trade items with each other, because trade generates great efficiencies relative to self-sufficiency.

For many countries, going without trade would be analogous to a household trying to be self-reliant. Imagine Finland, a country of about five and a half million people, trying to be self-sufficient. Even with millions of people, it would be difficult for Finland to make a decent fraction of the goods and services that modern households crave. The scale of production would be too small to justify many types of cars, and the more types of cars Finland made, the more expensive each would be, since they would not be able to take advantage of economies of scale. Finland would have to go without many types of food that would not be practical to grow there, or such foods would need to be grown in hothouses at great expense. Food costs would rise enormously as each crop had fewer benefits of scale. The wide variety of clothes, shoes, pharmaceuticals, furnishings, and electronics that we all take for granted would not be remotely feasible, either.

Indeed, many countries are closer to the economic size of US states, and going without trade for these countries would be similar to the state of Oregon (and its four million people) trying to live without trade. Eating nuts and berries (two excellent Oregon crops) would be fine for a while, and one could wash them down with Oregon's excellent pinot noir, but it stretches plausibility to imagine that Oregon residents would be content to make do without the thousands of products they have grown accustomed to, or that they could make all these products themselves. How could Oregon possibly make its own cars, planes, perfumes, clothing, computers, books, shoes, and the like? Surely Oregon is a richer state, and its residents enjoy higher standards of living, if it specializes in what it is relatively good at (nuts, berries, pinot noir, shoe designing, semiconductor research, aircraft parts, and so forth) and then trades its output for other goods on the broader market.

Intriguing early evidence suggests that trade may have even played a role in the evolution of humanity itself. Anthropologists and historians have puzzled about how *Homo sapiens* edged out the Neanderthals, despite the latter's superior strength, which should have provided a key advantage in the hunting and gathering economies of yore. Although this puzzle may never be completely resolved, one compelling theory suggests that trade was essential to the dominance of *Homo sapiens.*[1] Our ancestors had superior cognitive and social abilities, and this helped them develop trade networks. Through specialization and trade, early members of our species were able to conserve energy and better use their resources. Archeological evidence shows that *Homo sapiens* frequently possessed items that could only have been produced in regions far away from their communities, whereas Neanderthals relied solely on local products.

Going without trade is quite harmful to a country's wellbeing. For this reason, when the international community wants to punish a country for wrongdoing, it frequently withholds the benefits of international trade by imposing economic sanctions. If international trade were actually harmful to countries, then countries under sanctions might send thank-you notes to their antagonists! Instead, sanctions are often effective ways to alter governments' behavior, or to bring them to the negotiating table, since they are eager to partake of the benefits of unfettered trade.

Economic sanctions have been highly inconvenient, for example, for Russia's consumers. After Russia annexed Crimea in March 2014, the United States and the European Union used sanctions to freeze the assets of Kremlin-connected individuals and companies, and curtailed exports of military technology as well as key goods for Russia's oil industry. The sanctions, coupled with a fall in world oil prices in summer 2014, proved crippling to Russia's economy: per capita GDP shrank, the ruble's value swiftly declined, and the poverty rate increased. Russia refused to be cowed and enacted countersanctions that banned imports of beef, pork, fish, fruit, vegetables, and dairy products. This led to huge increases in food prices and a thriving black-market economy. (Even the Russian government couldn't avoid sanction-related suffering: the Ministry of Defense placed an order for homegrown "Russian iPads" at $6,000 a piece.)

One study calculates the collective impact of past economic sanctions to have been more deadly than the entire history of weapons of mass destruction, including large-scale acts of nuclear, chemical, and biological warfare.[2] The atomic bombs dropped on Hiroshima and Nagasaki killed about 125,000 people; chemical weapons have killed a similar number. Yet the United Nations found that Iraqi sanctions alone killed at least 239,000 children under the age of five. The sanctions placed on Iraq from 1990 to 2003 disproportionately affected the country's most vulnerable populations, increasing the price of food by 25,000 percent and holding syringes and other basic medical equipment hostage at Iraq's borders. As a result, thousands of Iraqis died of malnutrition, from infectious diseases, and due to the absence of essential drugs. Weapons of mass destruction generate universal fear and revulsion, yet the loss of human life due to these weapons does not approach the toll of sanctions.

Still, one might argue that the United States is such a big country that it does not need other countries. Going without globalization might be an option for the United States, even if it is not an option for countries closer in size to Oregon. Yet the case for international trade is also strong for large economies.

The United States could attempt to replace the goods we now import with domestic production, but that would give up the valuable benefits associated with trade, whereby we export the goods that we produce relatively efficiently in exchange for those goods that other countries make relatively efficiently. We *could* make our own coffee beans, winter fruits, and winter flowers, and we *could* limit ourselves to domestic sources of production for wine, steel, pharmaceuticals, and cars, but these decisions would have serious negative consequences, ultimately lowering living standards of all Americans. Next, let's see why.

Jobs, Jobs, and Jobs

If you wander through the aisles of Walmart, IKEA, or the Gap, you will see many, many imported products; in fact, it can be relatively rare to see American-made products in some US stores. Many Americans wonder: Why do we have to import these products? Why not instead produce T-shirts, jeans, furniture, and household items right here in the United States of America? Surely if we made these goods, there would be more factory jobs, more demand for those workers seeking such jobs, and resulting improvements in income equality.

First, consider the effect on the total number of jobs if we began to manufacture all the products that we now import. In June of 2018, the unemployment rate was 4.0 percent. Most economists believe this unemployment rate represents full employment. What does "full employment" mean? In a dynamic economy, some workers will always be between jobs, and some workers may be living in places where job opportunities are too few, but nationwide unemployment much lower than 4 percent would create upward pressure on wages and prices, resulting in inflation rather than additional job creation. Lower unemployment rates are simply not sustainable. Historical data support this idea; there are few years in the United States (or elsewhere) where unemployment has been lower than 4 percent.[3] Therefore, there is probably not much room to lower the unemployment rate further.

Some argue that labor force participation could be changed. Many people who are not in the labor force, however, have reasons for their nonparticipation. They are in school, or have retired early, or have chosen to stay home with children. These workers are unlikely to be lured into the labor force by the prospect of jobs making T-shirts or home furnishings.

Still, labor force participation is not constant over time. Over the period of 1980 to 1995, it rose about 2.5 percent in the United States (from about 64 percent to about 66.5 percent), in part due to women's increasing participation in the labor force. Since 2000, labor force participation has dropped by more than 4 percent (from about 67 percent to under 63 percent), with the steepest part of that decline happening during the Great Recession, and a more level trend in recent years (fig. 3.1).

It is clear that the Great Recession drove some workers out of the labor force, but demographic factors also contributed. Much of the recent decline in labor force participation is due to the aging of the population, since older workers are more likely to retire early. One factor that does not, however, appear to be a meaningful driver of labor force participation is international trade.[4] In years of rapid import growth, labor force participation has often grown, whereas labor force participation has fallen most in years of flatter import trends.

Thus, considering our low unemployment rate as well as the insensitivity of labor force participation to trade, even draconian reductions in imports would be unlikely to increase the number of jobs in the economy by more than a percent or two.

Yet it would take far more labor than one or two percent of the labor force to produce the goods that we currently import. In fact, one of the reasons we import the goods we do is that

Figure 3.1: Labor Force Participation is Not Driven Down by Imports

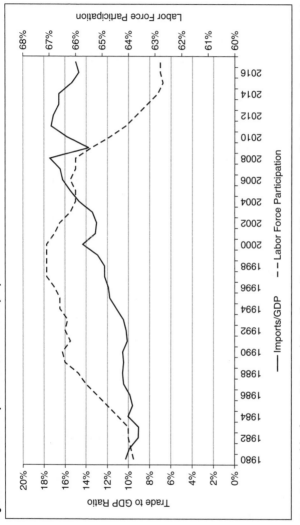

Notes: Data show labor force participation relative to the working-age population. Data sources: Federal Reserve Economic Data; World Development Indicators, World Bank.

these goods use labor intensively. Because of higher US wages, making these products abroad is far less expensive than it would be at home. To produce these labor-intensive goods here, we would need to move labor away from its current occupations and toward those industries where we would no longer be importing goods.

Which industries would shrink as a result, and would that be a good thing? Natural candidates would be export industries, since the very policies that reduced our imports would also reduce our exports. Our trading partners would be unlikely to sit on their hands while we raised trade barriers. If they raised trade barriers, too, that would directly reduce US exports. The prospect is unappealing because, in general, US export jobs are more desirable than most jobs: they pay higher wages and are associated with higher productivity growth.[5]

Even if we managed to avoid foreign retaliation, the greater cost of input goods (which had previously been imported) would reduce exports by hurting the competitiveness of American producers. Consider the commercial aircraft industry. The higher cost of aircraft parts would make American airplanes more expensive, lowering Boeing's worldwide market share relative to Airbus. US auto producers would similarly face higher prices for imported auto parts. Apple, Intel, and other globally integrated corporations would also see increased costs due to trade frictions.

Further, a US decision to cut imports would negatively affect our nation's own production, given that many products manufactured abroad draw on global supply chains in which US producers participate as suppliers. For example, in the goods we import from Mexico, a very large share of the value is made up of US content.[6] For that matter, it turns out that

Figure 3.2: Imports Help the Boeing 787 Fly

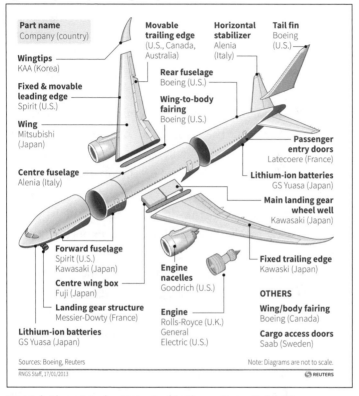

Part name	
Company (country)	

Movable trailing edge (U.S., Canada, Australia)

Horizontal stabilizer Alenia (Italy)

Tail fin Boeing (U.S.)

Wingtips KAA (Korea)

Rear fuselage Boeing (U.S.)

Fixed & movable leading edge Spirit (U.S.)

Wing-to-body fairing Boeing (U.S.)

Wing Mitsubishi (Japan)

Passenger entry doors Latecoere (France)

Centre fuselage Alenia (Italy)

Lithium-ion batteries GS Yuasa (Japan)

Main landing gear wheel well Kawasaki (Japan)

Forward fuselage Spirit (U.S.) Kawasaki (Japan)

Engine nacelles Goodrich (U.S.)

Fixed trailing edge Kawaski (Japan)

Centre wing box Fuji (Japan)

OTHERS

Landing gear structure Messier-Dowty (France)

Engine Rolls-Royce (U.K.) General Electric (U.S.)

Wing/body fairing Boeing (Canada)

Lithium-ion batteries GS Yuasa (Japan)

Cargo access doors Saab (Sweden)

Sources: Boeing, Reuters

Note: Diagrams are not to scale.

RNGS Staff, 17/01/2013

REUTERS

Reprinted with permission from Reuters Graphics, Thomson Reuters Markets LLC.

the US firms who are the biggest exporters are also often the biggest importers. It is difficult to reduce imports without creating collateral damage.[7]

Apple products provide another good example. A recent study suggests that both iPhones and iPads, typically assembled in China and imported from there, have only about 2 percent of their value added as Chinese labor input. Meanwhile, 58 percent of the value of the iPhone, and 30 percent of the iPad, are attributed to Apple's design and marketing activities in California.[8] Apple keeps most of its high-wage jobs, including engineering, design, finance, marketing, and management, in the United States. Putting a tariff on imports of "Chinese" iPhones and iPads would mostly harm American workers.

Narrowly domestic industries would also face cost increases from trade barriers. The American construction industry would face higher costs if it had to rely solely on domestic steel, and the result would be fewer sales. The retail sector would likewise find that higher-cost items result in fewer customers, causing that sector to shrink. In short, the new jobs in the sectors making goods that were previously imported have to come from somewhere. These workers will likely be drawn from other sectors that are shrinking, including both the export sector and narrowly domestic sectors like construction.

Much of the country is trade reliant, and exports originate from all US states.[9] A study by the Brookings Institution maps the regions that are most dependent on trade.[10] The country's biggest exporters are its cities; New York, Chicago, Los Angeles, Houston, Dallas, and Seattle together account for one quarter of all US exports. But many smaller cities and towns are even more trade-dependent, since trade represents a bigger part of their smaller economies. Four of the ten most trade-dependent towns are in Indiana; Columbus, Elkhart, Kokomo, and Lafayette all have export shares of income that exceed 30 percent.

If the United States embarked on policies that deliberately reduced international trade, there would surely be jobs created in some sectors and lost in others, but there is no reason to believe that the total number of jobs would change, since the unemployment rate is already as low as it can practically go and there is no evidence that reducing imports will increase labor force participation. The total number of jobs is driven by macroeconomic factors.[11] Meanwhile, trade restrictions would create serious disruptions, by reallocating job opportunities across sectors. This would create new groups of unemployed workers, buffeting the economy with additional shocks. As Paul Krugman put it, "It's like the old joke about the motorist who runs over a pedestrian, then tries to undo the damage by backing up—and runs over the victim a second time."[12]

International Trade and Economic Growth

There is absolutely no evidence that countries that are more closed to trade have higher employment, due to either higher labor force participation or lower unemployment rates. On the contrary, there is evidence that engaging in international trade boosts a country's economic growth and job creation. The simple bar chart below shows the economic growth rates of three groups of countries, categorized by their trade growth rates.

This chart follows the same method as a widely cited 2004 paper by economists David Dollar and Aart Kraay, who classified nations as mature-economy "rich countries," developing-economy "globalizers," or developing-economy "non-globalizers" and calculated the average of each group's real per-capita GDP growth over four decades. Here, we update their findings using World Bank data.[13] The globalizers among the developing economies consistently outperform the non-globalizers in terms of economic growth and, as

Figure 3.3: Countries that Trade More Have Faster Growth in GDP Per Capita

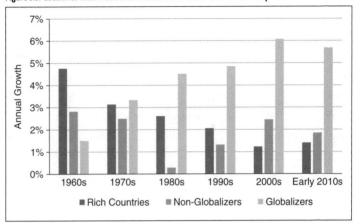

Note: Author's calculations based on World Bank data. Data source: World Development Indicators, World Bank.

shown in the next chart, employment. To be sure, correlation is not causality—but if trade were harming countries' economic growth or job prospects, we would expect to see very different patterns in these data.

Beyond trade, there are likely more important factors that determine a country's ability to sustain strong economic growth, including ones designed to build more inclusive economic and political institutions, as argued by Daron Acemoglu and James Robinson in *Why Nations Fail.* The argument here is not that international trade policy is the most important ingredient in sustained economic growth, but rather that there is no evidence that international trade is harming growth. Instead, it often appears to be helpful.

What do we really know about the relationship between international trade and economic growth? In general, analyses suggest a positive relationship between trade openness and

Figure 3.4: Countries that Trade More Have Lower Unemployment Rates

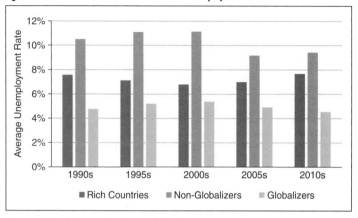

Note: Author's calculations based on World Bank data. Data source: World Development Indicators, World Bank.

growth, although the causal relationship is more difficult to show than mere correlations. Isolating the effects of openness is difficult, given that trade reforms tend to be enacted in moments of larger political reform.[14] Furthermore, the intangible consequences of more global openness are often inseparable from greater trade volumes. Yet no reputable paper has been able to connect increased openness with decreased growth. If trade has an effect on a country's trajectory, it appears to be a positive one.

Openness to the world economy has played an important role in one of the most encouraging developments in human history: the dramatic increase in worldwide living standards in recent years. This improvement in global living standards largely reflects progress in China, India, and other countries that have pursued policies conducive to economic growth and poverty reduction. In China, per-capita GDP was $1,500 in 1990; it rose to $13,400 by 2015, an enormous increase.[15] In

India, progress has also been substantial, with per-capita GDP growing from $1,700 in 1990 to $5,700 in 2015. Over the same time period, the number of people on the planet living below the World Bank poverty line (now $1.90 per day) declined from 1.96 billion to 700 million, a fall from 37 percent of the world's population to about 10 percent (fig. 3.5). Again, much of the improvement occurred due to economic growth in China and India (fig. 3.6). This astounding economic progress has been accompanied by gains in life expectancy, reductions in infant mortality, and improvements in educational attainment.

The World Bank poverty line is a very modest goal, $1.90 per day in 2011 dollars, but it measures something very serious: the amount of income needed to sustain the most basic needs of human survival. Between 1980 and 2012, the share of the Chinese population living in poverty fell from 88 percent of the population to 2 percent of their population (now about 1.35 billion people). One billion people were raised above the world poverty line. This is truly the most astounding economic progress in the history of the world.

Growth in India also resulted in big reductions in poverty. Although India's data are less complete, the data show that 54 percent of the population were in poverty by the World Bank standard in 1983. By 2011, the population had grown by 66 percent (to 1.26 billion), but the share in poverty had shrunk to 21 percent, saving about 400 million people from absolute poverty.

International trade is not solely responsible for these impressive achievements, but it has played a key role. It is unlikely that India or China would have been so successful in achieving their impressive growth rates if they had been closed off to trade; foreign ideas, capital, imports, and markets were essential

Figure 3.5: Growth in China Results in Huge Falls in Poverty Headcounts

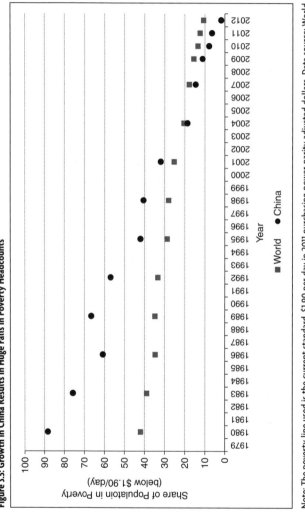

Note: The poverty line used is the current standard, $1.90 per day in 2011 purchasing-power-parity adjusted dollars. Data source: World Development Indicators, World Bank.

Figure 3.6: Economic Growth in China and India Has Been Spectacular

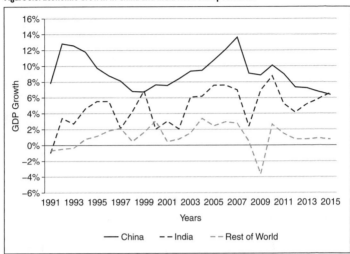

Data source: World Development Indicators, World Bank.

ingredients in their success. Indeed, adoption of foreign inventions and technology provide one reason why the economic growth of recent emerging economies has exceeded the growth of earlier economic transformations. It took the United Kingdom centuries to industrialize, but industrial revolution in the United States was faster, in part due to the adoption of earlier English inventions. Japan's industrialization proceeded at an even quicker pace, South Korea and Singapore accelerated from there, and China has been the fastest of them all.

How Do Countries Compete?

The gains from trade have been recognized for centuries. These gains hold even if wages differ across countries, and even if one country is more productive than its potential trading partners in making all things. This is the lesson of *comparative advantage*, an idea economist Paul Samuelson held up as exemplary of an economic insight that is both true and not immediately intuitive.

Consider first a simple example of a self-sufficient household with two family members, Karen and Peter. Karen is better at both of the key household tasks, hunting and gathering, but she is four times better than Peter at hunting and only two times better at gathering. One could argue that Karen should engage in both tasks, as should Peter. However, it is easy to show that if Karen spends all her time hunting and Peter spends all his time gathering, the household will have more of both products then if they did not specialize.[16]

Similar reasoning suggests that the college president should not shelve library books, even if she is better at shelving than anyone on the library staff. Her comparative advantage likely lies in fund-raising or management, where her skill superiority is even larger. The college will have more resources if she devotes her time toward these ends, and the books are shelved by someone else.

Exactly the same logic applies to countries. Imagine Japan is better at car production than China, in that Japanese workers make more four times more cars per year than their Chinese counterparts, and Japanese workers can also make bicycles with twice the speed of their Chinese counterparts. If Japan specializes in cars, and China in bicycles, then both countries can have more of both goods through international trade. These examples rely on comparative advantage rather than absolute advantage; gains from trade occur even when one country is better at everything, as long as its margin of superiority is not the same across all goods.

These ideas are familiar to students of introductory economics. The main insights stretch back in time to David Ricardo's 1817 work, *On the Principles of Political Economy and Taxation*. The Ricardian theory of trade is an oversimplified theory that neglects how gains from trade are distributed throughout society; this important issue is the topic of the next chapter. Still, the notion of comparative advantage provides powerful insights for understanding how trade affects countries.

One of Ricardo's essential insights is that international trade is not a zero-sum game. This is important to reassert, since the rhetoric of today's protectionists is not much different from the mercantilists of Ricardo's time; both hold a common belief that, in international trade, one country's gain is another country's loss. Historically, mercantilists argued that national power and prestige were dependent on a high volume of exports, a low volume of imports, and large stores of precious metals, or treasure. As articulated by East India Company director Thomas Mun, mercantilists seek for the country to sell more to "strangers" than consuming of theirs in value, so that the kingdom accumulates treasure.[17]

The mercantilist devotion to this doctrine has echoes in today's debate surrounding the trade deficit. But the logic of David Ricardo's theory of comparative advantage shows that, by specializing and trading, nations have access to a more diverse, cheaper set of goods. Every country can gain; there need be no losers. Going back to our simple example, when Japan makes cars and trades them for Chinese bicycles, both China and Japan end up with more products than if they each tried to make both products themselves.

In addition to showing the gains from trade, these simple theories show how high-wage countries can compete. Their higher productivity justifies their higher wages and makes their products competitive on world markets. In our example, Japanese workers earn more than Chinese workers *because* their productivity is higher. These theories also show how low-productivity countries can compete: their wages are lower, and that makes their products competitive, even when they produce fewer goods per year.

But what if high-productivity countries have low wages? Not to worry: productivity and wages are tightly linked (fig. 3.7). As a country's labor force becomes more productive (often due to investments in education and capital), wages rise.[18] In fact, Chinese wages have risen dramatically in recent years, precisely because of China's widespread productivity growth.

In summary, this chapter argues that countries have nothing to fear from international trade. Both rich and poor countries benefit from trade, as economic growth and efficiency are enhanced. This does not mean, however, that every individual in a particular country will gain from trade. Many may find themselves working in far more competitive conditions. Chapter 4 turns to these legitimate worries.

Figure 3.7: Countries with Higher Wages Have Higher Productivity

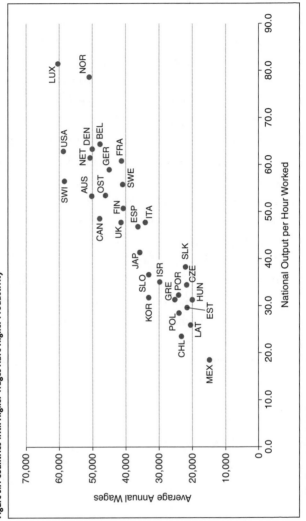

Note: The figure shows 2015 data. Data source: OECD Statistics.

Four

Winners and Losers from International Trade

While the basic logic of the overall gains from trade is undeniable, there are important features of the world that these arguments ignore. As countries open up to trade, their export sectors expand and their import sectors shrink. This Schumpeterian "creative destruction" entails serious transition costs, and may generate lasting changes in the distribution of income.

In the United States, international trade enlarges the sectors of our economy that make commercial aircraft, soybeans, medical instruments, integrated circuits, and software, while shrinking the sectors that make textiles, shoes, steel, and tires. In other sectors of the economy, the effect of trade is ambiguous, as we both export and import large quantities of cars, pharmaceuticals, manufactured goods, and machinery.

Sector contraction is painful. When people own equipment, buildings, or parcels of land that are well suited to producing a good that is increasingly imported, they are harmed by the increased foreign competition, and they may go out of business and lose much of the value of previously productive investments. When workers have skills that are suited to making products that are displaced by imports, demand for their labor decreases. They may experience lower wage growth, or even lose their jobs. Those that lose their jobs often have difficulty finding other jobs that use their skills and pay the wages they expect. Although other sectors are expanding, and other workers are receiving new job opportunities, this does not eliminate the real human costs associated with declining living standards and job loss in contracting industries.

Indeed, international trade is likely to have effects that worsen income inequality. In the United States, we export products that suit our advantages. Since the United States is well endowed with land that is ideal for many types of agricultural production, with a large capital stock that includes expensive, highly-mechanized farm equipment, and with technological knowledge about agricultural techniques, seeds, and fertilizers, it is unsurprising that we export many agricultural products.[1] Likewise, since the United States is well endowed with technologically sophisticated engineers, scientists, and computer scientists, and spends large amounts on research and development to enhance what those workers can do, it also exports goods that reflect these advantages, such as medical equipment and software.

At the same time, the United States has fewer low-skill workers relative to other countries, and goods like textiles, shoes, steel, and many manufactured goods may be produced abroad at lower cost. This reduces demand for domestic workers in these industries, and lowers their wages. Since low-skilled workers are more likely to be in import industries and high-skill workers are more likely to be in export industries, trade may systematically worsen the income distribution.[2]

International trade may also play a role, indirectly, in the rise of the top 1 percent share of the income distribution. Together with technological change, international trade enables those who are recognized as best in their field to sell their services and ideas to larger, global markets. If you are a top hedge fund manager, pop star, lawyer, or football player, technology can be used to codify and digitize your services, making it possible for you to sell what you do throughout the world. If you create a new search engine, social media network, or computing device, your profits expand dramatically if you can sell to a worldwide customer base. This creates outsized gains for those with the most unique human capital and the most entrepreneurial initiative, as well as those that are simply lucky. But paying these extraordinary returns to the "winners" in the world economy squeezes the returns for those with more common skills and less luck, as discussed in Chapter 2.

Harmful Effects on Wages and Workers: The Evidence

Job losses, particularly in the manufacturing sector, are undoubtedly difficult for workers, and evidence from the economics literature helps us understand why. Typically, manufacturing workers are both older and less educated than workers in other sectors, and this make job loss especially painful, since finding new jobs at similar wages is harder for older and less-educated workers. There is some evidence that workers in sectors with more import competition have both lower reemployment rates after job losses and greater earnings losses when they do find new jobs.[3] However, since domestic competition and technological change can also reduce manufacturing employment, it is difficult to pin down the precise degree to which manufacturing job losses can be attributed to increased imports.

Recently, a flurry of important studies have focused on quantifying the contribution of trade shocks to manufacturing job loss. For example, David Autor and his coauthors find that those commuting zones (clusters of counties that together constitute labor markets) where trade with China has increased most are the same zones in which job losses have been largest and wage growth has been most anemic.[4] They conclude that the shock associated with Chinese trade is large. Chinese imports account for about 1 million of the 5.8 million (net) job losses in manufacturing over the period 1999 to 2011—and if indirect effects on other industries are included, the number of job losses attributable to trade with China is twice as large.[5]

As it turns out, these intense "China shock" zones overlap heavily with the voting precincts that most heavily favored Donald Trump in the 2016 US presidential election. This election followed a long campaign season in which Trump (and Bernie Sanders, competing for the Democrats' nomination)

Figure 4.1: Areas of the United States Most Affected by the "China Shock"

Notes: Darker shading indicates more affected areas. Maps and research from the Autor, Dorn, and Hanson team are available at http://chinashock.info/. Reprinted with Permission from Dow Jones and Company, Inc.

Debating the China Shock

David Autor and his coauthors have made a small cottage industry of work researching the China trade shock, publishing many papers on the topic that emphasize the large magnitude of these harmful shocks.[1] Still, the question is not entirely settled. Scholars have pointed out that findings regarding the China shock's impact on employment may be sensitive to how the data are organized and whether adequate control variables were included.[2] There are also important concerns as to whether the effects of the Great Recession might cloud the effects of the China shock. And many question whether it is valid to add up every commuting zone that lost jobs to the China shock and describe that sum as the total effect of the China shock. For example, job losses due to trade likely caused policy-makers at the Central Bank to pursue looser monetary policy as a result, expanding employment elsewhere in the economy.[3]

---

1. These authors have a handy website that puts all the papers in one place: http://chinashock .info/. The site includes interactive graphics. Other important papers in this group include David Autor, David Dorn, and Gordon H. Hanson, "The China Syndrome: Local Labor Market Effects of Import Competition in the United States," *The American Economic Review* 103:6 (2013): 2121–2168; David Autor, David Dorn, Gordon Hanson, and Kaveh Majlesi, "Importing Political Polarization? The Electoral Consequences of Rising Trade Exposure," Working Paper 22637, NBER Working Papers, National Bureau of Economic Research, 2016.

2. See "Economists Argue about the Impact of Chinese Imports on America," *Economist*, March 11, 2017; Robert C. Feenstra, Hong Ma, and Yuan Xu, "The China Syndrome: Local Labor Market Effects of Import Competition in the United States: Comment," UC Davis, 2017; David Autor, David Dorn, and Gordon H, Hanson, "Response to Robert Feenstra, Hong Ma, and Yuan Xu's Comment on Autor, Dorn, and Hanson," MIT, 2017.

3. See similar arguments with Paul Krugman, "Trade and Jobs: A Note," Blog, *Opinion: New York Times*, July 3, 2016.

Meanwhile, even as job losses result from imports there may be job gains due to exports in other parts of the economy; that is, manufacturing job losses may be offset by job creation in agriculture or services.[4] Evidence suggests that companies (but not individual plants) that were more exposed to competition from China actually *increased* US employment. Lower Chinese input costs allowed greater competitiveness in areas that were complementary to those imported inputs. Some companies also reorganized their business activity to focus on areas that were less exposed to Chinese competition.[5] In short, adding up job losses due to the shock of an influx of Chinese imports captures only one part of the employment effects of trade. Like trade in general, the "China shock" is more likely to redistribute jobs than to change the total number of jobs.

4. See Robert C. Feenstra, Hong Ma, and Yuan Xu, "US Exports and Employment," UC Davis, 2017.

5. See Ildiko Magyari, "Reorganization, Chinese Imports, and US Manufacturing Employment," Columbia University Working Paper, January 2017.

frequently lambasted Hillary Clinton for promoting international trade through such agreements as the North American Free Trade Act (NAFTA)—given her affiliation with former President Clinton, who brought NAFTA into force in 1994—and the Trans-Pacific Partnership (TPP), negotiated by the Obama administration she served as Secretary of State. It appears that voters in locales where trade most harmed workers expressed their pain by voting for the candidate who promised trade restrictions and renegotiations of trade agreements. People often respond to harmful economic outcomes by seeking out polarized political positions, abandoning moderate politicians and parties.

Recent research reveals that the response to Trump's anti–Trade stance isn't an anomaly.[6] Well before his election, in the first decade of this century, areas of the United States that imported relatively high volumes of Chinese goods disproportionately voted moderate representatives out of office, in favor of ideologically extreme candidates of both parties. A consequence of economic disruption may be an increase in political polarization.

Political rhetoric, however, does not only respond to public opinion; it also drives it. Across the campaign season leading up to the 2016 election, opinion polls revealed big declines in the popularity of trade and trade agreements, despite the fact that wage growth that year was higher than in other recent years. Before the 2016 election, 58 percent of Americans described trade as a good thing, and only 33 percent labeled it as a bad thing. But by October 2016, those numbers had shifted to 45 percent saying good and 43 percent saying bad.[7]

The evidence that recent trade with China has had harmful effects on workers is important. Still, it is also worth considering the larger body of evidence on this question over the previous decades. Over the period that income inequality has been increasing, most research shows that trade has not been the primary cause of harmful labor-market results and inequality. Most economists put a larger share of the blame on technology, another important causal factor that works to increase demand for higher-income workers relative to lower-income workers.

Economists have spent decades bickering over whether trade or technology is responsible for the slow wage growth of American workers. Early studies produced three findings that appeared to absolve trade from responsibility: trade increased most in the 1970s, whereas wage stagnation and major upticks in income inequality occurred later; *all* industries showed growing use of skilled labor relative to unskilled labor, indicating that skill-biased technological change was a likely culprit; and the volume of imports looked insufficient to generate the large outcomes observed in labor markets (as documented in Chapter 2). China's emerging role in trade has challenged that earlier consensus, and the arguments among economists about the magnitude and importance of these findings continue. In the end, however, the preponderance of evidence suggests that international trade has had far less impact than technological change.

Further, it is important to remember that a great deal of economic disruption happens on an ongoing basis due to competition that is not international but rather domestic. In market economies, companies drive competitors out of business, new industries are born, and obsolete ones die.

Few companies today produce horse carriages, typewriters, or vacuum tubes; these products were displaced by automobiles, computers, and semiconductors. Large, big-box retail chains displace mom-and-pop stores, as customers appear to opt for lower prices over neighborly interactions. People stream their entertainment instead of hooking up cable TV boxes. Fancy coffee shops get sprinkled all over the country, while old-fashioned diners fade away. This creative destruction

Figure 4.2: Job Creation and Destruction, 2006–2016

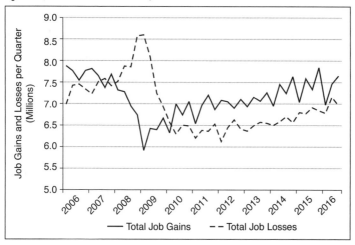

Note: The figure shows the US total nonfarm employment series. Data source: US Bureau of Labor Statistics.

always generates a lot of job loss and job creation. In fact, in the American economy, a single quarter typically sees over six million jobs created and six million destroyed.

This dynamic job creation and destruction is a result of capitalism itself, as new industries replace old industries, and competition (often domestic) causes some companies to expand as others contract. While such churn is disruptive, it is part of the process of reallocating labor to where it will be most productive.

Foreigners or Robots?

It is difficult to disentangle the effects of international trade from the effects of technological change, since both "foreigners" and "robots" bring substantial changes to labor markets.[8] Over the same period that international trade has grown, the economy has also experienced dramatic changes due to technological change, computerization, and the Internet. Back in 1980, few people or businesses regularly used computers, and no one relied on web pages, smart phones, and so forth.

It is amusing to describe to my students the technologies of my own college days. Thirty years ago, when I took my first economics course, I typed my papers on a typewriter. I used a pen to write letters on paper to my parents, which were delivered by the US Postal Service. I might have wanted to call a friend studying abroad, but it was prohibitively expensive; a single call could easily consume the monthly budget of a college student. If I needed the services of a business, I consulted a directory called the "yellow pages." Information on foreign economies was scarce. I found what I could in dusty volumes in the library, and entered the data manually into large and confusing computers; the cursor blinked in green against a dark screen, awaiting my commands.

Computers have since transformed all our lives. International phone calls, and even video chat sessions, are free to anyone with Internet access. Email makes communication nearly instantaneous throughout the planet. Information from foreign sources is a click away. Computers are friendly, and small, and computing power is staggeringly cheap. A college student's laptop has more computing power available than a *Fortune* 500 firm's supercomputer did a generation ago. A 1980s supercomputer (for example, the Cray supercomputer, costing over $20 million in today's dollars) was room-sized and had speeds inferior to today's iPhone.[9]

In the course of one generation, workplaces have been transformed almost beyond recognition; automation and computing

Figure 4.3: Manufacturing Output Increases as Manufacturing Employment Falls

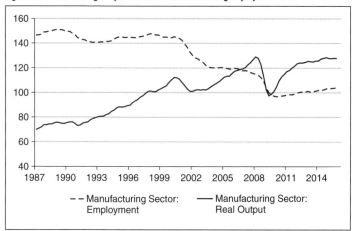

Numbers are indexed such that 2009 = 100. Data source: Federal Reserve.

have had dramatic effects on manufacturing jobs. As technology has spread and become less expensive, each manufacturing worker can produce a far larger quantity of goods. Since 1987, manufacturing output has increased by 83 percent, even as manufacturing employment has fallen by 29 percent.

Studies suggest that one result of this technological change has been to dramatically reduce the number of workers required in manufacturing in the United States. Technological change has swamped the effects of international trade; according to one study, 88 percent of manufacturing job losses are due to technological change.[10] More casual evidence also suggests that manufacturing in the United States is becoming increasingly automated. In a high-profile announcement in early 2017, for example, Ford Motor Company stated that it would add manufacturing jobs in suburban Detroit as part of its development of self-driving and electric vehicles. An analyst at the Center for Automotive Research noted: "Keeping a new technology near the engineers is an important thing, at least in the first generation." More broadly, he observed, "Each iteration of a facility becomes less like old-school manufacturing and more high-tech. That will ultimately mean fewer jobs."[11]

The decline of manufacturing jobs is nothing new. Over the past half-century, the manufacturing share of total US employment has declined at a notably steady rate. Technological change and structural changes in the economy would seem to be more important than trade shocks in driving this reduction in manufacturing jobs, since trade shocks were far from evenly distributed over this time period.

While technological progress in the past has been disruptive, it has not caused a reduction in the total number of jobs or a

Figure 4.4: US Manufacturing Employment Has Declined Steadily for Over Fifty Years

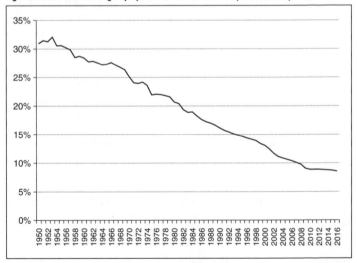

Note: This series shows the US manufacturing share of nonfarm employment. Data source: Federal Reserve.

higher unemployment rate. There have been many techno-logical revolutions that have ultimately enabled higher stan-dards of living and greater opportunities for workers, starting with the agricultural revolution that dramatically increased farm output per worker and freed labor to move to the cities, and later including revolutions in industrial processes like the assembly line. When work can be done more efficiently, that doesn't mean that the number of jobs has to fall, though jobs will be redirected. Two centuries ago, over three-quarters of the labor force worked on farms, whereas now less than 2 percent of the labor force works on farms.[12] Yet as agricul-tural productivity increased, that did not leave would-be farmers unemployed, since they could turn to job opportuni-ties in the cities.

Productivity growth in agriculture provided many gains. In 1960, Americans spent one-fifth of their incomes on food and did the vast majority of food preparation at home. Now, about one-twelfth of income is spent on food, and this includes ex-penditures on food preparation that used to be done (without pay) within the home.[13] Growth in manufacturing productivity similarly means that less of our hard work is needed to pur-chase most manufactured goods, such as cars, clothing, and furniture.

Yet, the technology revolution of recent decades still pres-ents a problem. It is not that it has reduced the number of jobs, but rather that it has systematically moved demand for labor away from some kinds of workers (those that can be replaced by computers and robots) and toward others (those whom computers and robots make more productive). Those who are displaced by computers are different from those who are helped by them. For instance, bank tellers, gas station attendants, secretaries, and factory workers have been replaced by ATMs, swipe-and-go self-service, computer typing and voicemail, and more mechanized factories. But engineers, software designers, scientists, movie stars, and financial managers are more productive, since they have computers to assist them in their endeavors. Computers make some workers more valuable, but they harm others, and those workers tend to be less well-off.

There are also concerns that the newest wave of technological change may have larger consequences for labor markets than prior technological revolutions, consigning a larger share of the working population to be "replaced" rather than "supported". Computers may now threaten job prospects on a much larger scale than before due to their ability to replace labor not just in terms of muscle effort, but also in terms of thinking and analytical ability. Regardless of whether artificial intelligence and other new forms of computing turn out to be truly distinct, continued technological innovations are likely to exacerbate trends of increasing income inequality.

Robots Abroad

As noted in Chapter 2, these troubling labor-market trends are not confined to the United States, or even to rich countries. Indeed, the fact that developing countries also experience these problems should give pause to those inclined to blame all rich-country troubles on international trade. If trade is reducing demand for US labor, it should be *increasing* demand for Chinese labor, and in turn increasing the labor share of income and reducing economic inequality in China.

The Race between Education and Technology

At the start of the twentieth century, the payoffs for high school and college completion were large. For example, young GE recruits in the 1920s were required to have a working knowledge of algebra, mechanical drawing, geometry, plane trigonometry, elementary physics, and practical electricity. From 1890 to 1970, US workers increasingly rose to the challenge, and educational attainment outran technological progress, creating a surplus of highly educated workers. In recent decades, that surplus has flipped to deficit, as students find themselves increasingly unprepared for a workplace saturated with modern technology. The spiraling costs of college are one reason why fewer people have gained the critical skills demanded by today's marketplace.[1]

The gap between the need for technology-savvy workers and the educational achievement of Americans has grown over the past four decades, due to flatlining rates of postsecondary educational attainment. This has hit industries that require highly-skilled technical labor particularly hard.[2] Estimates suggest that the United States will face a shortfall of five million workers in 2020, because 65 percent of jobs will require a postsecondary education. This possibility

---

1. There is also a gap between the skills employers value and the major choices of college students, with large deficits of workers in majors such as engineering and computer science. See Kelsey Gee, "Where College Seniors are Falling Short," *Wall Street Journal*, April 26, 2017.
2. For examples, see Jeffrey Sparshott, "The US Occupations at Greatest Risk of a Labor Shortage," *Wall Street Journal*, April 19, 2016.

has sent tech giants scrambling for solutions. For example, Google recently made and marketed apps and online tools for schools, intended to help bridge the gap between education and technology. Their work has ten million students in Google Classrooms, typing essays and solving word problems on Google Chromebooks. Despite such efforts to bring students up to speed, America's children are facing more of a marathon than a sprint.[3]

3. For a book-length treatment of this issue, see Claudia Goldin and Lawrence F. Katz, *The Race between Education and Technology* (Cambridge: Harvard University Press, 2009).

In fact, China has seen opposite trends, with increasing income inequality and a falling labor share of income. Similar trends hold for many other developing countries. What can explain this? It is likely that the computer revolution and technological change have increased the demand for those with the most skill, and reduced demand for those with the least skill, across all countries.[14][15]

Technological change has reduced the share of manufacturing employment in many countries, including several countries that are poorer than the United States. In Mexico, South Africa, and Turkey, the manufacturing share of employment has fallen in recent years; it has also fallen in Germany, Japan, the United Kingdom, Korea, the United States, and for the Group of Twenty (G20) countries on average.

Again, it is difficult to truly disentangle these two sources of labor market disruption, especially as international trade and technological change fuel each other. Globalization allows

Figure 4.5: Almost Everywhere, the Manufacturing Share of Employment is Falling

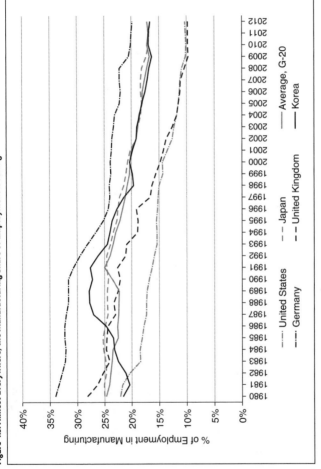

Data sources: International Labor Comparisons, US Bureau of Labor Statistics.

quicker technological diffusion, and competitive forces encourage labor-saving innovation. Technological change enables globalization by lowering communication costs and creating solutions to the logistical puzzles of global supply chains.

Monopoly and Excess Profits in the Global Economy

As Chapter 2 showed, excess profits also play an important role in this story of workers' woes. When entrepreneurs make risky and ingenious innovations, some get lucky and receive enormous returns. Among large corporations, there is substantial evidence of increased market power and corporate profits.[16] The most successful companies receive supersized returns to their investments, often in excess of 20 or 30 percent.[17] This has caused a large increase in cash stockpiles by corporations, as more and more of worldwide income takes the form of corporate profits.[18] In the United States, over three-fourths of corporate income is excess profits, and corporate profits are higher as a share of national income than they have been at any time in the past half-century.[19] [20]

Evidence indicates that the largest, most profitable companies use less labor per dollar of sales than do more typical firms; these "superstar" firms alone account for most of the falling labor share of income. As it turns out, a typical firm does not use less labor relative to a dollar of sales now than it did decades ago. But typical companies are far less important than they used to be.[21]

International business will be discussed in Chapter 7, but it is already clear that rising corporate profits bear some responsibility for both the declining labor share of income and rising inequality throughout the world. And, as we saw in Chapter 2, social norms, the declining role of labor unions, changes in tax policy, and other factors may also contribute to troubling labor outcomes.

Nonetheless, if workers are hurting, and international trade is playing a contributing role, some suggest that this is reason enough to put the brakes on globalization. After all, trade agreements are under governments' control, whereas social norms, technological change, and corporate market structure may be more difficult to change. And trade restrictions are more politically palatable than other remedies. Foreigners are an easy scapegoat; protectionist trade policy can appear patriotic.

Yet, such solutions harm the very workers they purport to help. Stepping back from international trade is both counterproductive and ineffective. Next, we'll see why, and discuss the path forward.

Five

Trade Politics and Trade Policy

Every person has two major roles they play in the economy: one as a producer and one as a consumer. In our producer role, we typically sell labor to an enterprise that makes a good or service—and it is in this role that international trade is often uncomfortable. Chapter 4 showed that international trade creates a tougher competitive environment; workers with less education are likely to be adversely affected by competition from countries with lower labor costs. If workers have less bargaining power, thanks to companies moving production abroad (or merely threatening to), they may also see restrained wage growth. Chapter 7 will discuss the role of multinational companies in far more detail.

Yet in our role as consumers, international trade is nearly unambiguously good. Reflect for a moment on the items you buy. Your cup of coffee, your fruit in winter, your clothing and shoes, your computer, your appliances, your car, and much else is less expensive because of international trade. Even if you buy domestic versions of these products, they are likely less expensive because they must compete with the foreign options available to consumers. If we were to raise trade barriers by enacting, say, 30 percent tariffs on foreign products, this would make most of the items we purchase more expensive, reducing the purchasing power of our wages.

International trade not only reduces the cost of the goods we consume, it also substantially increases the variety of goods we can access. In recent decades, the variety of imported goods has increased threefold. While it is difficult to quantify the value of increased choices for consumers, some scholars suggest that value is substantial.[1] This makes intuitive sense when one stops to contemplate the origins of one's purchases. It is nice to be able to buy flowers year around, and foreign varieties of wine and beer, to say nothing of the vast arrays of international foods, clothing, toys, electronics, and automobiles. International trade provides consumers with a rich abundance of choices.

While it is easy to appreciate the advantages associated with consuming international products, it can still, of course, be tempting to pursue protectionist trade policies to help industries that are hurting. Yet it is important to keep in mind the large costs associated with such policies. Across decades of studies, economists have consistently found that tariffs generate large collateral damage, and the jobs saved in protected industries often come at enormous cost to consumers. A review of thirty-one case studies found that protectionist measures cost consumers as a group, on average, over $500,000 per job saved.[2] A recent study of tariffs on Chinese tires (which ran from 2009 to 2012) found a cost to consumers of $900,000 per job saved in tire manufacturing. Unfortunately for American tire workers, less than 5 percent of these added costs to consumers showed up in their paychecks.[3] Meanwhile, workers in other industries were hurt as China retaliated; its tariffs on chicken parts harmed the poultry industry, causing exports to China to drop by 90 percent.

Tariffs are also one of the most regressive forms of taxation; there are three reasons why tariffs disproportionately burden those with lower incomes. First, tariffs do not burden income that is saved, only income that is consumed. Like other consumption taxes, such as many state sales taxes, tariffs therefore fall more heavily on poorer households. Poor and middle-class people often spend nearly all their income on meeting their consumption needs, saving little or nothing. Second, while tariffs *could* be higher on imported luxury goods, causing them to burden well-off households more heavily, that has never been the pattern in practice. On the contrary, tariffs have tended to be higher on the basic goods that are most widely consumed by poorer households.[4] Third, for poor and middle-class consumers, the share of total consumption made up of imported goods is greater than it is for richer consumers. Researchers have found that, across many countries, poorer consumers consume a higher fraction of traded goods relative to non-traded services than do richer consumers, and this pattern is particularly stark for Americans.[5] In the United States, tariffs take a bite out of the after-tax incomes of the poorest 20 percent of the population three times larger, in percentage terms, than they take from the top 20 percent.[6]

Consumers have a lot to gain from international trade, but consumers are often politically disorganized, and they are unlikely to form a vocal constituency in favor of open international trade. Instead, trade liberalization often proceeds based on other considerations. Export-oriented business interests, and globally oriented multinational companies, provide constituencies in favor of an open trading system. And policy-makers also pursue trade agreements toward political ends.

Back When Tariffs Paid for Government

Tariffs have played an important role in our nation's tax history, and indeed were the primary source of revenue to the US federal government until the early twentieth century. As the last decades of the nineteenth century, often referred to as the "gilded age," brought alarming increases in inequality, some policy-makers began to worry about the regressive nature of tariffs, which clearly placed greater burdens on working-class people. Rich "robber barons" faced light tax burdens; only a small portion of their income was spent on consumption goods subject to tariffs, and they were not subject to large property taxes. In *The Great Tax Wars*, Steven Weisman chronicles how the need to fund the government created intense political battles that ultimately led to the enactment of an income tax. In 1913, the Sixteenth Amendment to the US Constitution was ratified, clearing constitutional hurdles to levying taxes on income. The federal income tax was adopted the same year.

Myths about Trade Agreements

One interesting aspect of recent public debates in the United States is the huge emphasis that has been placed on trade agreements—both past agreements like NAFTA and proposed agreements like the Trans-Pacific Partnership (TPP). But many observers do not recognize what these agreements do, and how little these agreements affect US workers.

The United States generally has very low tariffs on almost all products. When a free trade agreement is signed, therefore, it typically involves very little tariff reductions by the United States, given that the tariffs were already low, and much larger tariff reductions by our trading partners. Free trade agreements are required by our international trade treaties (under the WTO or GATT) to move toward completely free trade, rather than lowering barriers partially. Imagine, then, that one country has tariffs that average 1 percent and the other country has tariffs that average 20 percent. A free trade agreement between the two will be inherently asymmetric as both countries remove tariffs.

As the United States has pursued various bilateral and regional trade agreements in recent decades, there was little change in our overall barriers, since we were already quite open to trade. In the case of NAFTA, for example, our tariffs averaged 4 percent while Mexican tariffs averaged 10 percent. Mexico also had a slew of other protectionist measures that were eliminated by the agreement.[7] This explains why those advocating for these agreements often celebrate the fact that they create a more "level playing field"; all members import products on the same basis, without barriers to trade. (Sports metaphors are quite common in this area. Let's move the ball forward and level the playing field before the clock runs down, shall we?)

The debate over NAFTA, both in the past and recently, has often produced more heat than light. NAFTA came into effect in 1994, although the United States had already been part of a free trade agreement with Canada since 1989. At the time, Ross Perot, a 1992 presidential candidate, predicted that NAFTA would generate a "giant sucking sound" as Mexico pulled economic activity out of the United States. Nothing of the sort materialized.

The elimination of tariffs had the greatest impact on the textile, apparel, automotive, and agricultural industries, but the years following the adoption of NAFTA showed minimal change for the US economy as a whole. Between 1994 and 2001, unemployment dropped from 6.9 percent to 4 percent, and 17 million jobs were added. In the years after NAFTA, only 5 percent of annual job turnover could be attributed to trade with Mexico; by contrast, 23 percent of turnover was the product of technological advancement.[8] NAFTA also did little to alter the aggregate trade balance, a measure far more responsive to domestic macroeconomic forces. (These are discussed in the next chapter.)

What does the evidence indicate more generally about trade agreements and trade? Surprisingly, many studies find trade agreements to have little effect on trade flows. For instance, controlling for the other variables expected to influence trade (such as the size of the economy and geographic factors), there is no evidence that WTO membership enhances trade.[9] Why? Simply put, actions speak louder than words. A country's decision to sign an agreement is far less important than that country's overall stance toward trade. Often, when countries like China join the WTO, they sign on to the agreement after years of policy changes that unilaterally opened their countries to trade. By the time they formally join the agreement, that action itself has little effect on their behavior, and thus, on their trade patterns.[10] In other words, foreign countries' domestic policy decisions are likely the dominant factor increasing trade flows in recent decades—on top of the facilitating factors of reduced transportation costs, and even more important, dramatically lower communication costs. Trade agreements play a relatively minor role.

For better or worse, many aspects of trade agreements actually have comparatively little to do with trade. For example, the TPP devoted much attention to intellectual property rights, labor standards, environmental standards, and currency manipulation. Whether these issues belong in trade agreements is an open question. In theory, there is no reason why issues outside trade cannot be included in trade agreements, but in practice, which issues should be included is often controversial.

What Should Trade Agreements Do?

Most agree that trade agreements are meant to liberalize trade among participant countries. There is less agreement about what else they should do. Some provisions of existing agreements have caused a great deal of controversy, including those that protect intellectual property rights. When the interests of highly profitable pharmaceutical companies are pitted against people in poor countries seeking affordable medication, many question if it is right to use a trade agreement to benefit the companies. Even larger controversy focuses on mechanisms for investor-state dispute settlement, which allows companies to sue governments through ad hoc arbitration proceedings; many argue these should be replaced by a reliance on domestic laws. In these two areas, current trade agreements strike many as too broad.

Yet despite these important examples, there are also ways in which *broader* agreements may make good sense. For example,

Shunning the Trans-Pacific Partnership

In a *New York Times* poll back in May 2015, 78 percent of respondents said they knew "not much" or "nothing at all" about the Trans-Pacific Partnership (TPP). Yet, within a year, the TPP had become a hot topic in the 2016 election season, drawing fire from both ends of the political spectrum. Shortly after taking office, President Trump withdrew the United States from the deal.

The TPP was negotiated by twelve countries along the Pacific Ocean: Japan, Malaysia, Vietnam, Singapore, Brunei, Australia, New Zealand, Canada, Mexico, Chile, Peru, and the United States. Combined, their economies represent 37 percent of global GDP and their populations number over eight hundred million people. The TPP's goal was to create a free trade area by eliminating tariffs over the course of several years. The agreement also contained provisions regarding digital commerce, intellectual property rights, human rights, and environmental protection. It expanded labor rights, dramatically increasing the number of people covered by enforceable labor standards. And it contained environmental provisions that addressed clean oceans, wildlife trafficking, and logging.[1] The inclusion of many of these provisions was a response to criticism of NAFTA; TPP was an opportunity for the United States,

---

1. For more detail on the agreement, see Council of Economic Advisers, *Economic Report of the President* (Washington, DC: United States Government Printing Office, 2015), 302–303.

Canada, and Mexico to renegotiate the terms of that controversial agreement.[2]

The TPP also had geopolitical intentions, as it was meant to create a group of partners with sufficiently strong relationships to counter China's growing regional influence. The US abandonment of the agreement generated ill will; Singapore's prime Minister stated that many countries would feel "damaged for a long time to come." In the meantime, China has increased investment in Southeast Asia through its One Belt, One Road infrastructure initiative, and the TPP is going forward without the United States. The remaining eleven countries signed the final agreement in March 2018; it has been relabeled the Comprehensive and Progressive Agreement for Trans-Pacific Partnership (CPTPP).[3]

Who really killed US participation in the TPP? Prime suspects extend beyond President Trump to include other 2016 presidential candidates, politicians across the ideological spectrum, and the public in its collective ignorance. Meaningful, inclusive debate on the substance of the agreement was virtually absent.

---

2. Several arguments in favor of US participation in the TPP are nicely summarized in a Council of Economics Advisers brief: Council of Economic Advisers, "Industries and Jobs at Risk if the Trans-Pacific Partnership Does Not Pass," Report, November 2016.

3. "Trading Places," *Economist*, January 27, 2018.

if countries are concerned about tax or regulatory competition, international agreements offer a means to avoid a "race to the bottom." Governments could use agreements to commit to higher standards, reducing global companies' ability to pit governments against each other.

Overall, the case for trade agreements is akin to the case for government. Individuals and companies can't solve important social problems without the rules and institutions of government: they would have no way to enforce contracts; transportation and communication would be far more costly; and they would lack the vital protections afforded by both the rule of law and the social safety net. Similarly, countries have grave difficulties pursuing areas of mutual interest without international agreements. Good agreements are important for setting the rules of the road, they play a vital role in preventing mutually harmful economic policies, and they promote peaceful, prosperous international relations. (Chapters 7 and 9 will discuss these issues further.)

It's All about Politics

Given that countries always have the option of liberalizing their trade regimes unilaterally, we might wonder why countries go through all the fuss of negotiating trade agreements. One answer is that, in addition to important rule-setting functions, trade agreements play important political roles.

First, trade agreements constrain future governments and may lead to a more open and free trading system than if countries were constantly revisiting their ideal trade policies based on the spirit of the moment. For example, consider the European

Union, which is a *customs union*.[11] Member states in a customs union agree not only to trade freely with members, but to devise and adhere to a common trade policy with respect to other nations.[12] Thus, when an EU member state elects a particularly nationalistic government, that government will be nearly powerless to raise trade barriers on either partner EU countries or on other nations. The only way to regain control of the nation's trade policy would be to exit the European Union— the very move that the United Kingdom is now undertaking, much to the dismay of many observers.

A similar political calculation surrounded China's accession to the WTO in 2001. Once China joined the WTO, that action committed its government to continued liberal trade policies. It also committed other WTO members, including the United States, not to discriminate against Chinese products.[13]

There is also a second way in which trade agreements advance political goals: they are often used to improve international relations among countries. Here again, the European Union project offers a good example. After centuries of conflict in Europe, the founders of the European Union explicitly sought to make countries more interdependent economically in order to make future conflicts less likely. One of the project's first steps was an agreement among the original six members (France, Germany, Italy, Belgium, Netherlands, and Luxembourg) to liberalize trade in coal and steel, essential inputs in military production. Agreeing to rely on each other's markets for these commodities was basically agreeing not to fight. More recently, the European Union has expanded to include many states that were formerly under the influence of the USSR. Countries such as Latvia, Lithuania, Estonia, Poland, Hungary, and the Czech Republic have embraced European integration as a way to become more closely linked to Europe and to be implicitly protected against potential external threats.

In the case of NAFTA, the United States also had strong political motives to expand the less-controversial Canada-United States Free Trade Agreement to Mexico. It was hoped that NAFTA would help make Mexico, a country that shares a two-thousand-mile border with the United States, more stable, more prosperous, and more democratic. And it was hoped that a more prosperous Mexican economy would also reduce undocumented immigration from Mexico to the United States. Establishing the counterfactual is never easy; we cannot know what would have happened in the absence of the agreement. Yet it is clear that NAFTA has had consequences that stretch far beyond trade.

For example, shortly after NAFTA took effect, Mexico experienced a macroeconomic crisis. The crisis itself had nothing to do with NAFTA; it resulted from macroeconomic problems in Mexico that included over-borrowing and an overvalued peso. When the Mexican peso swiftly depreciated in December 1994, Mexico struggled to finance short-term debts—including many denominated in US dollars that became more burdensome with the sharp decline of the peso. The crisis spread to other countries in a manner that was colorfully described as the "tequila effect." To help stabilize the Mexican economy, the Clinton administration authorized aid to Mexico via executive action. This action paid off; the Mexican economy recovered quickly from its crisis, and Mexico repaid the $12.5 billion it had borrowed from the federal fund in two years. But the decision was controversial at the time. Without the political connection cemented by NAFTA, it is unlikely that urgently needed support would have arrived.

As argued in the early days of the European Union, countries benefit from strengthening the motives for peaceful cooperation through closer economic relations. This adds an economic deterrent to conflict or war. When countries depend on each other as markets for their output, as suppliers of essential products, as sources of lending, or as destinations where assets earn less-risky or more-rewarding returns, they are less likely to erupt into violence when their interests conflict.

Consider the United States and China; the two are economically reliant on each other. The United States provides a large, rich market for Chinese products. We also provide a large and sophisticated market selling diversified financial assets, where Chinese savings can earn safe returns. China provides US consumers with large quantities of low-cost goods, and provides US companies with intermediate input goods that enable them to be more successful in world markets. China also provides a reliable source of funds, allowing the US government and private investors to borrow in larger quantities and at lower interest rates than they could otherwise. These economic interests are mutual, they are large, and they are likely to improve relations between the United States and China, reducing the chance that frictions will escalate into larger conflicts or war.

Can We Help American Workers by Restricting Trade?

The suffering of American workers is real. As Chapter 2 showed, wage stagnation, rising income inequality, and the declining share of labor income are enormous problems for the US economy. Beyond our borders, similar problems affect

Make Trade, Not War

The last great era of globalization ended with World War I. Rising nationalism and conflict abruptly ended a period of expanding international trade and migration. Only after the Great Depression and World War II had passed did countries work to build up international economic relations again, establishing the General Agreement on Tariffs and Trade (GATT) which eventually became the World Trade Organization (WTO), the International Monetary Fund (IMF), and the World Bank (originally to provide funds for war reconstruction).

Numerous studies have found that international trade is associated with reduced likelihood of political conflict. Several theories suggest mechanisms by which trade may promote peace. Trade is cheaper than war as a mechanism for increasing resources, trade increases the losses from conflict, and freer trade undermines domestic groups that favor protectionism and aggressive foreign policy.

One study finds that moving a country from the ninetieth percentile on a scale of protectionism to the tenth percentile is associated with a 70 percent lower probability of conflict.[1] Another finds that the least economically free states are fourteen times more conflict-prone than the freest states.[2]

---

1. Patrick J. McDonald, "Peace through Trade or Free Trade?" *The Journal of Conflict Resolution* 48:4 (2004), 547–572.
2. Erik Gartzke, "Economic Freedom and Peace," Annual Report, Economic Freedom of the World, Fraser Institute, Canada, 2005.

While causality is nearly impossible to establish, there is a robust negative relationship between proxies for nationalism, such as military spending and military personnel, and the importance of trade in economies. Countries that militarize, or whose trading partners militarize, trade less.[3] And nationalist sentiment is strongly correlated with more negative opinions about trade openness.[4] Closed borders, and closed minds, can hurt both prosperity and peace.

3. See Daron Acemoglu, and Pierre Yared, "Political Limits to Globalization," *American Economic Review* 100:2 (2010), 83–88.

4. See Anna Maria Mayda, and Dani Rodrik, "Why Are Some People (and Countries) More Protectionist than Others?" *European Economic Review* 49:6 (2005), 1393–1430; Kevin H. O'Rourke and Richard Sinnott, "The Determinants of Individual Attitudes towards Immigration," *European Journal of Political Economy* 22:4 (2006), 838–861; and Edward D. Mansfield and Diana C. Mutz, "Support for Free Trade: Self-Interest, Sociotropic Politics, and Out-Group Anxiety," *International Organization* 63:3 (2009), 425–457.

many other countries. Workers in China, Europe, India, and elsewhere are affected by these trends.

While international trade is not the only, or even the dominant, causal factor, it has played a role in the suffering of the American middle class. There are good reasons to suspect that trade with low-wage countries puts pressure on workers by making the environment in which people work more competitive. This lowers wages and reduces labor's bargaining power. At the same time, the United States is particularly well suited to making goods that require abundant capital, highly-skilled labor, research and development funds, and technology. As our export sectors expand due to trade, capital owners and highly-skilled workers benefit disproportionately.

Yet, not only US workers but workers throughout the world, including in less-developed countries, are experiencing lower labor shares of national income and increased income inequality. This leads one to suspect that international trade is not the only culprit in this story. The computer revolution, and the pervasive effects of technological change, are an essential part of the narrative. Computers displace some workers, yet they make others more productive, and this has important effects on the distribution of income, hurting the poorer members of society and benefiting those that are better off. Further, technology works together with globalization to swell the supersized returns of the most successful earners in the world economy, as they reap enormous benefits from selling their ideas to the entire world, squeezing the returns to others. Corporate profits and monopoly power are also on the rise, adding to these pressures.

The losers from these global trends are not happy, and they have responded by voting for those that promise populist interventions, such as erecting trade barriers, imposing penalties on firms that send jobs offshore, and renegotiating, or exiting, prior trade agreements. Yet the populists proposing to turn back the clock on globalization do not suggest turning back the clock on technological innovation. Surely, if we all threw away our computers, or even banned computing, that would be a quick way to increase demand for low-skilled workers and return to the economy of yore. Suddenly, there would be an enormous demand for labor to do the myriad tasks that computers used to do for us.

That argument is silly, of course. First, delaying techno-logical progress, let alone reversing it, is very difficult to do. (Though not impossible. Periods of war produce technological setbacks by destroying capital and reducing nonmilitary in-vestment.) Second, given that computers are recognized to provide so many benefits and efficiencies throughout the economy, and affect our daily lives in so many tangible ways, the idea of giving them up is inconceivable.

It is important to recognize that international trade and technological change generate twin tradeoffs. Both entail numerous efficiencies, large gains to consumers, and large sectors of the economy that "win." But both also create vocal groups of losers. Still, in contrast with technological change, globalization is more reversible, since we can easily take po-litical actions that would curtail or reverse it. Indeed, there are historical examples of this occurring. After the previous "golden age" of globalization (1870–1913), there was a period of war, economic depression, and backlash that substantially reduced trade, international investment, and migration. It would not be difficult for policy-makers to take actions that would reverse the present "wave" of globalization.

Supporters of international trade face a vexing political problem. Gains from trade are easy to ignore since consumers don't notice them, and they are diffusely spread throughout the economy. Gains in export sectors create firms that favor inter-national trade, but their workers may not easily associate their opportunities with the fact that their firms can sell prod-ucts worldwide. Yet losses due to import competition are easy to notice, as workers face lower wages or job loss. And, unlike computers, foreigners provide an easy target for blame. This creates big political problems for an open trading system.

Do Americans Like Trade?

Do Americans like trade? In short: it depends. Polling has, at some times, found relatively high favorable opinions of international trade. From 2015 to 2017, however, favorable trade ratings plummeted, despite these years' above-average wage growth and low unemployment. Likely, political rhetoric has shaped voter opinions. The erosion in favorable views about trade has been particularly strong among registered Republicans. In a 2017 survey about NAFTA, only 22 percent of Republicans thought that NAFTA had been good for the United States, whereas 67 percent of Democrats thought so. In 2000, the gap was much less wide, with 46 percent of Republicans and

Figure 5.1: Are Trade Agreements a Good or Bad Thing?

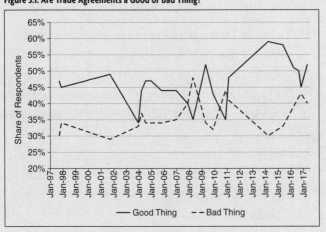

Data source: Pew Research Center.

49 percent of Democrats holding favorable opinions of NAFTA.[1]

It also appears that public opinion is driven less by self-interest than by personal views of what is good for society. For example, recent research suggests that the industry of the worker is not a predictor of their likely view of trade. But other political views are. Those expressing agreement with isolationist, nationalist, or ethnocentric views are more likely to have unfavorable views of trade.[2] Educational attainment also matters; voters reporting more years of formal education view trade more favorably.

---

1. Gallup Politics, "Americans Split on Whether NAFTA Is Good or Bad for US" February 24, 2017, http://www.gallup.com/poll/204269/americans-split-whether-nafta-good-bad.aspx.
2. N. Gregory Mankiw, "Why Voters Don't Buy It When Economists Say Global Trade Is Good," The Upshot, July 29, 2016; Edward D. Mansfield and Diana C. Mutz, "Support for Free Trade."

This political problem is daunting, but the case against protectionism remains strong. Giving up trade, or even reducing trade by instituting a 30 percent tariff or shutting down the trade-liberalizing components of international agreements, would create large costs for the US economy and US workers. In particular:

- Tariffs would harm consumers, with particularly harmful effects for low- or middle-income workers.
- Export industries would be hurt by the higher costs of intermediate products and the likely

retaliatory actions of our trading partners, hurting workers in those sectors.

- To replace the goods that would have been imported from low-income countries, labor would need to switch from other sectors, contracting other industries. This process would create its own shocks and disruptions.
- Since many other factors, including technology, monopoly power, and social norms, are also driving the woes of workers, it is unlikely that trade restrictions would be effective. This might lead to increased political pressures for even greater trade restrictions.

Importantly, the negative repercussions would also play out on the global stage. International relations would be harmed, and there would be fewer mutual dependencies tying countries together. Weaker international alliances and friendships would make it more difficult to solve international problems, and increase the chances of conflict.

Making Trade Work for Everyone

Between trade and technological change, it is difficult to tease out how much each should be blamed for the plight of workers—but in one important respect, it does not matter. Regardless of which is the bigger culprit, "solving" the problem by erecting trade barriers (or throwing away our computers) would generate a lot of collateral damage. There are much better, and more direct, ways to help workers.

Chapters 9 through 11 will lay out a policy agenda in far greater detail, but for now, the unifying theme is (perhaps unsurprisingly) to focus directly on workers themselves. Most directly, we can work to ensure that everyone benefits from changes in the economy that increase GDP. The tax system provides a powerful tool for achieving this end. By lowering tax burdens for those lower in the income distribution, and providing refundable tax credits for the least well-off, the tax system can help most Americans benefit from periods of economic growth. These tax policies are easily available to those with the political will to implement them.

At the same time, workers can be better prepared to compete in the world economy, and to use technological change to their advantage, if we invest in education. Educated workers make computers their assistants rather than their rivals. Good public infrastructure is another essential ingredient for making US workers productive. While some of these solutions take time to work, they are fundamentally important. In the meantime, workers who experience disruption can be supported by trade adjustment assistance (to help compensate workers for job loss caused by foreign competition), wage insurance (to support worker wages if they transition to lower paying jobs), and refundable tax credits (to boost worker wages at low incomes). Changes in labor laws and social norms also have roles to play in the ideal policy response to these important economic trends.

One key question remains. Absent the political will to help workers, are the gains from international trade still worth the losses? It is simple to show that the benefits from international trade exceed the losses overall, but it is also clear that some individuals will be harmed by trade. If the losers from trade are not compensated (because it is politically unpalatable to do so), is trade still worth the trouble?

While this question is more difficult to answer, there are some important insights to remember. First, we have the luxury of this debate in the United States, but for many countries, going without trade is not an option. They are simply too small to be self-sufficient. Second, there is no evidence that international trade is solely responsible, or even primarily responsible, for the labor market hardship of many workers. Many other factors, such as technological change, but also rents, market power, and evolving social norms and institutions, are all important. If we restrict trade in response, it is unlikely to make much of a dent in these larger labor market problems, but we will surely lose some of the gains from trade. Third, there is important evidence that trade produces many benefits—for export industries and their workers, for consumers (especially those of limited means), for international relations, and for the growth and stability of other nations. These are hardly inconsequential.

Trade agreements have been wrongly accused of creating worrisome labor market problems, but the fact is that such agreements can be part of the solution, offering policy responses to these developments. How? First, trade agreements should always take care to liberalize trade slowly, to slow the pace of economic disruption. (This, however, is not typically an issue for the United States, where trade barriers are already quite low.) Second, trade agreements can help promote workers' interests by containing provisions that support core labor rights and encourage the bargaining power of labor, as TPP attempted to do. By undertaking joint agreements on such matters, countries reduce the competitive pressures on governments to provide lax regulatory environments to attract mobile businesses. Third, trade agreements can be used as levers to help solve other international collective action problems, such as those related to climate change and tax competition. Given all the ways that international agreements can be a force for good, it is ironic (if understandable) that they have been so vilified in the public discourse.

Increasing income inequality amidst wage stagnation is the defining economic problem of our era. Responding is a challenge, but it is important to avoid responding in a simplistic manner that would harm ourselves and others. Trade restrictions are the wrong answer.

III

International Capital
and International Labor

The previous part of this book (Chapters 3 to 5) discussed the role of international trade in the American economy. While international trade can have serious downsides, trade provides great benefits to the American middle class, and therefore protectionist trade policies would harm the very workers they purport to help. There are much better ways to help American workers.

As Chapters 1 and 2 discussed, the economic success of the American middle class is of vital importance. The United States has experienced thirty-five years of middle-class economic stagnation, disappointed expectations, and increased income inequality. Chapters 9 to 12 of the book will discuss better ways to help American households, describing policy solutions that go *directly* to the problems of economic inequality and wage stagnation.

In this section of the book, Chapters 6 to 8 consider other aspects of globalization. While Chapters 3 to 5 focused on the movement of goods and services across borders in the form of international trade, Chapters 6 to 8 focus on the movement of capital and labor across borders. Chapters 6 discusses the international movement of financial capital (investments in stocks, bonds, and loans), Chapter 7 discusses the international movement of business activity by multinational corporations and offshoring, and Chapter 8 focuses on the movement of international labor through immigration.

Chapter 6 begins by considering international borrowing and lending. It turns out that international borrowing and lending are the root cause (and mirror image) of trade deficits and surpluses. Countries like the United States run trade deficits because they are spending more than they earn, borrowing the difference from abroad.

Six

Who's Afraid of the Trade Deficit?

There is some confusion about the US trade deficit. Politicians and reporters often breathlessly announce changes in the trade deficit to the public as if these trends were the gauge of the country's economic health. Yet in recent years, the trade deficit has shrunk when the economy did poorly, and increased when the economy did well. It turns out this is no mere coincidence. A country's trade deficit is simply not a good measure of its success or "competitiveness" vis-à-vis other nations. It is a phenomenon that solely reflects a country's savings tendencies, both private and public. This chapter will explain the origins of trade deficits and surpluses, and consider how they are influenced (and not influenced) by government policies. It will argue that reducing the trade deficit should not be a primary objective of US economic policy. At the same time, if we nonetheless insist on that goal, the most effective tools for trimming the trade deficit would be policies that address national savings, and in particular, steps that rein in budget deficits.

What Causes Trade Deficits?

The trade deficit is the difference between a country's exports and its imports. This chapter will make use of the terms *trade deficit* and *current account deficit* interchangeably; the latter is a broader, but closely related, concept.[1] In recent decades, the

United States has run a trade deficit in almost every year. However, as is quickly apparent from Figure 6.1, the years when the trade deficit was the largest are not the "worst" years in terms of the economy; in fact, recessions are associated with improvements in the trade deficit. (US recessions occurred in 1981–1982, 1990–1991, 2001, and 2007–2009.) For example, note the sharp reduction in the trade deficit in the wake of the 2008 financial crisis that ushered in the Great Recession. If reducing the trade deficit were the only goal, it appears that a recession would be the quickest way to achieve it!

Why do trade deficits improve in such circumstances? It is not because our businesses suddenly become more competitive than their rivals abroad—even if we could define which businesses are truly "ours" in an era of multinational corporations (a point we explore in the next chapter). Instead, the trade deficit becomes smaller because our demand for imported goods falls when US incomes fall, and that affects our trade balance, which is the amount of US exports minus US imports. Yet, to understand the roots of this link between the trade deficit and the economy, we need to step back a bit and ask why some countries run trade deficits and others run trade surpluses.

The origin of a country's trade balance is the imbalance between its savings and its investments, not the competitiveness of its goods or businesses. A country that invests more money than it saves, or whose government spends more money than it collects in taxes, must get the extra money for investment and government spending from somewhere, and it does this by borrowing from abroad. This borrowing is the mirror of the trade deficit; borrowing pays for the goods and services that are not produced at home.

Figure 6.1. Current Account Balances Do Not Indicate Economic Strength

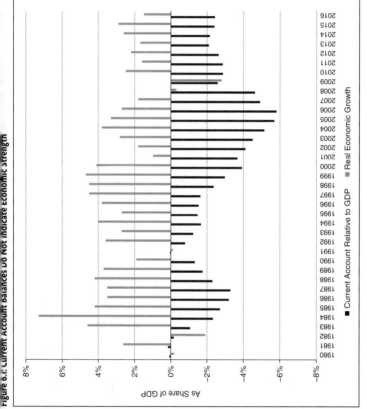

■ Current Account Relative to GDP   ■ Real Economic Growth

Note: As noted in the text, the current account is a closely related measure to the trade deficit.
Data source: Bureau of Economic Analysis.

Figure 6.2: Global Capital Markets Add Funds to the US Economy

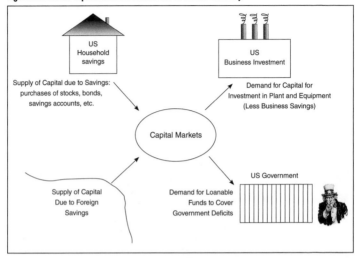

Some countries, including the United States, don't save nearly as much as they invest, and they also tend to run government budget deficits, the public equivalent of spending more than you earn. Together, these factors explain why the United States persistently borrows from abroad. Doing so allows us to consume a bit more than we are producing—lately, about 2.5 percent of GDP more. In contrast, countries such as China and Germany have higher savings relative to their investment desires, and have government budgets that are more balanced. As a consequence, they more often run surpluses.

Simply put, international financial flows (in the form of borrowing and lending) and international goods flows (in the form of exports and imports) are mirror images of each other. Countries that borrow, spending more than they earn, also import more than they export by the same amount. Countries that lend, spending less than they earn, also export more than they import, symmetrically (fig. 6.3).

The Simple Truth about Trade Deficits: It's All about Savings

Basic arithmetic, not abstract theory, explains why the trade deficit must be a straightforward result of two imbalances: that between private savings and investment and that between public taxation and government spending.

GDP (indicated here by the variable Y) measures the value added produced in a given economy in a given year; each year, government economists calculate this figure. It is the sum of expenditures by consumers (designated by C), companies investing (I, which includes new housing), the government's consumption spending (G), and foreign consumers buying American products (exports, EX), removing US spending on foreign products (imports, IM).

Thus, $Y = C + I + G + (EX-IM)$.

But consumption (C) is simply the amount of national income (Y) that is not saved (S) or paid to the government in taxes (T).

So $C = Y-T-S$.

If we plug the equation for C into the equation for Y, we find that:

$Y = Y-T-S + I + G + (EX-IM)$.

Rearranging, we find that the trade deficit is simply the sum of two other imbalances: the imbalance of savings and

> investment and the imbalance between taxation and government spending.
>
> $(EX–IM) = (S–I) + (T–G).$
>
> This simple equation is an accounting fact, not a theory, so it must hold. These facts are insightful explanations of why some countries run deficits and other countries run surpluses. Simply put, countries that save a lot relative to their use of loanable funds (investment) run trade surpluses, and countries that save little relative to their use of loanable funds run trade deficits.

What Policies Affect the Trade Deficit?

One interesting feature of this arithmetic is that it shows that trade deficits are not an outcome of how competitive our firms are. Nor do trade deficits depend on subtle trade policies. Imagine, for example, that we implemented a prohibitive tariff on Chinese steel as part of a trade dispute, and Chinese steel imports stopped entirely.[2] It is unlikely that the trade deficit would improve accordingly. First, we might simply import the steel from another country, perhaps at a higher price, which could *worsen* our trade deficit. Second, it is possible that our exports would fall, if foreign countries retaliated by pursuing similar trade policy actions of their own. Third, and crucially, the trade balance cannot improve unless there are associated changes in savings, investment, government spending, or tax revenue. It is not immediately clear that either private or public

Figure 6.3: Countries with Trade Surpluses Save a Lot; Those with Deficits Don't

China Has a Current Account Surplus.

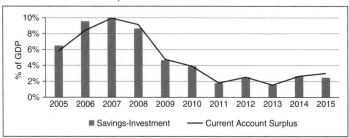

And So Does Germany.

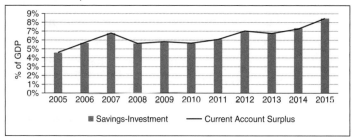

The United States Has a Current Account Deficit.

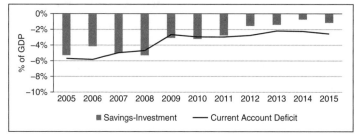

And So Does the United Kingdom

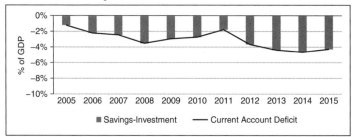

Data source: World Bank.

savings should increase. People and firms will not want to save more simply because Chinese steel has become inaccessible, and government policy-makers are unlikely to change budget balances in response. Even if investment fell as steel became more expensive, it is not clear that this would be a desirable outcome, since investment is the variable most positively associated with economic growth.[3] More likely, though, investment decisions would be unchanged by the revision in trade policy.

Indeed, countries with more trade barriers do not have smaller trade deficits than countries with fewer trade barriers. If anything, countries with higher tariffs have larger trade (current account) deficits (fig. 6.4).

Some suggest that, if the United States wants to reduce its trade deficit, it should pay more attention to the value of the US dollar in international markets. However, most major economies—the Eurozone (as a whole), Japan, the United Kingdom, Australia, Canada, and the United States—have floating exchange rates. In other words, the sellers and buyers of currency determine the value of exchange rates in the foreign currency markets, leaving little room for the Federal Reserve and other central banks to affect exchange rates in these countries. This is likely for the best, since monetary policy (the actions of the central bank) can then be devoted to more useful ends, like working to counter recessions.

The fact that other countries, including China and Switzerland, have managed exchange rate systems causes some observers to suggest that the US government take more active measures to deter foreign currency manipulation. To be sure, there are arguments for discouraging foreign currency

Figure 6.4: Protection Doesn't Help the Trade Balance

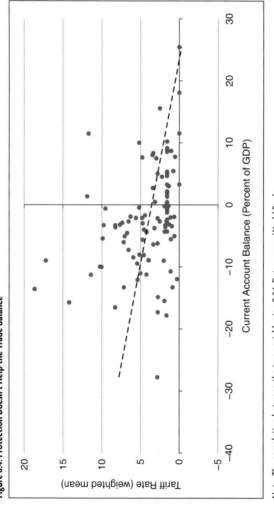

Note: The correlation between the two variables is –0.34. Data source: World Bank.

manipulation. Interestingly, however, China's latest currency interventions have actually been aimed at keeping the Chinese currency's value higher, not lower—and have thus reduced the competitiveness of Chinese exports![4]

If US government actors really want to improve the country's trade deficit, a more direct route would be to address the government's budget shortfalls. Any improvements in the matching of annual tax revenues to government expenditures should also improve the trade balance, assuming that private savings and investment decisions remain unchanged. When the government borrows less money, our national borrowing is less, and the United States as a whole comes closer to spending what we earn, shrinking both international borrowing, and the mirrored trade deficit, accordingly.

Other options for improving the trade deficit are far less appealing. We could take various policy actions to curtail investment (or plunge into recession), but this would be very bad for economic growth. We could attempt to boost private savings with tax incentives, as with today's 529 plans for tax-preferred college savings or 401(k) plans for tax-preferred retirement savings.[5] But doing this has had little overall effect in the past; savings tend to shift toward the tax-advantaged investment choices, but the level of private savings does not rise in aggregate. Further, any increase in private savings caused by tax breaks is likely offset by reductions in public savings, since tax incentives decrease tax revenues—and therefore drive up the budget deficit.

Is China a Currency Manipulator?

China frequently intervenes in their exchange rate market, and in past years, especially the period leading up to 2007, the Chinese currency was artificially undervalued as a result. While the undervalued Chinese currency fueled an export boom that helped lift hundreds of millions of Chinese out of poverty, their currency policy also fueled very large Chinese current account surpluses in the mid 2000s, adding to the US current account deficit in the process. Yet while these actions were important in the past, since 2014, China has often intervened to *increase* the value of their currency, thus reducing Chinese surpluses and other countries' deficits. China's current account surplus is far more modest than it was a decade ago.

Often, other countries intervene to increase, rather than lower, the value of their currencies. At several times in the past, the Mexican peso was overvalued, and Mexico tends to run a trade deficit with the rest of the world. (Although Mexico has a bilateral surplus with the United States at present.)

While currency manipulation might become a subject of future trade agreements, most countries target other goals (aside from the trade balance) when they set their monetary (and currency) policies, aiming for low unemployment, low inflation, and foreign debt sustainability. And at present, currency policy is small potatoes (and may even be helpful) when it comes to United States international balances.

Should We Even Care About the Trade Deficit?

So far we've seen that trade deficits are caused by imbalances in private and public savings and investment, and that the countries running trade deficits do so because their savings and tax revenues fall short of their investment and government spending, causing international borrowing, which is the mirror of the trade deficit. As a society, we are simply spending more than we earn, so our imports must exceed our exports accordingly. Therefore, protectionist trade policies are futile when it comes to affecting trade imbalances, since they do not affect their underlying causes. Government budget balances, meanwhile, have a direct effect on international borrowing and the trade deficit.

But one question remains unanswered. Should we even care about the size of the trade deficit and, therefore, aim to correct it with policy?

There are several reasons why running a trade deficit may actually be a wise thing to do. In the case of the United States, we have many investment opportunities due to our vibrant and entrepreneurial economy. Yet our citizens have notoriously low savings rates and are known instead for being world-class consumers. If the United States did not borrow on worldwide capital markets, interest rates would be higher, and fewer US investment opportunities would be possible. The US capital stock (plant and equipment) would be lower, and economic growth and living standards would also suffer, since investment is an important ingredient in raising worker productivity. Thus, international borrowing plays a vital role in the US economy.

Seen from the other side, the countries who run trade surpluses are also helped by engaging in international lending. In China and Germany, for example, there are ample savings but fewer investment opportunities (relative to their savings). By loaning money to other countries, they can secure higher returns for savers than they would earn by keeping their money in the domestic economy. Much like trade in goods, trade in financial capital (borrowing and lending) allows both nations to gain by following their comparative advantage. Impatient countries like the United States borrow at lower interest rates than they would experience without world capital markets, while patient countries like Germany save, earning higher interest rates then they would experience without world capital markets. Both countries can benefit.

However, from a borrowing country's perspective, there are still reasons to worry. Foremost among them is, of course, that the borrowed money must eventually be paid back; this will entail some subsequent period of lower spending relative to output in the future. Further, since financial markets can be abrupt in their determinations of whether assets are good investments, this can subject borrowing countries to excessively rapid swings from deficit to surplus. These rapid swings can create sudden changes in the exchange rate, even leading to deep recessions, with the associated misery of unemployment. Rapid reversals can also shift the allocation of the economy's resources across sectors too abruptly, creating large transition problems.

There are also less obvious dangers associated with running trade deficits. They likely change the composition of jobs in the economy, even if they do not change the total number of jobs.

A Modern Greek Tragedy

In 2007, the current account deficit in Greece was an astonishing 14 percent of GDP. In part due to its adoption of the euro in 2001, investors had initially been eager to loan to the Greek economy by buying Greek bonds and other financial assets. With euro adoption, there was no longer exchange-rate risk associated with Greek loans, and the Greek economy was booming after twenty straight years of economic growth.

When that boom turned to bust, however, investors soured on the Greek economy, and refused to loan additional funds to the country. The absence of a Greek currency with its own exchange rate did not help; Greece could no longer adjust its currency (formerly the drachma) downward to make Greek assets more attractive to buyers. Instead, Greece faced a solvency crisis, defaulted on its debts, and turned to the international community for repeated bailouts. The outcome in Greece has been tragic. Unemployment rates, which had dipped below 8 percent before the crisis, shot up to over 27 percent by 2013, and have remained over 20 percent for more than six years, causing riots and political turmoil. And while the current account did improve—even turning to a surplus in 2015—the rapid changing of the tides made for anything but smooth sailing.

Chapter 3 described how, when the economy is at full employment, international trade does not affect the total number of jobs, but it does affect their allocation, by adding jobs in export industries (such as airplanes, software, and soybeans) and taking jobs away from import industries (including shoes, clothing, and steel).

In a similar way, trade deficits affect job types. Economies running trade deficits produce less than they consume, borrowing the remainder from abroad. But there are some products (haircuts, restaurant meals, childcare, education, massages) that are difficult or impossible to replace with imports; these goods are *nontraded* goods. Goods are nontraded if there are prohibitively high transportation costs associated with moving them across borders. Few people would travel to India or Mexico for their haircuts, even if they are less expensive abroad! So, even if a country is borrowing from abroad to consume more than they produce, they cannot import the extra haircuts and restaurant meals. Therefore, in countries running persistent trade deficits, the nontraded goods sector must expand relative to the traded goods sector. This changes the types of jobs in the economy.

This also implies that transitions from trade deficits to trade surpluses will entail reallocations of workers and resources away from the nontraded goods sector toward the traded goods sector. This could cause temporary unemployment of barbers, waiters, construction workers, and others. Due to the serious pain associated with making such transitions quickly, it is ideal for countries to make more gradual changes in the size of their international imbalances. Sound financial regulation can help reduce the risk associated with rapid reversals, by making sure that capital inflows are directed toward productive investments rather than speculative ones.

All that said, there is *no* relationship between the trade deficit and the *total* number of jobs, or the unemployment rate. As seen in the figure at the beginning of the chapter, the trade deficit is typically the most negative when the economy is strong, and unemployment rates are low. The recessions that cause higher unemployment also improve the trade deficit through lower spending, and thus fewer imports.

Is the US Trade Deficit Sustainable?

International borrowing and lending can make both countries better off, and international borrowing benefits the United States by allowing us to borrow at lower interest rates, increasing capital investment, worker productivity, and standards of living. Yet countries that borrow do have to pay back their borrowed funds eventually, and rapid transitions from deficit to surplus can be quite painful. In the case of the United States, crucial questions arise. Is our trade deficit sustainable at current levels? Do we face an abrupt transition at some future time, and if so, how do we manage that risk?

Observers worried that the US economy was approaching an unsustainably large trade deficit in 2006, when the current account deficit approached 6 percent of GDP. As it turns out, the trade deficit came down rapidly in the years following, due to the Great Recession. But there are still reasons to suspect that a large deficit might be more sustainable for the United States than many countries. First, the United States is home to a disproportionate share of the world's marketable securities and financial instruments. As such, it attracts a disproportionate share of global savings, in comparison to our share of world GDP. This makes it easier for the United States to finance our trade deficits by borrowing from abroad.

Second, when a country's trade deficit becomes unsustainable, participants in international capital markets become more reluctant to loan money to the country. This reduced demand for the debtor country's assets will reduce the demand for the debtor country's currency, causing it to depreciate. (The depreciation prevents capital inflows from drying up, since it makes assets more attractive to foreign buyers.) This process can be destabilizing for countries that borrow in foreign currency since the value of their debt repayments increases as their currency depreciates. However, virtually all US borrowing is denominated in US dollars, so currency depreciation is less troublesome for the United States.

Third, the importance of the US dollar in world financial markets, and our floating (market-determined) exchange rate, make it more likely that future transitions from deficit to surplus, or to smaller deficits, will be relatively smooth. Since we are not intervening in currency markets to alter the value of the dollar, we do not need to worry about dramatic, sudden depreciations of our currency (which sometimes happen if countries can no longer "defend" their choice of exchange rate under managed currency systems). If investors decide US assets are less safe or rewarding then they were previously, dollar depreciation will follow, but not in a sudden, crashing way, assuming the fundamentals of the US economy are not dramatically altered. (A default on US debt, or a dramatic large-scale international conflict, could change that assessment.)

Finally, the net international investment position (which measures the difference between foreign-owned US assets and US-owned foreign assets) of the United States has not been deteriorating rapidly. The total amount that Americans owe foreigners is a relatively modest share of GDP, about 40 percent at present. Thus, the real burden of repayment should not be excessive.

All of that said, it is still important to rely on sound financial regulation to ensure that our financial system is channeling funds toward productive investments.[6] Making sure that financial institutions are adequately capitalized and not "too big to fail," paying attention to risks associated with the parts of the financial system that are less subject to regulation (the "shadow" banking sector), and reducing the distortions that encourage excessive leverage in the economy are all important steps toward reducing financial frailty in times of economic stress.

In summary, the trade deficit is the flip side of international capital mobility; when a country imports more than they export, they also borrow to make up the difference. Countries with trade deficits borrow funds that are paid back in the future. While the benefits of international borrowing and lending are similar to the benefits of international trade, there are also dangers and vulnerabilities that result from international borrowing and lending.

There are different ways to view the US trade deficit. Spending more than we earn does not seem like a good thing, but our international borrowing also reflects the strength of US investment opportunities. Absent international borrowing, our economy would have fewer funds for productive investment. Further, the last several years have shown relatively

Trump and the Trade Deficit

At numerous points in the 2016 presidential campaign, candidate Trump pledged to decrease the US trade deficit, and as president, Trump has continued to place trade deficit reduction at the center of US trade policy, often focusing in particular on bilateral trade deficits.[1]

Bilateral trade balances are a particularly silly target for U.S. trade policy, since they are shaped by comparative advantage in a way that is perfectly natural. Simply put, the countries that provide our desired imports (for example, oil) may not coincidentally happen to be the same countries that desire our exports (for example, aircraft). Moreover, bilateral trade data are inherently flawed, since internationally sourced components are not separately measured. For example, if China imports computer parts from Singapore, assembles a computer, and then sells it to the United States, the entire product will show up as a US import from China, even if most of the import's value was supplied by Singapore.

Even if the focus is the overall trade deficit, as this chapter explains, trade policies are likely to have no effect. For example, bowing out of the Trans-Pacific Partnership may change the pattern of trade between different countries

---

1. For example, in the administration's July 2017 articulation of objections for the renegotiation of NAFTA, the paramount objective with respect to trade was to "improve the US trade balance and reduce the trade deficit with NAFTA countries." See Office of the US Trade Representative, "Summary of Objectives for the NAFTA Renegotiation," Report, July 17, 2017.

without changing the overall levels of US imports and exports. Similarly, tariffs on products from particular trading partners can lead to more expensive imports from other countries, as well as reduced exports due to retaliatory actions abroad. Importantly, none of these trade policies affect the fundamental macroeconomic factors (savings, investment, and the budget balance) that drive countries' trade balances.

However, it is likely that the broader economic policies of the Trump administration and Congress affect the trade deficit in important ways, through the savings imbalance channels above. In particular, the Administration and the majority in Congress have enacted tax law changes that dramatically increase the size of the budget deficit. According to the Congressional Budget Office, these tax law changes add $1.8 trillion to deficits over the coming decade.[2] These increasing budget deficits will worsen, rather than improve, the trade deficit.

In short, the Administration's trade policies will likely have little effect on the trade deficit, and its budget policies are likely to make it worse. If Trump truly cares about the trade deficit, he should focus on fiscal discipline, lowering the budget deficit.

---

2. $300 billion of this total is due to additional debt service because of the additional borrowing due to lower tax revenues. See Congressional Budget Office, "Estimated Deficits and Debt under the Conference Agreement of H.R. 1," January 2, 2018, https://www.cbo.gov/publication/53437.

modest US trade imbalances, so it is likely that the United States is on a sustainable path. Reducing trade deficits should not be an urgent policy priority at present. And, a focus on *bilateral* trade deficits is even more misguided.

If policy-makers insist on making the *overall* trade deficit a goal, however, one thing is clear. To reduce the trade deficit, trade policy interventions do more harm than good, both in terms of reducing the gains from trade and in terms of their ineffectiveness in addressing the trade deficit. A more straightforward policy to reduce the trade deficit would be to focus on the budget deficit. The budget deficit is within the control of the federal government, and it has an important causal effect on the trade deficit.

Seven

Multinational Corporations

Globalization is not just about the cross-border flows of goods, services, and financial capital discussed in Chapters 3 through 6. It is also about international business, and the wide reach, large size, and market power of the world's global companies. Of course, multinational corporations are hardly a new phenomenon. Important international companies with market power have been around at least since the days of the Hudson Bay and East India trading companies.[1] But in recent decades, the scale and sweep of the world's largest corporations have increased dramatically.

This chapter first describes the phenomenon of multinational corporations. Multinational companies are (typically) headquartered in one country, but their operations span many countries. Parent companies, and their affiliate children throughout the world, are both big players in the world economy, undertaking the vast majority of all international trade. Global companies are typically the most successful and innovative companies in the world, and their global production processes achieve staggering efficiencies.

The international mobility of global corporations creates important challenges for government policy-makers, workers, and citizens. How can national governments tax and regulate companies that span international borders? How do laborers retain bargaining power in negotiations with employers that are more agile than they are? How do consumers make sure that the market power of these global corporations does not work against their interests? This chapter ends by discussing how economic policy can be modernized to address these concerns regarding global businesses, while still fostering a strong and successful business environment.

The Growing Importance of International Business

The scale and importance of international business activity has increased over recent decades. Global foreign direct investment—a measure of multinational company business investment—slowed during the Great Recession and its aftermath, but the importance of global firms is as great as it has been at any point in recent history (fig. 7.1).

The difference between foreign direct investment and the international capital mobility discussed in Chapter 6 is captured by the word *direct*. The purpose of such investment is to maintain direct control over a foreign asset, rather than just earn returns from it. If Apple invests in an Irish subsidiary, for example, the American "parent" company owns and controls the Irish affiliate, Apple Ireland—whereas if I buy a share of Diageo, the UK-based multinational corporation that produces Guinness beer, I do not control this company; I only receive dividends (and capital gains) from its profits.

In the United States, multinational corporations contribute mightily to the national economy as sources of both outward and inward foreign direct investment. The country is home to some of the world's largest and most important global companies, whose affiliates operate throughout the globe, and it also hosts many affiliates of foreign-headquartered

Figure 7.1: Stocks of Foreign Direct Investment (In or Out) Are Growing

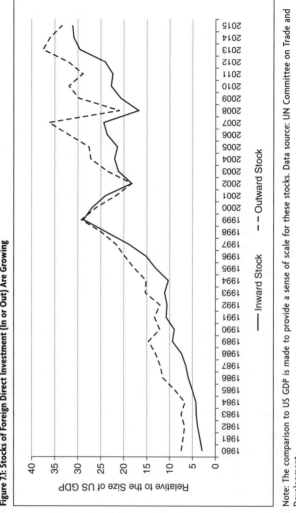

Note: The comparison to US GDP is made to provide a sense of scale for these stocks. Data source: UN Committee on Trade and Development.

multinational companies. Currently, stocks of foreign direct investment (the market value of all foreign investments) are quite large, equivalent in size to about one-third of US GDP.

For the United States, the scale of operations of foreign affiliates is far larger than the scale of international trade. Sales of goods and services by the affiliate "children" of US parent companies abroad were $7.4 trillion in 2014, an amount 43 percent of the size of US GDP, and much higher than US exports, which were $2.4 trillion in 2014. In the opposite direction, sales of US affiliates of foreign parent multinational companies were $4.4 trillion in 2014, an amount 25 percent the size of US GDP; in comparison, US imports were $2.9 trillion in 2014.[2]

Multinational Firms Control Most International Trade

Multinational companies play a prominent role in the broader globalization story. The scale of their operations is much larger than the size of international trade, and beyond that, multinational companies themselves conduct the vast majority of international trade. In 2014, US parent multinational companies exported $314 billion to their affiliates abroad and $488 billion to unaffiliated entities, accounting for 49 percent of that year's goods exports; the same companies also accounted for 39 percent of US goods imports. Foreign multinational companies are also big traders. In 2014, the US affiliates of foreign-headquartered multinational companies accounted for 30 percent of all US imports and 26 percent of all US exports.[3]

Global firms tend to be systematically different from domestic firms. They are larger and have more market power; they are more productive and grow faster; they have broader

Figure 7.2: Multinational Companies Do the Vast Majority of All US Trade

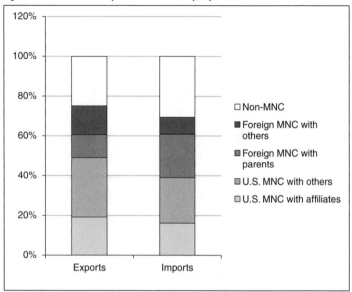

Note: Data are for 2014, the most recent year with data available. Data source: US Bureau of Economic Analysis.

international supply networks, and are often both the world's largest importers and the world's largest exporters.[4] Looking at the list of the top 1 percent of US exporting companies, 36 percent of them also appear among the top 1 percent of US importers. Of the companies on the list of top importers, 53 percent are also top exporters (fig 7.3).

These facts have profound implications for the consequences of protectionist trade policies. Even if it were desirable to encourage exports and discourage imports, which Chapters 3 and 5 argue against, protectionist policies are likely to hurt the very same firms that they help, while simultaneously raising consumer prices and creating adjustment costs for the larger economy.

Figure 7.3: The Top US Exporters and Importers Are One and the Same

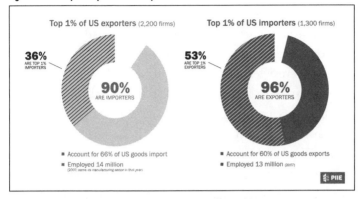

Source: J. Bradford Jensen, "Importers Are Exporters: Tariffs Would Hurt Our Most Competitive Firms." Peterson Institute for International Economics. December, 2016. Reprinted with permission from Peterson Institute for International Economics.

Who Are They? Who Is Us?

Multinational corporations also confuse questions regarding companies' nationality. Indeed, the most global companies act as if they have *no* nationality, as they spread their activities throughout the globe. In some cases, companies even split their headquarters activities across multiple nations.[5] The very definition of a headquarters has been muddied: is it where the company's stock is listed, where the company's tax residence is, or where the company's management and control take place? And what if management and control are scattered around the globe?

As Chapter 3 discussed, the production processes of many goods have become increasingly globalized, due to technological advances and the increased openness of many countries to international trade. Multinational companies use international supply chains to produce a single product across multiple countries. Boeing 787 airplanes are made up of complex parts sourced from the United Kingdom, Japan, Sweden, Australia, Canada, Korea, France, Italy, and elsewhere.

If one were determined to alter the US trade balance through one's car purchase, it wouldn't be immediately clear how to do so. Is it better to buy a Ford car that was designed in Michigan and assembled in Mexico with parts from Canada, Japan, Ohio, and China? Or a Japanese car that was designed in Japan and built in Ohio, also with parts from many countries? A 2011 analysis finds that the Ford Fusion has 20 percent American parts and the Honda Accord has 80 percent American parts, despite the fact that Ford is an American car company and Honda a Japanese one.[6]

While it is possible for a car buyer with nationalistic inclinations to find a content label listing the countries from which the largest sources of value originated, many other consumer products present a deeper mystery. One country of origin is stamped on the product, yet given globally fragmented production processes, it might not be the country where the majority of the product's value was created. For example, iPhones imported from China have far more American than Chinese content. This can make trade data misleading, since such data capture the full prices of goods as they cross borders, not merely the value added in the sending country. A value-added measure of trade would make the US trade deficit with China far smaller.[7]

The Benefits of Large Global Firms

Multinational businesses come with tremendous advantages for both workers and consumers, and these are important to acknowledge before we turn to the policy challenges surrounding them. First, global corporations may heighten competition in many markets. When foreign firms enter the US market, or when US firms enter foreign markets, competition increases and domestic firms lose market power. Many countries of the world are far smaller than the United States, and these competitive effects may be especially important for them. Imagine if a country the size of Norway or Costa Rica had to rely on domestic firms for all of their mobile phones or airlines; they would likely be at the mercy of monopoly providers. It is unlikely that the scale of the country would support multiple domestic companies, so the Norwegians and Costa Ricans are better off due to the competitive influence of foreign companies. Even in large countries like the United States, foreign firms often provide useful alternatives to domestic firms. They are also a source of job opportunities, new technologies, and new products.

The world's largest multinational corporations are typically successful for a reason. They make good products, and they spread information, technological progress, and innovation. They also provide variety to customers throughout the world.

For example, the world's most profitable company in 2016 was Apple Computer. The popularity of its products is undeniable. Many consumers enjoy using Apple's shiny, sleek products and shopping in stores that look like glass boxes. The products are famously user-friendly; a preteen can set up computing functions that used to puzzle PhD engineers. Apple's innovative products have inspired its competitors to make

Made in America (Thanks to Italy and Japan)

Jeep workers at the sprawling Toledo Assembly Complex in Ohio are quick to voice their economic patriotism: local efforts to "keep Jeep" in town are just one expression of a fierce loyalty to American products. Over 90 percent of the parts needed to produce fifty thousand Jeeps in Toledo each month are sourced from communities within fifteen hundred miles of the plant. But the ownership of this classic car presents a twist in the quest to "buy American": since 2014, Jeep and its parent company Chrysler have been part of the Fiat family.

After completing its total acquisition of Chrysler, the Italian, London-headquartered Fiat Automobiles became the seventh-largest automaker in the world. Its Jeep Wranglers topped Cars.com's 2017 American Made Index, joined by four Honda-produced vehicles. Six out of the ten "most American" cars (based on the source of their parts) are made by foreign firms. Large foreign involvement in American auto production is part of larger foreign direct investment trends; the United States receives more foreign direct investment than any other country, at $391 billion in 2016. The United States is also the largest source of foreign direct investment, sending $299 billion abroad in the same year.[1]

---

1. See UNCTAD, *World Investment Report 2017* (Geneva: United Nations Conference on Trade and Development, 2017); 2016 is the most recent year with available data.

better, more user-friendly, products. And Apple's concern with maintaining its dominance has kept it ceaselessly seeking out additional ways to please its worldwide customers. Its products have spurred innovation both upstream (to parts suppliers that make their chips and screens) and downstream (as users utilize their devices as inputs to their own production processes).

As it turns out, Apple is also an exceptionally profitable company; its worldwide profits in 2016 were $45 billion. Many of these profits were booked offshore in tax havens. While much corporate tax avoidance is perfectly legal, it does indicate that our tax system is not working as advertised. Profit shifting diverts tax revenue from government treasuries, presenting a big challenge for policy-makers. (The recently enacted U.S. tax legislation, discussed further below, will not solve this problem.)

In short, the large, multinational companies that drive international business generate many benefits. But they also present important policy concerns regarding market power, effects on labor, regulatory competition, and tax competition. The next sections address these four areas of concern.

Concern 1: Multinational Firms are Becoming Larger and More Powerful

The concentration of economic activity in the hands of the largest and most powerful multinational companies has been increasing. McKinsey Global Institute calculates that the top 10 percent of the world's public companies earn 80 percent of the profits. Companies with more than $1 billion in revenues account for 60 percent of revenues and 65 percent of market capitalization.[8]

Two Global Giants on the New Silk Road

The Chinese company Alibaba got its name from the *Arabian Nights* tale of "Ali Baba and the Forty Thieves"; it evokes images of loaded caravans and vast treasure troves. Globally, the name now conjures internet marketplaces rather than souk stalls, but the treasure remains. The Alibaba Group is the largest e-commerce firm in China, and it handles a greater volume of transactions than eBay and Amazon combined. In 2017, the company launched in Singapore, Malaysia, Hong Kong, and Taiwan as part of an effort to reach two billion customers over the next fifteen years. If trends persist, Alibaba's sales will soon exceed the dreams of even the forty thieves; the company's 2016 Singles' Day shopping festival was the biggest one-day retail event ever, hitting gross merchandise volume of $17.7 billion.

Alphabet, Google's parent company, is pursuing knowledge and profit as relentlessly as Alibaba. Much of Google's (and thus, Alphabet's) revenue comes from search advertising. Alphabet controls 88 percent of the search advertising market, and in one recent quarter alone (ending March 2017) it drew profits of $5.43 billion. Big money means big projects, which come under Alphabet's "Other Bets" division: the company has entered the broadband business (Google Fiber), the home automation space (Nest), and the self-driving phenomenon (Waymo and X). For Alphabet and Alibaba, the new Silk Road is made of silicon.

Annually, *Forbes* produces a ranked list of the largest two thousand public companies in the world (based on evaluation of their sales, profits, assets and market value). Comparing these lists reveals the increased profitability of the world's largest companies in recent years. From the 2004 to the 2018 list, combined profits of the top two thousand companies increased over 400 percent, while sales of these companies increased about 200 percent. Although the sales of the top two thousand global firms increased at a rate commensurate with world GDP growth over this period, profits increased much faster—despite the collapse of profits in the years surrounding the Great Recession. By 2017, the *Forbes* Global 2000 collectively made a profit of about $3.2 trillion on $39 trillion in sales.

There is substantial evidence that market concentration is on the rise. In most sectors of the economy, the share of revenues earned by the largest firms is increasing. So are *excess profits*—profits above the normal (market equilibrium) return on capital—which are typically associated with firms' market power. The market returns of the most profitable companies are larger than ever before, rising dramatically relative to those of typical firms (fig. 7.4).[9] In the United States, estimates suggest that excess profits make up three-fourths of total corporate profits.[10]

Concern 2: The Power of Global Companies Creates Downsides for Workers

The multinational nature of large firms, as well as their dominant position, gives them more bargaining power with respect

Figure 7.4: The Most Successful US Companies Pull Away from the Pack

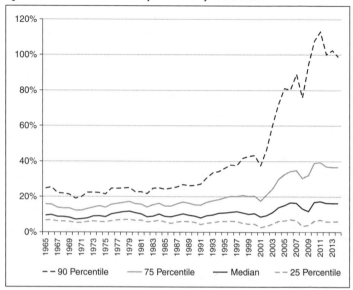

Note: Lines show the performance of US firms in terms of their return on capital invested, excluding goodwill, in percentages. Source: Jason Furman and Peter Orszag, "A Firm-Level Perspective on the Role of Rents in the Rise in Inequality," presented at "A Just Society" Centennial Event in Honor of Joseph Stiglitz, Columbia University, October 16, 2015.

to suppliers, labor, and even governments. Intriguing new research by a team of researchers at MIT, Harvard, and the University of Zurich has established a relationship between the rising market dominance of large companies and the declining labor share of income.[11] They find evidence that technological change increased the concentration of market share in the hands of a small number of companies, and they show that these mega-companies have lower labor shares of income than typical companies. (There are fewer workers relative to other factors of production.) Thus, as the world's largest corporations become more and more dominant, and account for a larger share of national income, the labor share of income falls accordingly, since these companies use fewer workers to produce a given value of output.

Declining labor shares have also been associated with large increases in cash stockpiles by corporations.[12] More and more of worldwide income takes the form of corporate profits and retained earnings, disproportionately held by a small number of highly successful companies. In the United States, corporate profits in recent years are higher as a share of GDP than they have been at any point in the last fifty years, in either before-tax or after-tax terms. Since 1980, corporate profits after tax have increased dramatically, from about 6 percent of GDP to over 9 percent of GDP.[13]

And the cash stockpiles of the world's most successful companies are not necessarily fueling the sorts of investments that ultimately benefit workers by raising their productivity. In fact, greater market concentration has been associated in recent years with lower investment.[14] Many prominent macroeconomists worry about an excess of savings relative to investment—among them, Ben Bernanke, who worries about a "savings glut," and Larry Summers, who is pessimistic about "secular stagnation."[15]

When companies earn outsized returns, this squeezes the returns for other factors of production throughout the economy. Workers in the most successful firms often do just fine, but as more and more of national income accrues to the most successful firms, workers in other companies experience greater competition and lower real wage increases.

David Weil has argued that the workplace is becoming increasingly "fissured" so that non-core tasks (such as janitorial services and payroll processing) are often outsourced to other companies, and even offshored to other countries. These more routine jobs face intense competition; employers with lower profit margins and a labor-intensive product have intense pressure to keep labor costs under control.[16]

The increased market power of the world's largest multinational corporations has important consequences for both efficiency and economic inequality.[17] In terms of efficiency, one can never be certain that companies with market power make economic decisions that are consistent with the social interest; they might squelch innovations by less powerful competitors, or hike prices excessively in the absence of sufficient competitive pressures.

There are also large implications for wealth and income inequality. Among workers, pay disparities are exacerbated by the fact that the most successful companies' workers are more highly compensated. More important are the rents generated by the market power of these companies, which disproportionately accrue to the well-to-do.[18] Company shareholders and executives take the lion's share of the excess profits associated with market power, and capital gains and dividends are far more concentrated in the hands of those at the top than labor income is.[19]

In part due to large corporations' market power, but also due to social norms and tax policy, CEO pay has skyrocketed in recent decades. Since the late 1970s, CEO pay has grown by over 900 percent (in inflation-adjusted dollars), and it now averages $15 million a year. CEO pay is three hundred times that of typical company workers, a ratio that has increased tenfold just since 1980, when CEOs earned thirty times the average salary of their companies' workers.[20]

Concern 3: How Can National Governments Regulate Global Firms?

Supersized global companies raise concerns about harmful effects on consumers due to market power. Still, there are policy tools available to willing governments. Antitrust laws, while made and enforced at the national level, often have global reach. The Federal Trade Commission and the US Justice Department have authority over all companies that wish to operate in the United States, or sell to US consumers, regardless of the nationality of their corporate headquarters.

Similarly, the European Commission has authority over those companies that wish to sell in the European market. Indeed, they have asserted this authority in many high-profile cases. When Boeing and McDonnell Douglas were planning their merger, the Europeans were initially unwilling to allow it, fearing anticompetitive effects on the global commercial aircraft market. (The two companies could have merged anyway, but they would have risked their access to the large and wealthy European market by ignoring the objection.) Only after meeting several preconditions set by the European Commission, including the voiding of previously negotiated long-term contracts with airlines, was the merger allowed to proceed. The Europeans have also challenged the competitive practices of Microsoft, Google, and other major US multinational corporations.

Jurisdictions with large and rich markets, like the United States and the European Union, have the ability to regulate multinational companies, since companies have strong incentives to keep their access to such markets. Smaller countries, like Belgium and Costa Rica, may have less power over large firms. This provides an additional rationale for larger regional agreements like the European Union, beyond the previously noted gains from international trade and smoother international relations. European Union member countries like Belgium have more sway over global companies if they work together as part of a larger, supranational market.

At the same time, given the mobility of international businesses, there are concerns about national governments competing to attract them. For example, if multinational mining companies respond to environmental regulations by forsaking countries with environmental regulations in favor of countries that allow environmentally hazardous production methods, that can lead to a "race to the bottom," where countries try to outdo one another by lowering regulatory burdens and cutting taxes in hopes of winning businesses' favor. Evidence suggests that a race to the bottom may be of particular concern in the case of extractive industries such as oil drilling and mining, especially in developing countries. In the past, this race to attract extractive industries has led to excessive resource depletion and toxic pollution, made all the more painful by disappointing gains in job creation and economic growth.[21]

It is important to note that disparate environmental regulations do not necessarily trigger a race to the bottom. For example, a multinational company that needs to comply with a higher-standard jurisdiction may find it more cost-effective to use one uniform production method throughout its operations. By employing the cleaner production method in lower-standard jurisdictions, it helps to spread cleaner technologies and methods throughout the world. In just this way, higher clean air standards in California caused US automotive companies to improve their environmental performance throughout the entire US market. It was more effi-cient to adopt cleaner technologies for all vehicles sold in US states than to use a more "dirty" technology for less strin-gent states.

Another example concerns global shipping. While it is easy to register a ship in many jurisdictions, and some locations provide options with scant regulation and very low fees, ship-ping standards have nonetheless not collapsed. Ships registered with stricter rules receive benefits that those sailing under "flags of convenience" do not: fewer port detainments, more fish market access, and smoother labor relations with dock workers. This has caused a "race to the middle" in shipping standards, as low-standard registries have raised their stan-dards to give registered ships the same benefits.[22]

Concern 4: Can National Governments Tax Global Firms?

The possibility of a race to the bottom in corporate tax policy is also a very real concern. In response to the mobility of mul-tinational corporate investment, many governments have sought to create more attractive tax environments to lure in-vestments, jobs, and tax revenues to their jurisdiction. These efforts have led to steady declines in corporate tax rates in re-cent decades (fig. 7.5).

Despite the declining tax rates, corporate revenues have been relatively flat in many peer countries, leading some to sus-pect that tax competition is not a concern. However, it is important to remember the very large rise in corporate profits over this period, which would otherwise imply that corporate tax revenues should be increasing.

Figure 7.5: Corporate Tax Rates Are Falling Across Peer Countries

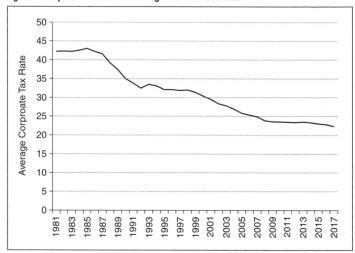

Note: The figure shows the average OECD-country corporate tax rate at the central government level. Data source: OECD Statistics.

While there is evidence that investment and employment are sensitive to tax rate differences among countries, their responsiveness to favorable tax environments is far less than the responsiveness of the corporate tax base itself. For US multinational corporations, the location of economic activity across countries is primarily determined by the sorts of factors that should matter: market size, customer purchasing power, educated workforces, and well-functioning institutions.[23] For example, when looking at where U.S. multinationals locate jobs, whether measured in terms of payroll or job headcount, the biggest markets in the world are the ones that attract activity (fig. 7.6).

Countries like the United Kingdom, Canada, Germany, and China are economic powerhouses; it is not surprising that they

Figure 7.6: Where Are the Jobs for US Multinationals? The Usual Suspects: Big Markets

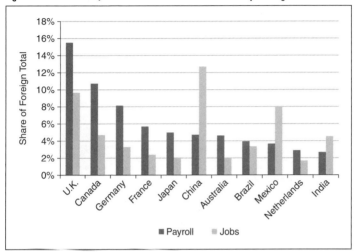

Note: Calculations are based on data for US multinational companies. This figure shows the eleven countries with the biggest job and payroll shares. Data are for 2014, the most recent year with available data. Data source: US Bureau of Economic Analysis.

attract substantial US multinational activity. For similar reasons, the United States has also, in recent years, received more foreign direct investment than it has sent abroad.

When it comes to the distribution of the corporate tax base, however, US multinational companies are extremely tax-sensitive. Over half of all foreign profits are earned in just seven tax havens with effective tax rates under 5 percent: the Netherlands, Luxembourg, Ireland, Bermuda, the Cayman Islands, Switzerland, and Singapore. These countries have a combined population smaller than that of California. Of the top ten affiliate-profit countries, only three (the solid bars in Figure 7.7) are not tax havens.

How is it that a country the size of Bermuda, with a population of about 65,000—roughly the same size as the student

Figure 7.7: Where Do US Multinationals Book Their Profits? Tax Havens

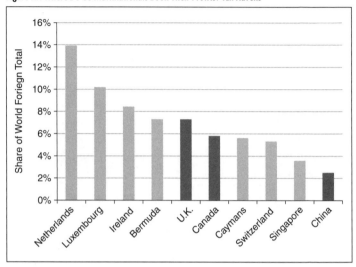

Note: Calculations are based on data for US multinational companies. This figure shows the ten countries with the biggest income shares. Data are for 2014, the most recent year with available data. Data source: US Bureau of Economic Analysis.

body of Ohio State University—ends up with $94 billion in profits, representing 7 percent of all foreign profits of US multinational firms, and about $1.5 million per resident?[24] The profits of US multinational affiliates in Bermuda are sixteen times the size of Bermuda's economy.[25] It is simply implausible that such profits were truly "earned" in Bermuda; instead, they were shifted to Bermuda for tax purposes, since Bermuda has a 0 percent corporate tax rate. Similarly implausible levels of profits are reported in the other tax havens on the list: the Cayman Islands, Luxembourg, the Netherlands, Switzerland, Singapore, and Ireland.

Multinational corporations shift profits abroad through a variety of mechanisms. For example, they can underprice goods sold from high-tax affiliates to low-tax affiliates, and overprice goods sold from low-tax affiliates to high-tax affili-ates; this makes the low-tax affiliates appear more profitable.[26] They can also transfer intellectual property to affiliates in tax havens through cost-sharing agreements or other mechanisms; the profits from utilizing the intellectual property then accrue in the haven jurisdiction. Another method is to change the structure of financing across a company's affiliates such that the high-tax affiliates have more interest deductions and the low-tax affiliates have more interest earnings. Finally, compli-cated chains of ownership and hybrid corporate structures can be used to create income that goes untaxed in *any* jurisdiction; recent press accounts have described many instances of com-panies creating "stateless income" using such techniques.[27]

In my research, I find that profit shifting by multinational corporations is a large and pervasive problem, costing the US government over $100 billion per year at present, and other governments collectively about $200 billion per year.[28] Cor-porate tax base erosion has not gone unnoticed by govern-ments, the press, and the international non-governmental organization (NGO) community. One response was the re-cent "Base Erosion and Profit Shifting Project" of the OECD and G20 countries, which produced nearly two thousand pages of suggested guidelines for governments seeking to stem the profit shifting problem. While this attempt to tackle tax avoidance should be commended, it is unclear that these efforts will be enough to stop tax base erosion. A more sys-tematic overhaul of company taxation is likely necessary. Below, I suggest how we might modernize the US tax system to make it more suited to the global economy.

Modernizing Economic Policy in a World of Global Companies

Multinational corporations are successful in generating value, innovation, and activity, often to the benefit of larger society. Yet international business also creates policy concerns in the four areas just discussed. This section will consider ways to modernize economic policy to adapt to the sophistication and international mobility of today's global companies.

Many useful policy responses are unilateral; as the next section will show, they do not require cooperation with other countries. But other good policy responses involve combined efforts. For example, international agreements can help governments counter the pressures of policy competition. By agreeing on frameworks of core labor and environmental standards, and by working together to stem tax base erosion and tax competition, countries can avoid the downsides of competitive pressure. Rather than face a prisoner's dilemma, where everyone suffers by acting individually, they can reach binding commitments that produce better outcomes for all.[29]

Working together on international agreements need not imply policy harmonization. For example, countries can, and likely should, choose different minimum wage rates and tax rates. Poor countries cannot afford rich-country minimum wages, and citizens may have different preferences regarding the size and role of government. But there are still substantial gains to be had from avoiding beggar-thy-neighbor policies; often, there are situations where agreements can improve outcomes for all participants.

Britain's decision to leave the European Union and Donald Trump's election on a platform of isolationist policies were both steps in the opposite direction. International trade agreements like the proposed Transatlantic Trade and Investment Partnership (T-TIP) and supranational arrangements like the European Union are just the sort of institutions and agreements that work against policy competition.

The T-TIP, now indefinitely stalled, was intended to be a high-standard trade agreement between the United States and the European Union. There was an emphasis within the agreement on ensuring high labor standards, environmental protections, and consumer protections.[30] Given recent political developments on both sides of the Atlantic, the likelihood of this agreement going forward is remote at best. Meanwhile, the European Union has recently reached a trade agreement with Canada; this agreement is noteworthy for fostering cooperation in several areas, including competition policy, regulatory cooperation, sustainable development, labor rights, and environmental policy. The agreement has provisions specifically prohibiting either side from lowering its labor or environmental standards to boost trade.[31]

In the future, agreements like T-TIP can do much to modernize economic policy to suit a global economy. The world's largest businesses have globally integrated operations that span borders. Governments need to acknowledge that reality, and adjust their policy choices accordingly.

While some environmental problems can be addressed effectively at a national or subnational level, others require larger, international efforts.[32] The largest and most important example concerns the world's greenhouse gas emissions, which drive climate change and profound damage to the planet's ecosystems. The Paris Agreement of 2016 was a crucial step, as countries worked together to set policy goals toward addressing this problem. (Chapter 10 will discuss why a carbon tax is a useful way for the United States to respond to the world's largest environmental problem, while also raising essential tax revenues that allow for lower tax rates elsewhere in the tax system.)

Labor issues are also of concern. There is substantial evidence that the share of world economic output accruing to capital has increased dramatically in recent decades. Rising corporate profits and corporate savings are an important part of that story, as are labor unionization rates, which have been steadily falling throughout the world (fig. 7.8).

How globalization will affect workers' rights in developing countries is uncertain; global influences can help as well as hurt. Economic growth typically leads to higher wages and greater labor rights. For example, child labor tends to fall dramatically as countries become richer, regardless of their political commitments to ending child labor.[33]

In many areas—labor rights, environmental policy, and tax competition—there are common concerns associated with competitive pressures across jurisdictions. What if mobile firms move their operations toward those countries with the lowest standards and lowest tax burdens? What prevents a race to the bottom? International agreements can be a key part of the toolkit.

Also, some purely domestic policy responses affect other countries in positive ways. For example, antitrust laws provide a useful way for governments to counter excessive market power in the hands of too few companies, helping to protect consumer interests and to provide a healthy, competitive market for smaller firms. US and EU antitrust laws affect both domestic companies and companies from other countries that

Figure 7.8: Steady Declines in Union Jobs in the United States and Abroad

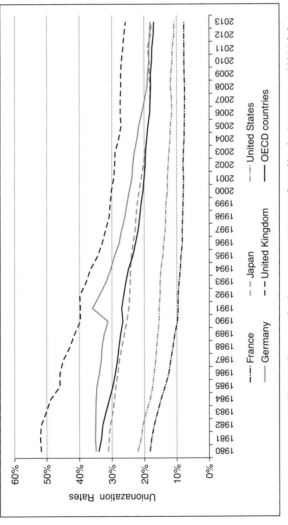

Data sources: OECD Statistics; Jelle Visser, "Union Membership Statistics in 24 Countries," Monthly Labor Review, January 2006; Lyle Scruggs and Peter Lange, "Where Have All the Members Gone? Globalization, Institutions, and Union Density," The Journal of Politics 64:1 (2002), 126–153; David G. Blanchflower, "A Cross-Country Study of Union Membership," Dartmouth College Working Paper, March 2006.

want to serve their markets. Effective antitrust enforcement benefits other countries, since ensuring competitive outcomes in large markets will also have broader pro-competitive effects in the larger world economy.

It is also possible for one country's corporate tax base protections to have positive effects on other countries' tax bases, as well. For example, a minimum tax on income booked in tax havens reduces the incentive for multinational companies to shift profits away from higher-tax jurisdictions toward tax havens.

An Agenda for Unilateral Action

Even absent international agreements, there is much that can be done by the United States on a unilateral basis—and, given the size and power of the United States, these actions can be quite effective. The following agenda is built on three key items.

Item 1: Do Not Resort to Tax-Cutting and Regulation-Gutting

The threat of international competition is often held up as a rationale for reductions in tax rates or regulatory burdens. Yet, in the United States, we should avoid the pressure to lower our regulatory and environmental standards. While standards should be efficiently designed and continuously streamlined, there is no reason to roll them back. The United States has a long history of successful global corporations that continues to the present day. Even before the tax cuts of 2018, there was no need to ease tax or regulatory burdens to attract investment or economic activity. For example, across fifteen years of *Forbes* Global 2000 rankings, the United States is consistently home to a disproportionate share of the world's largest corporations. Our economy is about one-fifth the size of the world economy—16 percent in purchasing power parity (PPP) terms and 22 percent in US dollar terms—yet we have larger fractions of the world's top two thousand firms: 28 percent by count, 33 percent by sales, 37 percent by profits (consolidated worldwide), 24 percent by assets, and 44 percent by market capitalization (fig. 7.9).[34]

Some observers caution about the threat of *corporate inversions*, which occur when companies restructure to change their headquarters locations for tax purposes. Despite a few highly publicized instances of corporate inversions, however, there is little evidence that corporate inversions are a sizable problem.

Figure 7.9: US Share of Forbes Global 2000 Firms (and World GDP), 2016

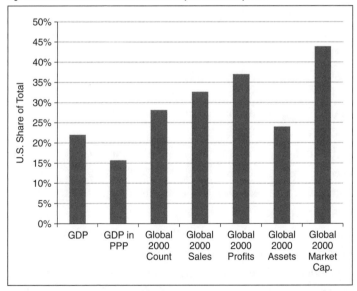

Note: Data on top companies are for 2016; the Forbes 2017 Global 2000 list reports 2016 data. The first two columns show the US share of the world economy; the following columns show US shares of Forbes Global 2000 companies, by different measures. Data sources: World Bank; *Forbes* 2017 Global 2000.

The US-headquartered share of the *Forbes* Global 2000 (in terms of sales, profits, assets, or market capitalization) has been increasing slightly in recent years, despite the growth of China and India. Recent US Treasury regulations in 2015 and 2016 were effective in reducing tax-motivated inversions, although some of these regulations have been challenged, and the current administration is rethinking this regulatory stance.[35] Nonetheless, there are easy legislative solutions to corporate inversions that do not require a race to the bottom in corporate tax rates.[36]

Further, it is important to have adequate tax revenues to ensure that the United States remains an attractive place to invest. Good public infrastructure, good institutions, the rule of law, well-educated workers, and investments in research and development are all important foundations for the economic success of US companies, and they all require tax revenues to sustain. And while regulations can always be improved, lax regulation is not a recipe for economic success. On the contrary, there is substantial evidence that insufficient financial market regulation was instrumental in generating the Great Recession of 2008.

Further, our corporate tax system was already competitive, even before the rate cuts enacted in 2018 due to the legislation commonly referred to as the Tax Cuts and Jobs Act (TCJA).[37] Our corporate tax system most certainly had serious problems, but a high tax burden on multinational corporations was not one of them. While it is true that the US statutory rate of 35 percent was indeed high relative to peer nations, this is not the relevant measure of multinational corporate tax burdens. Due to their aggressive use of corporate loopholes, many US multinationals had effective tax rates in the single digits, far lower than that statutory rate. Also, US corporate tax revenues are consistently lower than the corporate tax revenues of our peer trading partners, by about 1 percent of GDP. Part of the revenue shortfall is explained

Trying to Take a Bite Out of Apple

The European Commission's ruling against Apple provoked strong feelings in Ireland, with news headlines like "If Apple won't pay tax what hope is there for civilisation?" and worries about sovereignty among Irish members of parliament. In August 2016, EU Competition Commissioner Margrethe Vestager ordered Apple to pay the Irish government €13 billion ($14.5 billion); she and the Commission claimed that "sweetheart deals" struck in 1991 and 2007 allowed Apple to escape taxation on the billions of profits earned by Apple's Irish subsidiaries. The corporation had an effective tax rate of 0.005 percent on its European profits in 2014.

While Ireland's corporate tax rate is low, at 12.5 percent, Apple's less-than-single-digit rates have more to do with other components of tax regimes that allow corporations to move profits frictionlessly throughout Europe and beyond, often ending up in island havens with zero tax rates. Shifting massive profits through a network of subsidiaries isn't unique to Apple; many US multinational companies have haven operations. As of 2017, American companies stored over $2.5 trillion of earnings overseas.

Figure 7.10: After-Tax Corporate Profits Are At Fifty-Year Highs

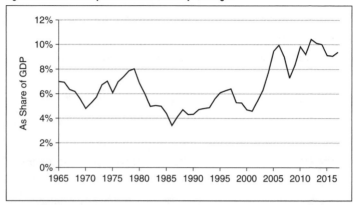

Data source: Federal Reserve.

by profit shifting to tax havens, and there are also other reasons for weak US corporate tax revenues.[38]

Indeed, US multinational companies are global leaders in tax avoidance, causing concerns abroad about their aggressive tax planning and reduced tax payments. For example, European Union officials have recently argued that US multinational corporations have received excessive amounts of tax relief from EU member states.

In the end, corporate after-tax profits are doing very well. While our economy isn't perfect, our corporations are generating greater after-tax profits than ever before (fig. 7.10).

Item 2: Protect the Corporate Tax Base from International Profit Shifting

The corporate tax is our only systematic tool for taxing capital income. It cannot be easily replaced with individual level taxation.[39] The corporate tax is also a highly progressive feature of

What Not to Do: The Tax Cuts and Jobs Act

In late December 2017, Congress passed the Tax Cuts and Jobs Act (TCJA). This legislation is discussed in more detail in Chapter 10; here I focus on the corporate tax provisions that pertain to multinational companies. The legislation did not seek a revenue-neutral business tax reform as had previously been proposed by plans from both the Obama Administration and Dave Camp, the Republican chairman of the House Committee on Ways and Means from 2011 to 2015. Instead, the TCJA provides about $650 billion in corporate tax cuts over ten years; there is a small revenue loss due to the international business tax provisions.[1]

The main international business provisions are summarized below, comparing the law before and after the TCJA with a revenue-neutral reform proposal.

This simple table omits many complexities, but the law lowers the corporate rate dramatically, and the international provisions of the law encourage profit shifting by adopting a territorial tax system, no longer applying US tax to foreign income. While there are also provisions to discourage profit shifting, captured by the colorful acronyms BEAT and GILTI, the Joint Committee on Tax estimates that the international provisions will actually lose revenue

---

1. This ignores the revenue associated with the one-time tax cut on prior unrepatriated earnings.

Table 7.1   Before and After the Tax Cuts and Jobs Act

	Before TCJA	**After TCJA[1]**	**Revenue-Neutral Reform Proposal[2]**
Statutory corporate rate	35	21	25–28
Rate on foreign income earned in haven without tax	0 until repatriation, then 35	0 until you reach a threshold of excess profits, then 10.5	Ideally, closer to the US rate (19 in Obama plan)
Rate on foreign non-haven income	Foreign rate until repatriation, then US taxes, allowing foreign tax credit	Below US rate if blended with haven income[3]	Foreign rate, unless foreign rate is too low, then minimum tax rate

Notes:

1. Under the TCJA, the corporate rate may be somewhat lower if the firm has above-normal profits generated by export sales. However, that provision (the FDII) is likely to be challenged by trading partners since it is not compatible with WTO obligations.

2. This column reports the author's estimate of what a true revenue-neutral tax reform would entail, based on an overview of the Camp and Obama proposals as well as recent developments. For more detail on what a revenue-neutral business tax reform might look like, see Kimberly Clausing, Edward Kleinbard, and Thornton Matheson, "US Corporate Income Tax Reform and Its Spillovers," IMF Working Paper WP/16/127, July 2016.

3. Since the TCJA uses a global minimum tax, tax obligations in higher-tax countries can offset the minimum tax due on haven income. Therefore, companies can blend their haven and non-haven foreign income, reducing the bite of the US minimum tax. (80 percent of the foreign taxes paid are creditable.)

relative to current law.[2] This is difficult to do, given the vast scale of the current profit shifting problem.

While there is a minimum tax that applies to tax haven income in the TCJA, haven income is still taxed at half the US rate, and taxed only above a 10 percent return on tangible assets. This generates a perverse incentive to shift tangible investments offshore to soften the bite of the minimum tax. In addition, since the minimum tax applies on a global basis, income earned in all foreign countries is tax-preferred relative to income earned in the United States, since high-tax foreign income acts to cushion companies from minimum tax due on low-tax foreign income.

In the end, once the dust clears, the legislation provides large corporate tax cuts, large revenue losses, and a far less progressive tax system. It also fails to make progress addressing our profit shifting problem. Most disheartening, the large deficits created by the bill will make future business tax reforms far more difficult.

---

2. These estimates are the December 15 conference agreement estimates provided on the Joint Committee on Tax website. Again, this ignores the revenue raised by the temporary repatriation provision. Under prior law, those earnings were taxable upon repatriation at the US rate, but the TCJA deemed these prior earnings repatriated, and taxed them at a special lower rate of 8 or 15.5 percent, payable over eight years.

our tax system, since it falls more heavily on relatively concentrated sources of income, such as capital income and rents. While the corporate tax may harm workers somewhat, it burdens workers far less than most alternative taxes, such as the payroll tax, labor income taxes, or consumption taxes.[40]

The question, then, is how to design a better corporate tax that is more suited to a global economy. To stem profit shifting to tax havens, we should stop the tax system's favoring of foreign income. Prior to the Tax Cuts and Jobs Act (TCJA), we allowed the deferral of US taxation on foreign income until it was repatriated to the United States. Post TCJA, we tax haven income at half the US rate, and completely exempt from tax the first ten percent of the return on assets. Rather than either of these approaches, we should tax foreign income as it is earned at the normal rate (allowing a tax credit for foreign tax). Doing so would remove the tax incentive to shift profits to tax havens as well as the tax disincentive to repatriate income.[41]

An alternative, more incremental, step would be to institute a per-country minimum tax that would tax foreign income as it was earned, not allowing deferral of US tax on income earned in the lowest-tax countries. A per-country minimum tax is more effective than the global minimum approach of the TCJA, since it avoids incentivizing all foreign income relative to US income.[42] This incremental step would in fact be a big move in the right direction, since about 98 percent of profit shifting is toward countries with tax rates below 15 percent.[43] Other helpful steps would include stronger rules to limit "earnings-stripping" (aimed at preventing artificial financial arrangements that shift profit out of the US tax base) and other measures designed to discourage corporate inversions, such as an exit tax.[44]

A more fundamental reform would be to require worldwide corporate tax consolidation. This would require a multinational firm to report all income and all expenses in a single, consolidated return, allowing foreign tax credits for foreign taxes paid. Losses could also be used to offset income throughout the global enterprise. This sort of reform would better align our tax system with the reality of globally integrated corporations.[45]

A more novel approach would be to tax all global corporations the same way we tax national corporations in US states, by a system called formulary apportionment. Instead of asking Intel to separately account for its income and expenses in Oregon, Oregon (like all other states that tax corporate income) assigns some fraction of Intel's national income to the state, based on the fraction of Intel's national economic activities that are in Oregon. (Different states use different formulas to make this assignment.) Historically, this system has offered a way around the vast complexity of separately accounting for income in each individual state when a business's operations are well integrated across states.

The same logic would apply to globally-integrated businesses that have difficulty accounting for income in individual nations when their operations are truly global. This difficulty establishing the source of income also generates ample tax avoidance opportunities, as companies seek to book income in the most tax-advantageous locations. To apply formulary apportionment, the United States would tax firms like Intel, Nike, Apple, Bayer, or Honda based on their global income. The fraction of their global income taxable in the United States would be based on the fraction of the company's real economic activity conducted in the United States—as reflected by payroll, jobs, or sales—versus elsewhere in the world. Real factors such as employment and sales are far simpler to measure than income, given the accounting fictions involved in reporting income under the current system. Currently, we require accountants to specify the location of income, despite the fact that income often has no easily-established source due to the efficiencies associated with multinational business activity as well as the intangible nature of much modern economic value.[46] This ambiguity amounts to an open invitation to assign profits to tax havens. A system of formulary apportionment would be much more difficult to game, since determining the location of customers or employees is relatively clear-cut.[47] This system has worked well in subnational contexts in the United States, Canada and elsewhere.[48]

In comparison to our pre-TCJA tax system, any of these reforms could be accompanied by a lower statutory rate and still yield greater revenue, since our corporate tax base has been so leaky due to profit shifting to tax havens. Post-TCJA, tax rate increases may be needed, since it is unclear we can afford the large net business tax cuts of the TCJA. In the interests of revenue, efficiency, progressivity, and tax administration, it is vital to have a predictable and healthy US corporate tax.[49] With that goal in mind, discouraging international profit shifting must be a priority.

Item 3: Pay Attention to the Fundamentals

In discussions about the competitiveness of US multinational firms, corporate interests often emphasize tax burdens as a determinative influence. Yet, as noted above, even the pre-TCJA statutory rate of 35 percent had more bark than bite; American multinational firms are often able to achieve very low effective tax rates. More important to US corporate success in a global economy are healthy economic fundamentals. While we often take such things for granted, they are essential to the success of US businesses and the workers within them. An incomplete list of such fundamental factors follows.

Sound macroeconomic policy. Managing economic fluctuations and keeping US debt and deficits at sustainable levels requires sound macroeconomic policy—guiding the actions of both the central bank (monetary policy) and the US government (fiscal policy). Macroeconomic policy-makers make changes in the money supply and the budget balance in light of economic conditions to dampen recessions and avoid costly periods of unemployment or inflation. (Unfortunately, the TCJA moves in the opposite direction, since it expands the budget deficit at a time when the economy is already quite strong. Since these tax cuts increase our national debt, they will make it more difficult to respond to the next recession.)

Sound financial regulation. The financial system is the bloodstream of the economy. Financial markets (stock markets, bond markets, and the banking system) provide essential funds for companies. These markets are essential to the functioning of our economy. They help companies fund new investments or meet payroll, and they help individuals borrow for home purchases and college educations. When the financial system flounders, this can have large spillover effects on the real economy, as we saw when the 2008 financial crisis gave way to the Great Recession. Adequate financial regulation is essential. This means ensuring sufficient capitalization of financial institutions; not allowing institutions to reach a point of being "too big to fail"; containing the larger financial system (such as "shadow banks") within the regulatory system; and making sure that risks to the larger economy are well understood and managed.

Robust infrastructure. A healthy and well-functioning infrastructure is fundamental to economic success; it facilitates the smooth flow of goods, services, and ideas. Public investments in roads and bridges, ports and airports, and computing and internet access are likely to pay large dividends, especially given our decades of underinvestment in these areas.

Investments in basic science and research. America's lead in science and technology resulted from important investments in basic science and research. Government funding for basic research through the National Science Foundation, the National Institutes of Health, and institutions of higher education is essential to this success.

A prepared workforce. Preparing workers for the jobs of tomorrow is essential. The education system needs to be well-funded and well-designed to equip people to make the best of a working world that is experiencing rapid technological change. Buttressing workers' bargaining power through adequate labor laws and protections is also important.

A policy agenda that addresses these fundamentals will be discussed in greater detail in Chapter 9.

This chapter began with the observation that the world's largest multinational corporations come with many benefits: they make good products; they innovate, adopting and spreading cutting-edge technologies; and they make investments in both production and in their own workers. They have astounding global reach, conduct the vast majority of all international trade, and achieve staggering efficiencies. Yet they also present policy challenges relating to four concerns: they are becoming larger and more powerful; their power creates downsides for workers; their global scope creates regulatory challenges for national governments; and their mobility can cause excessive corporate tax cuts that serve no nation well. While these concerns are challenging, there are ways to modernize economic policy to adapt to the technological sophistication and international mobility of today's global companies. The United States can address the downsides of today's multinational corporations, without endangering our dynamic business environment.

Eight

Immigrants, We Get the Job Done!

In the recent Broadway musical *Hamilton,* the immigrant origins of our nation are celebrated.[1] We learn the story of Alexander Hamilton, one of the founding fathers and the nation's first treasury secretary. Hamilton was an orphaned immigrant from the West Indies who, as the song goes, "got a lot farther by working a lot harder, by being a lot smarter, by being a self-starter." This narrative of a striving, foreign-born hero fits with a long American tradition of celebrating the scrappy beginnings of many of our national heroes. The idea of the American dream is that, if you work hard, your merit and drive will take you to the top of American society; your country of origin, your parents, and your inheritance (or lack thereof) are not determinative.[2]

We are a country with a long immigrant past. The 98 percent of US citizens that are not Native American can be traced to immigrants, distinguished only by how long it has been since they or their forebears arrived. Yet, while the United States is a nation of immigrants, it is also a nation conflicted about immigration. Waves of backlash have occurred throughout our history. Our immigration policies have moved in fits and starts, with periods of liberal immigration followed by periods of more restricted immigration. As successive cohorts of immigrants arrive, those preceding them too often view the new ones as somehow less desirable than those that came before.

Figure 8.1: Immigrant Source Countries to the United States in 2015

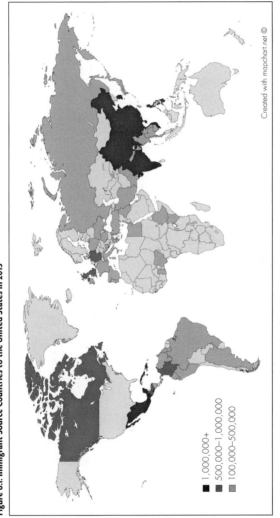

1,000,000+
500,000–1,000,000
100,000–500,000

Created with mapchart.net ©

Note: The map shows where immigrants residing in the United States in 2015 were born. Data source: US Census.

As this chapter will describe, it is almost impossible to imagine the American economy without immigrants. They have been a foundational part of our economic success in history, and their positive contribution continues today. In contrast, the negative effects of immigrants are typically overstated, especially relative to the large gains for the economy as a whole. This chapter shows that the benefits from increasing immigration are likely to be substantial. Given the present pressures on the US economy, a less restrictive immigration policy would make good sense.

A Nation of Immigrants

While immigration has increased in recent decades, as a share of the population, it is still shy of historic peaks around the turn of the twentieth century. While the absolute number of immigrants is larger than in times past, the share of immigrants in the population is a better indicator of their importance. As Figure 8.2 shows, immigrants are now about 13 percent of the population. These data, and the remainder of this chapter, define immigrants as any US residents who were born abroad.[3]

While immigrants are less than one-seventh of the population, they have an outsized effect on many key areas of the US economy. For example, they are disproportionately entrepreneurial; both in the United States and elsewhere, immigrants are more likely to found businesses than native populations.[4] A 2012 report shows that more than 40 percent of America's *Fortune* 500 companies were founded by immigrants or their children—including the oldest on the list, Bank of New York

Figure 8.2: Immigrants are Increasingly Important, But Still Less So than in Early 1900s

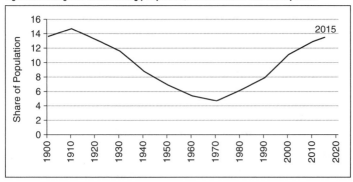

Data source: Migration Policy Institute; US Census.

Mellon, founded in 1784 by Alexander Hamilton.[5] Other important American companies with immigrant founders include Google (now part of Alphabet), AT&T, Goldman Sachs, Kohl's, Nordstrom, Qualcomm, and DuPont.

Immigrants have a big role in successful business start-ups. Forty-four of the eighty-seven private start-ups that are now valued at over $1 billion were started by immigrants, and sixty-two of these companies have immigrants as key members of their management team.[6] Between 2006 and 2012, immigrants started one-third of the US venture capital–backed companies that became publicly traded, a total of ninety-two companies.[7]

It is nearly impossible to imagine Silicon Valley without immigrants. Google, Instagram, Uber, and eBay were founded by immigrants, and the role of immigrants in the region extends far beyond these companies. As of 2014, 46 percent of Silicon Valley's workforce was foreign-born. The share is even larger for workers between the ages of 25 and 44, and it rises to a whopping 74 percent of workers hired for their math and computer expertise in that age bracket.[8] These workers also extend opportunities for American-born workers. Heavily immigrant "math-analytical" teams are often overseen by US-born management. Their mathematical prowess complements the linguistic and cultural fluency of native-born Americans in a pairing of specializations that makes both groups better off.[9]

Immigrants tend to spur innovation in their communities, and they are much more likely to invent.[10] A large number of immigrants come to the United States to study and work in fields associated with innovation. National Science Foundation data indicate that over 240,000 temporary visa holders were seeking graduate degrees in science and engineering in 2015. These visa-holding students were 31 percent of all graduate students in science, 64 percent in computer science, and 57 percent in engineering.[11] One study concludes that foreign-born workers in scientific fields were responsible for between 30 and 50 percent of US productivity growth between 1990 and 2010.[12]

The children of immigrants are also more likely to achieve prominence in their fields than the population at large. And they have positive effects on their entire counties: the greater the proportion of foreign-born residents in a county, the more children grow up to achieve great success in their fields.[13] And while Nobel Prizes are not the paramount measure of economic success, it is instructive to observe how many US-based Nobel laureates have been immigrants. In 2016, Bob Dylan, who was awarded the Nobel Prize in Literature, was the only US winner who was American-born. Six other prizes, in scientific fields, went to researchers based at US institutions who were foreign-born. Over the years from 1977 to 2015, academics associated with American institutions won an astonishing 65 percent of all Nobel Prizes in scientific fields (Chemistry, Medicine, Physics, and Economics), but a minority (46 percent) of those prizes have gone to American-born recipients.[14]

There has been a rapid increase in the education levels of new immigrants in recent years, with 48 percent of arrivals from 2011 to 2015 holding college degrees (a higher percentage than prevails among native workers).[15] Yet while many immigrants are highly educated, others comes to the United States with less education. Still, low-skill immigrants also make important contributions to American society, and many have skills that are complementary to those of the US workforce. Low-skill workers typically fill jobs for which the supplies of US-born workers are scarce, working as agricultural laborers, construction workers, or domestic assistants. While their children may grow up to be the founders of billion-dollar startups, less educated immigrants are more likely to found smaller businesses like restaurants, salons, cleaners, or home repair shops. These small businesses are also a source of economic activity and job creation.

A colorful example comes from Huy Fong Foods, whose spicy Sriracha sauce inspires fanatical devotion. The $60 million company was founded by Vietnamese immigrant and entrepreneur David Tran. Tran is also a refugee; in the late 1970s, Tran and his family escaped from Communist-controlled South Vietnam aboard the *Huey Fong*, a Taiwanese freighter for which he named his new business in 1980. Tran exclusively uses California peppers (grown a few miles from Huy Fong's Irwindale, CA headquarters) and manufactures every component of the famed Sriracha sauce on site. Tran has turned down almost two dozen offers to relocate, and he is committed to keeping his sauce an entirely American creation. He says that it constitutes a debt repayment, given that the United States was the only nation that welcomed him.

Immigrants Boost Growth

Immigrants bring tremendous gains to the US economy, and these gains come in several forms. Entrepreneurship and innovation create a more vibrant economy with stronger productivity growth, job creation, and dynamism. Immigrants increase economic growth not only directly, by increasing the number of workers in the economy, but also indirectly, by increasing the productivity of the economy as a whole. As a National Academy of Sciences panel report concludes, "the prospects for long run economic growth in the United States would be considerably dimmed without the contributions of high-skilled immigrants."[16]

Immigrants often bring skills that are not found in large quantities in the domestic population. By adding immigrants to the mix, native workers can benefit from working with people whose skills complement their own skills, and this can lead to greater economic prosperity.[17] Specialization patterns may change in response to immigrants in useful ways. For example, if highly skilled immigrant engineers provide engineering expertise, native workers may move into marketing or design work that complements the work of the engineers. This specialization fuels innovation by both groups and allows for greater adoption and diffusion of new technologies.[18]

Immigrants also lower prices for all sorts of goods, including construction work, domestic services like child care and food preparation, and agricultural goods, and these lower prices enhance the purchasing power of native workers. Immigrants provide inexpensive household labor that frees others to use their work time most effectively. And, since immigrants are more mobile, they help smooth labor market adjustments, by increasing labor supply in areas of strong demand and reducing labor supply in weaker areas.[19]

Immigration Solves Demographic Challenges

Immigrants are an important answer to the demographic challenges faced by many rich countries like the United States. (In fact, these demographic problems are far more pressing in some rich countries, such as Japan, precisely because they have smaller immigrant populations.) It is a very common pattern, across time periods and regions of the world, that as countries' incomes grow and people get richer, there is a marked decrease in childbearing, slowing population growth (fig. 8.3).

Over time, slowing population growth raises the number of retirees relative to workers, putting large stress on government budgets due to both the larger old-age spending (such as Medicare and Social Security in the United States) and the smaller tax payments of the retired. This budget squeeze puts a higher tax burden on the current generation of workers. Older populations also reduce economic growth since a smaller fraction of the population is working. These demographic changes have been a source of much economic trouble in many countries.

For example, Japan has a very old population, with nearly 0.8 elderly persons for every person in the labor force; Italy has 0.5 elderly persons for each person in the workforce. Canada

Figure 8.3: In Rich Countries, Women Have Fewer Babies

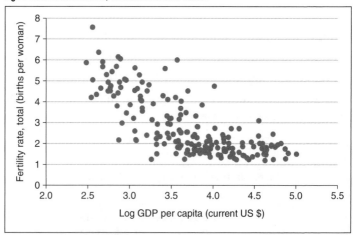

Note: Data are from 2015. Data source: World Development Indicators, World Bank.

and the United States have healthier trends, even if both countries also face demographic pressures from the retirement of the baby-boom generation (fig. 8.4).

The United States has been blessed with higher population growth than many peer countries, and our demographic challenges, while large, are smaller than those in Italy and Japan. What is the source of this advantage? Simply put, recent waves of immigrants. Over the next fifty years, immigrants and their children are projected to account for the vast majority of US population growth, thanks in part to immigrants' higher fertility rates.[20]

In many advanced economies, plummeting birthrates have left policy-makers scrambling for solutions to the budget imbalances and slower growth that result from an aging population. In Japan, the population started to decline in 2004 because of low birth and immigration rates. If Japan's 2016 fertility rate

Figure 8.4: In Japan, the Elderly Are 80 Percent the Size of the Labor Force

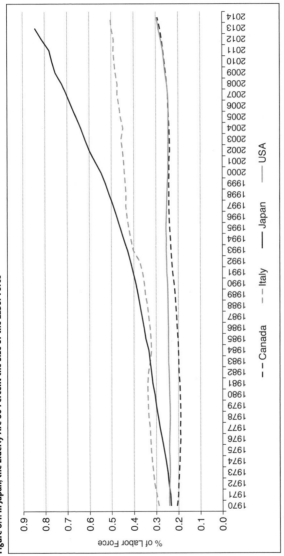

Note: The figure shows the elderly population relative to the size of the labor force.
Data sources: OECD; World Bank.

(projecting an average of 1.46 births per woman across their childbearing years) were to continue, sustaining the current population would require an influx of 650,000 immigrants per year. If neither immigration nor fertility rates increase, Japan's population will fall by two-thirds, to approximately 42.9 million people, over the next hundred years. Such demographics make for unsustainable budget pressures and dramatically reduced economic growth.

In contrast, the Canadian government has responded to demographic pressures by recognizing that immigrants fill an important need, and all of Canada's current labor force growth can be attributed to immigration. The foreign-born, or "new Canadians," now comprise one-fifth of Canada's population, a proportion that increases to one-half in the country's largest city, Toronto. Population growth via immigrant arrivals is roughly double growth via reproduction, and the Canadian government hopes to raise immigration rates even higher.

The Immigrants Themselves

Many benefits accrue to the United States from immigration, but it is important to remember the immigrants themselves, whose benefits from migration can also be enormous. As one testament to the benefits of migrating to the United States, consider the number of applicants for the annual visa lottery. Fifty thousand visas are awarded annually by lottery to migrants from countries that do not have large US immigrant populations.[21] Even though this excludes the very populous countries of China and India, over fourteen million people applied for entry through this lottery in fiscal year 2018. While probabilities vary wildly based on country of origin, overall chances were less than 1 in 290.

This enthusiasm for immigration results in part from large wage differences. The average foreign worker from a less-developed country can expect to increase their wages fivefold by moving to the United States. Some countries of origin, such as Nigeria, Yemen, and Haiti, have a greater than tenfold wage increase for equivalent workers in the United States.[22] (These calculations account for the traits of the workers and consider solely the wage effects resulting from where workers are located.)

For typical migrants, their productivity, wages, and living standards will be much higher in the destination country than in their origin countries. There are multiple reasons for these differences, but they largely result from superior resources in the destination country: better production facilities, more equipment, more advanced technology, superior infrastructure, and more sound and stable institutions. Institutional differences cover a lot of ground, but there is ample evidence of their importance in determining which countries are rich and which are poor.

Economists Daron Acemoglu and James A. Robinson provide a compelling argument for the importance of institutions in their book *Why Nations Fail*. They explore the geographically and culturally continuous community of Nogales, which is broken in two by the US-Mexico border: on the American side, incomes are higher, lifespans are longer, and educational outcomes are better. Acemoglu and Robinson argue that these differences stem from the countries' different political and economic institutions.

According to Acemoglu and Robinson, countries have either inclusive or extractive political institutions; inclusive ones are defined by their pluralism (they address the demands of diverse citizenries) and by their centralization of power, while extractive ones fail to meet either or both of these conditions. Inclusive political institutions support and promote mass participation and opportunity, whereas extractive ones take wealth from one group for the benefit of another.

Over the course of a nation's history, what may start as small institutional differences can become very big ones through the dynamics of virtuous or vicious circles. Immigrants moving from poor countries to rich countries are typically leaving extractive institutions for inclusive ones; their greater productivity in the destination countries reflects the myriad advantages of the wealth around them.

Trillion-Dollar Advantages

Because of the large difference between what migrants earn in their origin countries and what they could earn in the United States, there is a tremendous efficiency case for allowing more migration. Labor mobility is far more restricted than product mobility, and this creates the equivalent of large (typically over 400 percent, and sometimes over 1,000 percent) effective barriers. The average foreign worker from a less developed country receives a fivefold wage increase by moving to the United States.

The distortions from trade barriers are not even comparable. The typical US tariff barrier is closer to 3 percent, and even the exceptionally distorted sectors of the US economy (for example, sugar) have trade barriers that are equivalent to 80 percent protection.[23] Since distortions associated with limiting labor mobility are much higher, the benefits from reducing these barriers are also much higher. This led Michael Clemens to quip that immigration barriers are leaving "trillion dollar bills on the sidewalk."[24] Indeed, the efficiency gains from reducing barriers to labor mobility are estimated to be many multiples that of reducing the barriers to trade, perhaps around fifty times the size.

Since benefits from immigration are so immense, this implies that it will be easier to compensate anyone who is hurt from immigration with these extra benefits, while still leaving large net benefits for those who gain from immigration. There are also fewer concerns with unfair competition than there might be with international trade, since immigrants are subject to the same tax laws, environmental standards, and other regulations as domestic workers.

So What's the Problem? Concerns about Immigrants

When immigrants join the domestic economy, there are many positive economic consequences. There is more output and economic growth. There are more gains to those who benefit from immigrant labor, including their employers, consumers of goods that are consequentially less expensive, and other workers whose skills complement immigrant skills. And, of course, the immigrants themselves benefit. Yet many in the United States are concerned about negative consequences from too much immigration. This section will discuss three common worries about immigration, arguing that they are largely overstated.

Worry Number 1: Negative Economic Effects on US-Born Workers

The effects of migrants on labor markets are never precisely known; studies on this question have variable answers. Systematic overviews of work in this area, however, suggest that effects on native workers are typically very small, and more likely to be positive than negative overall.[25] Still, immigration may bring harmful effects to those US-born workers who most directly compete with immigrants in labor markets. An increased supply of labor in a given labor market, if other factors are held constant, will tend to lower wages. Yet it is not always the case that other factors are held constant. For example, immigrants may themselves create labor demand if they are forming businesses, innovating, and more generally increasing economic activity. Since we cannot theoretically predict the effect of immigrants on native worker wages, we need to turn to the actual experience.

Ideally, we would be able to establish the effect of immigration on native workers through a careful examination of the data. One method is to compare areas or time periods with greater immigration to areas or time periods with less immigration, and examine how wage outcomes for native workers vary. There have, indeed, been such comparisons—and usually they have failed to find any negative effects from immigration. This type of analysis, however, is not able to isolate the effects of variations in immigration levels from other factors. Since immigrants choose where and when to migrate, and are more likely to go to places (and in times) with ample job opportunities, that confounds understanding of the relationship between their swelling numbers and labor-market outcomes. For example, if migrants choose to go to booming regions knowing there will be plentiful job opportunities, there could appear to be a positive correlation between immigrants and native workers' wages, even if the immigrants did not cause the underlying positive economic conditions.

Careful analyses of these questions have failed to generate a clear consensus among economists. Some argue that there are negative effects on lower-skilled native workers in the United States.[26] In general, the workers found to be most harmed are those who are most similar to the incoming immigrants. The most harmed group is often the previous wave of immigrants, and there is also some evidence that high school dropouts are harmed. Still, other studies find positive wage effects, even for low-skilled workers.[27] On the other hand, the positive effects of high-skilled immigrants on wage growth, even that of other high-skilled workers, is far less ambiguous. The associated increases in productivity and innovation have beneficial effects, and high-skilled immigrant workers appear to complement most other workers, although native workers may be left worse off in very narrowly defined labor markets.

An especially valuable way to study this question is to analyze "natural experiments" where immigration suddenly surged in particular places due to unusual circumstances. One such experiment came courtesy of the Mariel boatlift, as discussed in the accompanying text box.

Another text box discusses the natural experiment set up by the Bracero Program to bring in migrant agricultural workers in the mid-twentieth century. When native workers compete directly with immigrant labor, they may fear that

The Mariel Boatlift: An Opportunity for Cubans, and Economists

On April 20, 1980, Fidel Castro announced that Cubans who wanted to emigrate to the United States could leave the island from the harbor town of Mariel. Approximately 125,000 did, and about 50 percent of the *Marielitos* settled permanently in Miami. The "Mariel boatlift" was an enormous opportunity for Cubans hoping to escape Castro's communism. Also excited were economists, who were presented with a natural experiment to examine the impact of immigration on native labor markets. The influx of *Marielitos* swelled Miami's labor force by about 7 percent and its low-skill workforce by approximately 20 percent. Yet, in a 1990 study, David Card found that the admittance of the *Marielitos* had "essentially no effect on the wages or employment outcomes of non-Cuban workers in the Miami labor market."[1]

George Borjas challenged this finding in a 2017 paper.[2] Borjas focused on the wages of Miami's least-educated male workers (those who did not finish high school) before and after the Mariel Boatlift, and found that they had fallen between 10 and 30 percent. He concluded that the lower wages of high school dropouts in Miami were likely due to

---

1. David Card, "The Impact of the Mariel Boatlift on the Miami Labor Market," *ILR Review* 43:2 (1990), 245-257.
2. George J. Borjas, "Still More on Mariel: The Role of Race," Working Paper 23504. NBER Working Papers. National Bureau of Economic Research, 2017.

the Mariel supply shock. Aside from the *Marielitos*, it is hard to imagine other explanations.

Yet a new study by Michael Clemens and Jennifer Hunt provides an alternative explanation for Borjas's finding.[3] The impact of the *Marielitos* on low-skill wages can be attributed to a data collection quirk: in 1980, Miami's census surveyors sought to improve their coverage of black male Americans. The less-than-high-school sample Borjas analyzed experienced a doubling of black males during this period. The lower wages of black workers, coupled with the entry of low-skill Haitians, were responsible for the differences between the findings of Borjas and Card. While discussions over the "right amount" of immigration may be far from over, it looks like the *Marielito* ship has sailed. The evidence points to unchanged wage and employment outcomes from the boatlift.

3. Michael A. Clemens and Jennifer Hunt, "The Labor Market Effects of Refugee Waves: Reconciling Conflicting Results," NBER Working Paper 23433, National Bureau of Economic Research, 2017.

their wages will suffer as a consequence. Yet, in some cases, migrant labor may have few native substitutes; immigrants largely do jobs that would otherwise be done by machines, or not done at all.

To sum up, it is possible for immigration to have negative economic effects on existing US workers, particularly teens and recent immigrants. Yet a few key points should be kept in mind. First, even if negative effects fall on previous cohorts of

Do Immigrants Do Unwanted Jobs?

Opponents of immigration often claim that immigrants take job opportunities from willing Americans, depressing wages in the process. In agricultural labor markets, this claim doesn't match the reality on the ground. Michael Clemens, Ethan Lewis, and Hannah Postel examine the impact of the 1942 Bracero Program on American farm workers.[1] *Bracero* is Spanish for "manual laborer" or, more literally, one who works with his arms. The Bracero Program consisted of a series of US laws granting about half a million Mexican laborers each year permission to perform seasonal work on America's fields between 1942 and 1964. During the Kennedy administration, the program was ended, due to fear of reduced native job opportunities. Yet the data show that the program's termination had no effect on the wages or employment of natives. It did not yield additional job opportunities for native workers; instead, farmers altered their crop mixes in favor of fruits and vegetables that could be picked mechanically, adopting technological innovations that bracero labor had kept at bay.

Today, about half of America's crop farmworkers are undocumented immigrants. In California's Central Valley, where annual crop output is worth $35 billion, that share

1. Michael A. Clemens, Ethan G. Lewis, and Hannah M. Postel, "Immigration Restrictions as Active Labor Market Policy: Evidence from the Mexican Bracero Exclusion," NBER Working Paper 23125, National Bureau of Economic Research, 2017.

reaches 70 percent. Lately, undocumented worker crack-downs have resulted in labor shortages. Immigration from Mexico is on a downward trend, and growers watch with dismay as their crops rot in place. The shortage presents employment opportunities that very few American workers are willing to take. A 2013 paper by Michael Clemens studied the North Carolina Growers Association (NCGA). Before using the guest worker program (which offers foreign workers seasonal contracts), the NCGA must prove it has made an effort to recruit Americans. In the years 1998 to 2012, when farms needed thousands of workers each season, applications from US-born workers never surpassed 268. And in that peak year, 2011, only seven Americans stayed for the whole growing season—while their Mexican counterparts boasted a retention rate of 90 percent.[2]

2. Michael A. Clemens, "International Harvest: A Case Study of How Foreign Workers Help American Farm Crops Grow—and the American Economy," Partnership for a New American Economy and the Center for Global Development, 2013; Michael A. Clemens, "The Effect of Foreign Labor on Native Employment: A Job-Specific Approach and Application to North Carolina Farms," Working Paper, 2013.

immigrants, those groups are likely still better off for having moved to the United States. Given the large wage benefit they received on arrival, slower subsequent wage growth due to new waves of immigration still leaves them with dramatically enhanced living standards. Second, to the extent that high school dropouts are hurt by unskilled migration, the best way to help such workers is not to restrict immigration; skill upgrading and education would benefit the native population more. Third, there is very little evidence of any negative effects associated with skilled immigrants. Given the large positive contributions of skilled immigrants to the entire economy, it is quite likely that their net effect is also positive for the vast majority of groups.[28]

Worry Number 2: State and Local Budget Stress

Immigrants tend to be highly concentrated in particular regions of the country. Over the period 2010–2016, 34 percent of all immigrants were destined for just five cities: New York, Miami, Los Angeles, Houston, and Washington, DC.[29]

Figure 8.5: Immigrants Are Very Concentrated in Some US Cities

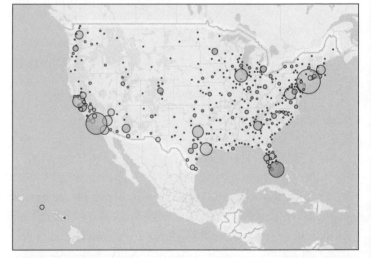

Note: The figure "US Immigration Population by Metropolitan Statistical Area (MSA), 2011–2015" was originally published on the Migration Policy Institute's Migration Data Hub at www .migrationpolicy.org/programs/migration-data-hub. Reprinted with permission from the Migration Policy Institute.

This concentration of immigrant populations can cause budget strains for governments, but figuring out the budget impact of immigrants is harder than it looks. Studies often compare immigrants' tax contributions with their use of government services, but service use can be difficult to calculate. For example, should one assign to immigrants the typical cost of running the government, including national defense, even if the national defense budget does not rise with population, but depends instead on overall military needs and strategies? Since national defense is very expensive, estimates of the fiscal impact of immigrants will depend on whether one assigns them their per-capita share of spending on defense, or instead the additional spending due to their presence, which is near zero.

Also, if immigrants are a budgetary drain, receiving more in government services than they pay in taxes, but their children are a budgetary boon, paying far more in taxes than they receive in benefits, how should the effect of the immigrants be tallied? Should we assess the contribution of only the immigrants themselves, or acknowledge that their arrivals have long-term effects? This is an important question, since the children of immigrants grow up to earn substantially higher incomes than their parents, and pay a lot more in taxes.

Especially hard to gauge are the fiscal impacts of undocumented immigrants. A recent study concluded that undocumented immigrants generate close to $12 billion annually in state government revenues, mainly by paying sales and excise taxes.[30] Establishing their use of government services is more difficult, however. Due to their lack of legal status, they are ineligible for many services, but estimating their use of other services remains tricky.

Finally, do we account for the positive effects of immigration on economic growth in these analyses? Immigrants have important effects on productivity and job creation, yet there is no easy way to take these factors into account in budget estimates.

Despite the measurement difficulties, there are a few consensus findings. While immigrants do not appear to have large negative effects on the federal budget (and their impact is often positive if government spending is assigned to residents based on what public services they are actually using), immigrants do appear to have negative impacts on state and local government budgets in the locations where first-generation immigrants are most concentrated.

Children of immigrants ultimately have a more favorable fiscal impact than their parents; the National Academy of Sciences Panel Report estimates a net cost to state and local budgets of $1,600 for a first-generation immigrant, whereas second-generation immigrants provide a net benefit of $1,700.

In general, immigrants have similar budget effects as natives if they are otherwise similar in terms of age and educational attainment. If anything, immigrants have more positive budget impact since their children earn higher incomes and make higher tax payments than the average US-born citizen.[31] While the immediate fiscal impacts of low-skilled immigrants are negative due to their lower socioeconomic status, these effects disappear as immigrants assimilate and wages increase for subsequent generations. Meanwhile, for high-skilled immigrants, even the initial negative impact is reduced or eliminated.

Worry Number 3: Cultural Concerns

At root, much of the backlash against immigration often has cultural themes, rather than narrowly economic ones. There are competing narratives regarding how immigrants fit into American society. Traditionally, we celebrate immigrant assimilation into American society with the image of the "melting pot." One way to interpret this metaphor is to think of America like a large stewpot, where the resulting soup is more delicious due to the combined influence of many ingredients. In that sense, there is no truly American culture other than that which emerges from a combination of all of our constituent parts. Examine an American coin. On it, you will find an early national motto inscribed: *e pluribus unum.* Out of many, one. Our one American society is the product of many influences, and many would agree that it is stronger and better as a consequence.

For example, is there such a thing as American cuisine? Some foods are particularly popular in the United States, but these foods typically had their true origins elsewhere: pizza from Italy, tacos from Mexico, hot dogs from Germany, and so forth. Even apple pie is not particularly American, despite the slogan. Apples suitable for cooking were not found in North America until they were brought over by later colonists, and pies have been around since the ancient Egyptians at least. Combining them was hardly an American invention.

In 2000, I lived in Brussels, Belgium, at the heart of the European Union. I often shopped at a grocery store which posted little flags to help people find food from different countries, perhaps useful to the many European Union bureaucrats who lived nearby. One day, I caught sight of the stars and stripes, and I eagerly approached the flag in the aisle to see what truly American food awaited me. What was there? Mexican food. Tortillas, beans, salsas, peppers, and so on—all of which I did indeed miss from home.

The four largest cities in the United States at present, and the only cities with more than two million people, are New York City (population 8.6 million), Los Angeles (4 million), Chicago (2.7 million), and Houston (2.3 million). These are also cities with huge immigrant populations. Foreign-born residents make up 38 percent of Los Angeles's population, 37 percent of New York City's, 29 percent of Houston's, and 21 percent of Chicago's—all far above the national average of 13 percent.[32]

What would these cities be like without immigrants? It is impossible to imagine. Part of what makes these cities such wonderful engines of economic activity and cultural offerings is their incredibly diverse immigrant populations. So much of our art, music, food, fashion, design, and innovation come from the vibrant mix of immigrants and natives in our biggest cities.

Areas with more immigrants also tend to be fond of their immigrant populations, whereas areas where immigrants are thinner on the ground are more skeptical. The states with the highest immigrant concentrations are California (27 percent), New York (22 percent), New Jersey (21 percent), Florida (19 percent), Hawaii (18 percent), Texas (16 percent), and Massachusetts (15 percent), whereas mountain, plains, and southeastern states have lower concentrations.[33] In public opinion polls, immigrants are viewed more favorably precisely in the places where they live, even among the native-born population.

Figure 8.6: Immigrants Are Least Popular Where They Are Rarely Found

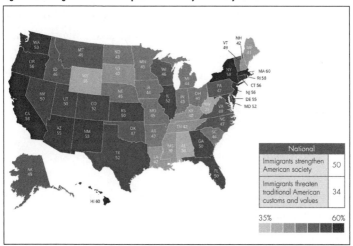

Source: PRRI 2015 American Values Atlas. Reprinted with permission from Public Religion Research Institute.

Yet there are several cultural worries about immigrant populations. Some worry that they will not assimilate, keeping to themselves and not learning English. There are concerns that they will bring cultural norms from their home countries that will weaken US institutions and rule of law. Some worry about crime, due to the low socioeconomic status of some immigrant populations and the fact that some immigrants are here illegally. (This presumably shows that they are willing to break laws, although their lack of legal status may generate more reluctance to commit crimes due to concerns of detection and deportation.) Increasing terrorism, while an extremely low-incidence threat, produces its own set of anxieties.[34]

In reality, there is little evidence of negative effects of immigrants on the quality of American institutions (such as property rights, the rule of law, and so on); if anything, the relationship between the immigrant share of the population and measures of institutional quality is positive.[35] Also, immigrants are less likely to commit felonies; immigrants have half the share of felonies relative to their population as the US population as a whole.[36] And indicators point to, if anything, faster assimilation by immigrants than a century ago.[37]

Immigration, the Global Economy, and International Relations

Immigration may encourage international trade and international business between countries.[38] There is much evidence that international trade and finance are less globally integrated than one might expect. Distance and transportation costs are not the only inhibitors of trade and investment. Poor information and communication are also impediments. Immigrants may increase trade and foreign investment by strengthening ties and information flows between their origin and destination countries. Immigrants may also have preferences for different goods; this contributes to the flow of new goods into the destination country, often influencing the tastes of natives.

International business may also be a driver of migration flows. Multinational firms often post workers outside of their home countries; in fact, several prominent global companies employ half their workforces outside of their countries of origin. Skilled workers are particularly likely to be sent abroad, and innovation often involves global teams of knowledge workers.[39]

Immigration flows strengthen ties between the United States and other countries. When immigrants leave their origin countries to seek new lives in the United States, they continue to communicate with their home countries, talking to friends and family, sending money home, and sometimes visiting in person. Immigrant experiences in the United States affect perceptions of the United States abroad, and personal relationships across borders generate groups of people who understand multiple societies.

Immigrants also bring American society into contact with other countries and cultures. There are new ideas, new cultural events, and new foods; American traditions expand to include Chinese New Year, Diwali, and Cinco de Mayo celebrations. In the classroom, foreign students help American students understand the world beyond their borders. In my economics teaching, I see this often. As foreign-born and domestic students share their experiences and ideas, viewpoints widen and become more thoughtful.

These sorts of ideas drive the Fulbright Program, established in 1946. The program enables scholarly exchanges between the United States and other countries. Its alumni testify to how the experience of living and studying abroad expands minds and fosters mutual understanding. About 8,000 Fulbright grants are awarded each year, allowing students and scholars in 160 countries to pursue educational opportunities and cultivate cultural understanding. Alumni have gone on to win Nobel Prizes (59), MacArthur Foundation Fellowships (71), and Pulitzer Prizes (84). Thirty-seven have become heads of state. There was a political calculation involved in the program's creation, as early advocates hoped awardees would absorb and broadcast American values. Still, scholars attest to the ever-mutualistic nature of international exchange.

More generally, the growing international mobility of people helps develop a common sense of humanity and shared interest as global citizens. Ultimately, people who understand each other better help to create commonalities among governments and nations, furthering peace and prosperity.

What Immigrants Leave Behind

One worry about immigration is that high-skilled immigrants may reduce the success of their origin countries by creating a "brain drain." At first glance, this seems a highly plausible concern. Since the United States benefits from the talents of these capable people, surely their talents are missed in their home countries. Yet some key considerations may allay this concern.

First, immigrants traditionally remit some portion of their larger paychecks to family members left behind. For example, in 2015 Indian-Americans, a group the size of 0.2 percent of India's population, earned an amount equal to about 8 percent of India's GDP. India was estimated to receive $69 billion in remittances (from multiple countries) in 2015, over 3 percent of GDP. Mexico received about 2 percent of GDP in remittances from the United States in 2015. As a source of funds, the influx of remittances can be vital to the economy of the home country.[40]

Second, the mere possibility of emigration may raise the perceived benefits of education in the origin country, as potential emigrants compete for scarce visas. This spur to educational attainment increases the capabilities of those that remain in the country, benefitting productivity growth.

Third, evidence suggests that brain drain effects on the home country are limited. For example, there are not worse health outcomes in countries that have larger health-worker outmigration.[41] Skilled immigrants send home substantial funds, helping to make up for their absence, and most studies of the effects of brain drain on production in the origin country yield estimates that are quite small.[42]

A Better Immigration Policy

The United States attracts many types of immigrants: workers of various skill levels seeking better economic opportunities, refugees fleeing persecution and war, family members seeking to be reunified with their relatives in the United States, and foreign students who come for an education but desire to remain in the United States. Most immigrants enter the United States legally, and new undocumented arrivals have dwindled in recent years. About eleven million people, however, reside in the United States who first entered the country illegally or overstayed their visas; this population is a little less than one quarter of all immigrants.

Our immigration policy has changed infrequently over the decades. A notable change of priorities occurred in 1965, when a nation-based quota system was repealed in favor of prioritizing family reunification. Two decades later, the 1986 Immigration Reform and Control Act set up a system of employer sanctions for hiring undocomented immigrants, increased resources for border enforcement, and provided amnesty for undocumented immigrants residing in the United States. Since then, changes to our immigration system have been smaller, including changes in visa allotments and the creation of the diversity category of visas in 1990, provisions that made it more difficult for immigrants to access welfare benefits in 1996, and laws that tightened documentation and reporting requirements as well as immigration rights in 2003 and 2005.

In recent years, many middle-class voters have come to feel threatened by changes in the world economy, yet opinions about immigrants are more positive than negative (fig. 8.7). As this chapter has argued, that should be the case. Immigrants have an overwhelmingly positive effect on the economy as a whole. This is not to say, however, that immigration policy cannot be improved. Below, I offer three ideas.

Automatic Green Cards for Foreign-Born Graduates of US Universities

The United States has shortages of workers in science, computer science, and engineering, areas that are essential to the productivity growth and entrepreneurial future of American industries. Foreign-born workers have a huge role to play here: they are more likely to innovate, they are more likely to found businesses, and they have a disproportionate influence in scientific fields.

The United States makes available 140,000 employment-based slots for permanent residency each year. Also, the H1-B visa program allows businesses to sponsor high-skilled workers for temporary visas; current law allows up to 65,000 of these visas each year. While there is an overlap between the recipients of such visas and foreign-born students who come to study in the United States, typically foreign students are allowed just one year after leaving school to work in the United States before they are required to return home.[43]

As noted above, many foreign students seek graduate degrees in science and engineering fields in the United States, and of course there are also a large number of foreign-born

Figure 8.7: US Opinions of Immigrants Are More Positive than Negative

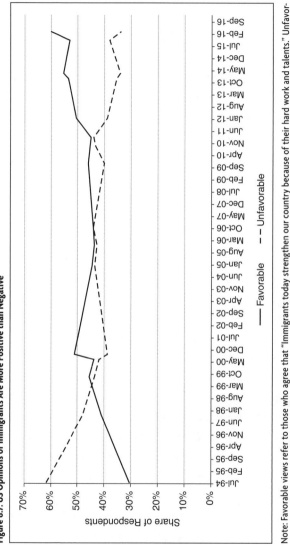

Note: Favorable views refer to those who agree that "Immigrants today strengthen our country because of their hard work and talents." Unfavorable views refer to those who agree that "Immigrants today are a burden on our country because they take our jobs, housing, and health." About 10 percent of respondents indicate both, neither, don't know, or provide no answer; these answers are excluded. Data source: Pew Research Center.

students doing their undergraduate work in the United States. During the 2015-6 school year, American colleges and universities hosted over one million international students, comprising 5 percent of the nation's student body. Why do so many foreign-born students study in the United States? Simply put, our higher education system is the best in the world. While our K-12 education is not stellar, all leading rankings of world universities put a large and disproportionate share of US institutions at the top. These institutions are an incredible source of strength for the US economy.

The United States is the world's most attractive destination for international students, even as the United Kingdom and other Anglophone countries gain ground. US institutions are particularly popular with Chinese and Indian students; of those studying abroad, 41 percent of Chinese students and half of Indian students choose the United States for their degrees.

Foreign students must meet both the admission criteria of our institutions of higher-learning and the requirements necessary for a student visa. Most of these students face very competitive processes in order to qualify for study in the United States, and international student tuition amounts to billions of dollars of service exports for the United States. International students typically study diligently and perform well in their classes. Many of these students desire to stay in the United States after graduation.

It is counterproductive for the United States government to send graduates of US colleges and universities home after only one year of work in the United States. While some of these foreign-born graduates eventually qualify for employment-based visas, many do not, and they are therefore required to return home despite their often strong wish to stay in the United States.[44]

One could argue that such restrictions suit the interests of the origin countries of these students, since the students can return home and apply their education to the betterment of their homelands. Yet it is clear that these restrictions are not in the economic interest of the United States. Why exclude such a well-educated and diligent population, and cut ourselves off from the additional benefits these graduates would provide in terms of productivity, innovation, and entrepreneurial energy? They speak English well, are culturally assimilated, and have skills our employers desperately need.

One possibility is a policy whereby graduates from a list of accredited and selective institutions of higher education would automatically qualify to start the process of receiving their green cards for permanent residence in the United States. (After, they would be free to seek US citizenship through the usual process.) If such a policy increased the number of foreign students too steeply, reducing slots at US universities for native-born students, limits could be set accordingly, or the US education system could expand.

Of course, there are other ways to increase skilled immigration, such as simply increasing the number of H1-B visas. Many highly qualified workers are forced to leave the country because they are not successful in the H1-B visa lotteries. One in eight tech workers in the United States is here because of an H1-B visa, and there is a shortage of native workers with the skills required in math, science, and technical positions.[45] Still, there are serious arguments that the H1-B program would benefit from reforms in the allocation process.[46]

A Balanced Immigration Policy

While the above policy would bring more highly-skilled immigrants into the United States, a balanced immigration policy would serve our economy's many needs for immigrants. There are both efficiency and moral arguments for admitting less-skilled workers who have lacked opportunities abroad. In terms of efficiency, these workers gain immensely from a change in location for themselves and their descendants, and these large gains provide a compelling argument for migration.

From a moral perspective, Americans have frequently taken pride in welcoming diverse populations from around the world, including those fleeing adversity at home. The inscription on the pedestal of the Statue of Liberty, near Ellis Island (the point of entry for many previous generations of immigrants), captures this spirit well.

> Give me your tired, your poor,
> Your huddled masses yearning to breathe free,
> The wretched refuse of your teeming shore.
> Send these, the homeless, tempest-tost to me,
> I lift my lamp beside the golden door!

Something would be lost if we replaced this sentiment with a plea to send instead "your PhD researchers, your doctors, your investors with millions to invest, the well-dressed elites of your glittering shore." While there is much to be gained from inviting highly-skilled immigrants, there is also a moral imperative to continue the American tradition of welcoming those less fortunate.

In recent decades, our immigration policy has emphasized family reunification as a goal, and while this is an important priority, it should not be the only driver of our immigration populations. In 2016, 68 percent of the immigrants admitted to the United States as lawful permanent residents were admitted based on family ties; of that group, 70 percent were spouses, minor children, or parents.[47] While the argument is strong for reuniting such immediate family members, it is perhaps less imperative that more distant relatives (such as adult siblings) be prioritized at the expense of greater access for those fleeing persecution or war. For example, there are over five million refugees due to the Syrian conflict.[48] This massive number of refugees has created a migrant crisis for the European Union, affecting many of our closest allies. There is a strong argument for the United States to continue opening its doors to these "huddled masses yearning to breathe free," with the usual precautions regarding screening and national security.

Thus, I recommend reorienting immigration policy, holding steady family reunification visas, or perhaps cutting the number of non-immediate family member visas slightly, but expanding both lottery admission for new immigrants from other countries and refugee admission, on net allowing a modest (perhaps 30 percent) increase in the total numbers for these groups.[49] In addition to the efficiency and moral reasons for expanding these immigration flows, the additional labor force would help the United States with upcoming demographic challenges. These workers are likely to complement the skills of American workers, resulting in few harmful effects on US-born workers. Also, recent research suggests that refugees begin making a positive net contribution to government budgets within nine years of arriving, a swift transition for those huddled masses.[50]

Compassion toward Undocumented Immigrants

Of the forty-three million foreign-born people in the United States, a little less than 25 percent are here illegally.[51] While undocumented immigration is publicly perceived to be a large problem, evidence indicates that the net flow of undocumented immigrants from Mexico, the dominant source country, has in fact turned negative, and the total number of undocumented immigrants residing in the United States has fallen.[52]

While enforcing the border controls of the United States is necessary, greater expenditures in this area are unlikely to be cost-effective. Spending on border patrol exceeds spending on all other Federal criminal law enforcement activities combined. There are likely more cost-effective ways to discourage undocumented immigration.[53] This is especially likely since, in recent years, more undocumented immigrants have overstayed visas than entered without documentation.[54]

For those undocumented immigrants already in the country, I would suggest providing a path toward citizenship, as suggested by Obama Administration and congressional leaders in prior immigration reform plans such as the DREAM Act. Providing a path to citizenship does not benefit only the undocumented workers; it also benefits the US economy as a whole. Documented workers are likely to pay more in tax revenue than they receive in benefits, helping the federal budget.[55] Giving workers legal status also gives them a greater incentive and ability to invest in learning and skill-building, allowing them to contribute more to the economy and reducing wage competition for the lowest-wage workers.

A Pragmatic and Compassionate Immigration Policy

These policy suggestions blend pragmatism and compassion. Americans mindful of their own immigrant ancestors may be motivated by the compassionate side of these policies. There is a strong moral case for treating fellow human beings kindly. Yet this compassion need not come at the expense of native workers. There is ample evidence that immigrants are a boon to the economy, helping spur innovation, productivity, business creation, and job growth.

Small segments of the workforce may be harmed by new immigrant flows. Since the benefits from immigration are so large, however, there will be ample additional resources available to help groups that are hurt. In this respect, the case for immigration is even larger than the case for trade, since the efficiencies associated with free product mobility have already been largely achieved, whereas there are still enormous restrictions on labor mobility.

In sum, immigrants are viewed favorably in the United States for good reason. We should continue to have a sensible, pro-growth, pro-immigrant policy stance. Like other types of international economic integration, immigration provides huge benefits that we'd be wrong to turn down. While the current political climate has policy-makers looking for quick and easy solutions to middle-class discontent, tighter immigration restrictions are a bad idea. The fourth part of this book will lay out a better path forward.

IV

Securing the Future of the Middle Class

The prior chapters have argued that globalization is a force for good. Global trade makes countries richer, raising living standards and benefiting consumers. International capital mobility can make both borrowing and lending countries better off. International business is a source of efficiency and innovation. Immigration is one of America's greatest strengths, both historically and currently. Immigrants play an essential role in economic growth, innovation, entrepreneurship, and relieving demographic pressures.

There are also worries, however. After several decades of middle-class wage stagnation, economic insecurity is a serious problem. Income inequality has increased dramatically, and the role of labor in the economy has changed fundamentally. This has raised skepticism about globalization. Many worry that the benefits of participating in the global economy are not worth the costs.

The next big American debate concerns this question. Will we keep our economy open to the world around us, fostering international economic relationships across borders and accepting immigrants into our country? Or will we work to erect barriers, stemming the flow of goods, services, capital, and people, both into and out of the United States? In times of hardship, economic stagnation, and inequality, it may be tempting to choose the closed path. Foreigners provide a convenient scapegoat for our problems; rallying around the flag makes people feel united against an external threat.

Easy answers are not always right. Sometimes, they are dangerous. Closing borders and injuring international economic relationships are both perilous moves. Raising import prices causes standards of living to decline; trade barriers disrupt many industries. Damaged international ties reduce mutually beneficial economic relations and weaken international cooperation. Fewer immigrants mean fewer new businesses, slower innovation, heavier demographic burdens, and the tarnishing of our image as a hopeful land of opportunity.

Importantly, restricting immigration, trade, and international business is more likely to harm workers than help them. Such restrictive policies come with unintended consequences, large collateral damage, and disruption. Further, such policies respond to only a small fraction of the influences that have caused labor market disruption in recent decades. For example, technological change is an important factor; automation and the rise of computerization and the internet have changed workers lives dramatically. Many other factors are also at work, including evolving social norms, changes in tax policy, the larger role of companies with market power, and the role of "superstars" in winner-take-all markets. Thus, not only are trade and migration barriers likely to generate harmful side effects, but they are also likely to be ineffective in addressing workers' economic problems.

In this fourth part of *Open*, I put forward a positive policy agenda for responding to the economic stagnation of the middle class and the recent dramatic increases in income inequality. These are not small problems, and they require bold, yet sensible, responses. While the necessity of responding to these problems is obvious to most observers, too many of the proposed solutions are either timid or foolish.

The positive policy agenda of the following chapters works to bring together a pro-growth, pro-jobs, pro-middle class alliance that is clear-eyed about what works in the global economy and compassionate about what doesn't. It draws on the American traditions of rugged individualism and self-sufficiency, but also on the American traditions of openness and caring. It relies on markets to do what markets do well, recognizing that government must ultimately be responsible for civilization itself; we need rules and sound public policies for a good society.

Chapters 5 through 8 included policy suggestions regarding globalization itself: trade, international capital mobility, international business, and immigration. These suggestions preserve what is working about the global economy while also making necessary changes to modernize economic policy in order to meet the challenges of today's technologically sophisticated global economy.

The suggestions in Chapters 9 through 11 are about meeting the needs of the middle class directly and effectively. They tackle the challenging problems of middle-class stagnation and income inequality described in Chapter 2. These suggestions preserve the many benefits of open economies; I do not suggest closing borders or erecting walls.

Instead, the policies go straight to the problems of American workers. Chapter 9, 10, and 11 deal with three aspects of this policy response. Chapter 9 focuses on strategies to help workers meet the demands of the global economy. Chapter 10 describes how a grand bargain for true tax reform can both help American workers and modernize the tax system, making it more suited to a global economy. (The tax law changes that went into effect in 2018 make true tax reform even more necessary; these changes largely work against the principles I articulate in Chapter 10.) Chapter 11 describes a new partnership with the business community, one that embraces the global economy and provides an excellent business environment, but also raises expectations for social responsibility on taxation, labor, and competition.

Bold and responsible solutions require a reshaping of our politics, and that is a particularly tall order. We are suffering from a dangerous polarization in this country, with a far right of the political spectrum that too often sees government as the source of every problem, and a far left that too often sees business interests as the source of every problem. Each camp is skeptical of the other, and each curates its own news, commentary, and view of reality, aided by the personalized information delivery of the internet.

Income inequality and economic stagnation contribute to this polarization, as both the left and right see vindication of their disparate views in the same economic events, becoming more deeply entrenched in their original positions. As a result, we elect legislators who are less likely to compromise in order to govern, and government itself functions poorly, reinforcing the sense that something in Washington is deeply dysfunctional. This polarization is dangerous. It leads to either paralysis or,

Steps toward a More Equitable Globalization

Equipping Workers for a Modern Global Economy (Chapter 9)

- Better utilize trade agreements to counter policy competition, keeping an open world economy
- Help workers meet the demands of the world economy through wage insurance, free community college, and greater economic security
- Support community adjustment to trade and technology shocks
- Solidify economic fundamentals needed to compete in the world economy, by increasing funding for education, research and development, and infrastructure

Tax Policy Suited to Our Modern Global Economy (Chapter 10)

- Strengthen the earned income tax credit for lower-income workers, helping those at the bottom prosper
- Retain and strengthen progressive tax system, to ensure that all benefit from the modern global economy
- Tax all types of income earned by the same person or business at the same rate, regardless of form or

location; close loopholes, including international tax avoidance

- Address climate change and keep tax rates lower with a carbon tax
- Bring together stakeholders in a grand bargain to reform the tax system

A Better Partnership with Business (Chapter 11)

- An embrace of the global economy
- Simple, fair regulations
- A simple, fair tax code; more transparency on taxes
- More transparency on pay structure and labor inclusion
- More robust antitrust laws

worse, the embrace of seemingly quick and easy solutions to our problems, solutions that will only end in frustration for voters, workers, and citizens.

The conclusion of the book, Chapter 12, places the above policy suggestions within a larger discussion of politics. If this is the way forward, how are we to achieve it?

Nine

Equipping Workers for a Modern Global Economy

In this chapter, I suggest four key steps to better equip workers for a modern global economy. We should promote better trade agreements that enable policy cooperation, further international prosperity, and pay attention to the downsides of globalization. We should take serious steps to help US workers adjust to the demands of the world economy and technological change. We should assist communities that have been harmed by trade and technological shocks. And we should shore up economic fundamentals to promote shared prosperity. These four ideas all work to ensure the prosperity of American workers in the global economy.

Better Trade Agreements

Better trade agreements can achieve important goals. First, they can bring nations closer together, fostering peace and prosperity throughout the globe. The past several decades have witnessed more global economic progress than has taken place in any equivalent period in the history of humankind. We should not turn our backs on this progress. We should celebrate these gains, while making sure that those harmed by the forces of economic change are made whole.

Second, good trade agreements can help governments work together on important global problems that require coordinated solutions. We live in a world where many key economic forces and policy problems are global, yet government policies are made at the national (or even subnational) level. Climate change, for example, is a truly global problem that affects all people, and actions in one country affect the entire planet. Tax competition and regulatory competition are also global problems. If the countries of the world lose tax revenue to tax havens, or if environmental regulations cause dirty production to migrate as a consequence, these are problems that clearly cross borders.

Good, smart trade agreements can be part of the solution to these problems. The benefits of international trade provide carrots that draw nations to the bargaining table, where they can mutually benefit by cooperating to solve problems such as climate change and international tax evasion. Good examples of countries coming together to make progress have already included the Paris Climate Agreement (COP21) and the OECD / G20 project on Base Erosion and Profit Shifting. While each of these agreements marked only a step toward solving a big problem, every journey begins with a single step. These are clear moves in the right direction. Going alone is not enough.

While issues such as climate change and tax competition are not central to international trade, there is no reason why trade agreements can't be flexible enough to support an international response to these problems. In the past, trade agreements have often included non-trade issues. Despite legitimate concern about prioritizing some non-trade inclusions (intellectual property rights, investor-state dispute settlement),

COP21: A Pale Blue Dot in the Balance

The Paris Climate Conference (officially known as the Twenty-First Conference of the Parties, or COP21) has a serious goal: to save the planet from catastrophe. Under the Paris agreement, more than 190 countries made emissions-reduction plans, called INDCs (intended nationally determined contributions). These plans aim to prevent the planet from warming by more than two degrees Celsius, the agreed-upon threshold for avoiding cataclysmic change, although under the plans submitted so far, global temperatures are likely to increase a more threatening three degrees. INDCs have no binding power, and rely on individual participant governments to pass legislation and implement their commitments. Under the agreement, nations will be required to share their progress every five years starting in 2023, allowing the international community to take stock of progress.

Even as President Trump announced that the United States would withdraw from the agreement (a four-year exit process), COP21 still boasts a list of almost two hundred participant nations and includes China, the world's biggest emitter today. The importance of meaningful, internationally-coordinated environmental regulations is difficult to overstate. The future of the planet is at risk.

A Prisoner's Dilemma in Tax Avoidance?

Perhaps the most celebrated result in the discipline of game theory—the study of strategic interaction—concerns the prisoner's dilemma. Two prisoners are separated, and each is promised a lighter penalty if they confess to a crime, implicating their partner. In this famous game, both prisoners end up confessing, and facing harsher punishments, since it is in their individual interest to confess, regardless of the choice their partner makes (confessing or not). Yet it is the criminals' *mutual* interest to coordinate, so that neither confesses.

Tax competition presents a similar game, with both governments and multinational companies acting as strategic players. Each country has an individual incentive to lower tax rates and provide loopholes, in an effort to attract multinational corporate activity and a larger tax base. Companies respond by moving profits into tax haven jurisdictions and even generating income that goes untaxed in any jurisdiction. If governments instead coordinate to stem tax base erosion, they can achieve a more favorable outcome. Companies would have fewer ways to avoid taxation, and governments would be able to collect revenues from more stable tax bases.

Such cooperation need not imply that countries choose the same tax rate. Rather, they can coordinate actions to shut down the easy methods of tax base erosion that have become so common lately. Recently, the Organization for Economic Cooperation and Development, together with the G20, worked on an international project to stem corporate tax base erosion and profit shifting. After several years of negotiation and the drafting of nearly two thousand pages of suggested guidelines, more than seventy ministers met in June 2017 to sign a multilateral convention to implement tax treaty measures related to the project. While this is far from an end to the prisoner's dilemma, it is certainly a step in the right direction.

trade agreements can and should be about more than trade. Countries can cooperate to avoid the harmful aspects of tax and regulatory competition, and trade agreements provide a natural forum for such cooperation. Indeed, it is odd that trade policy has been traditionally dealt with multilaterally, but tax policy has not.[1]

In addition, while trade agreements have not been the cause of worrisome labor market trends in the United States, such agreements can be part of the policy response to them. First, trade agreements should take care to liberalize trade slowly, to slow the pace of economic disruption. Second, trade agreements can help promote workers' interests by containing provisions that support core labor rights and encourage the bargaining power of labor, as the Trans-Pacific Partnership (TPP) attempted to do. By undertaking joint agreements on such matters, countries reduce the competitive pressures on governments to provide lax regulatory environments in hopes of attracting highly mobile businesses.

Helping Workers Meet the Demands of the World Economy

Setting appropriate rules for the world trading system is important, but even more important is giving workers the tools they need to succeed in our modern global economy. More should be done for workers that are experiencing disruption due to trade or technological change. Several policy solutions are promising. First, much can be done through the tax system. The earned income tax credit (discussed further in the following chapter) is one of our best anti-poverty tools, and it is has support across the political spectrum.[2] Under the earned income tax credit, workers with low incomes receive a tax credit for every dollar that they earn. Unlike many traditional anti-poverty programs, this program encourages work by increasing the reward for work for low-income workers.[3]

Also, wage insurance has been tried on a small scale, but it could be substantially expanded. Since 2015, there has been a small program known as Reemployment Trade Adjustment Assistance (RTAA). If a worker loses a job due to trade and accepts a lower-paying job, the program pays that worker 50 percent of the difference between their old and new incomes, up to a maximum of $10,000. The program is limited to workers over fifty years of age earning below $50,000 at their new jobs, and it applies only to workers who are certified to have lost their job due to trade pressures or international shifts in company operations. In 2015, 413 Trade Adjustment petitions were received, and 57,600 workers were covered and eligible for some type of trade adjustment.[4] Only a small fraction of those workers received wage insurance.

While linking such assistance to trade disruption may help build political support for international trade, that linkage minimizes the economic pain caused by other types of economic disruption, including technological change. The certification required to receive wage subsidies through RTAA also likely goes too far in limiting access to this type of assistance. Losing one's job to a robot is not less painful than losing it to a surge in imports, and losing one's job at age forty-five is as disruptive as losing it at age fifty-five. Wage insurance should be expanded to cover more workers and more causes of job loss. Care can be taken to avoid abuse by requiring some threshold-level of job experience and placing time limits on benefits. Like the earned income tax credit, wage insurance encourages work and reemployment. It also reduces the chance that workers become disengaged from the labor force, permanently lowering their economic prospects.

There may also be an important role for relocation assistance. The US economy is large and diverse, and economic conditions vary a great deal by region. As discussed in Chapter 4, trade shocks can often be quite localized, affecting particular areas much more heavily than others. The same is true for technical change. Even as some areas of the country experience negative shocks, other areas are doing well, and some areas even face labor shortages. It may be useful to help workers move to places with more abundant opportunities, and to help workers acquire the skills needed to succeed in those new jobs.

In recent years, for example, the Dakotas have boomed, due to the oil industry expansion after fracking techniques allowed oil extraction in new areas. As of mid-2017, North Dakota had the nation's lowest unemployment rate, at 2.3 percent; South Dakota's 3.3 percent rate is also unusually low. The boom in the Dakotas has been so substantial that the region has suffered from labor shortages. Menards (a home improvement chain) even resorted to flying in workers each week from its Wisconsin base, and putting them up in North Dakota hotels.

Relocation assistance is not a panacea, however. Workers may be limited in their ability to pack up and move by the fact that the same negative economic shock that affected them also took its toll on housing prices in their locale. When housing prices fall, mortgage holders can easily end up owing more money on their homes than those homes are worth. This makes relocation difficult—and strengthens the case for prudent lending practices, consumer protection such as the CFPB (Consumer Financial Protection Bureau), and community-level assistance.

Our swiftly churning capitalist economy creates ever-changing labor demands and therefore frequent needs for worker training. Community colleges fill a vital role in providing education and credentials throughout workers' lives. Community college education should be expanded and subsidized, reducing tuition. Ideally, community college would be free of cost altogether. Even if some tuition is retained, workers who have recently lost their job (after some experience threshold) should automatically qualify for tuition-free community college for the following three years. As of this writing, ten states, including California, are considering free community college legislation, following the successful implementation of programs in Tennessee, Oregon, and Minnesota. For example, Tennessee's Promise program, adopted in 2015, funds two years of community college or technical school enrollment; it created a 30 percent increase in community college enrollment and a retention rate 16 percentage points higher.

More broadly, community colleges fill a vital role in providing higher education to students who are not seeking a traditional four-year college experience. In the fall of 2015, 24 percent of full-time undergraduates attended community colleges, and 49 percent of all students who received their bachelor's degree in the 2015–2016 academic year had attended a two-year institution previously. Also, students who begin their college educations at community colleges have success at four-year programs that is similar to that of traditional students entering these programs from high school.

Community colleges also fill important needs by helping older workers refresh their skill sets. Community colleges typically tailor their programs to local job markets, offering specialized classes for workers hoping to improve their résumés. The dramatically lower costs of community college make higher education more affordable; the average cost of a year of community college was $3,350 in 2014–2015.

Finally, workers need more security. Progress has been made in giving all Americans access to affordable health insurance—which should not depend on employment, as it often did in years past—but we still have a long way to go. The Affordable Care Act (ACA) was a huge step in the right direction, but we should work to improve rather than weaken it. When Congress recently repealed the individual mandate requiring Americans to purchase health insurance, it weakened the entire structure of the ACA.[5] Economic insecurity is also tied to consumer indebtedness. We should bolster the Consumer Financial Protection Bureau (CFPB), which works to help protect consumers from financial instability. More generally, financial regulation must be strong enough to keep the financial system stable, supporting sustainable economic growth.[6]

Better Community Adjustment

The best response to economic disruption is to help those individuals who are directly harmed. Sometimes, however, entire communities have been hurt by trade shocks and technological disruption. Policies directed at these communities, such as investments in infrastructure and education, can be quite useful. These investments are likely to help attract business activity.

The Federal government can also play a bigger role helping communities adjust. By its very nature, the federal government helps smooth shocks across regions: it collects less in federal taxes from regions that are not doing well economically, and at the same time spends more on means-tested programs and unemployment insurance in regions that are experiencing downturns. Research finds that the federal tax system reduces the negative impact of lower incomes by one-third or more, while automatic federal spending increases have a smaller beneficial effect due to their smaller size.[7] When regions experience unusual economic downturns or shocks, it would be wise to increase federal spending, particularly on infrastructure and education needs.

Staying Competitive in the World Economy

Our modern, global economy generates important policy challenges related to competition among jurisdictions. But the most essential ingredients for competitiveness are found at home. These fundamental factors are essential to an economy's success, regardless of their degree of economic openness.

A Revitalized Rust Belt: Pittsburgh 2.0

Pittsburgh, Pennsylvania has transformed itself from a rust belt industrial town into a revitalized, diversified city. After the steel industry's decline sapped the region of fifty thousand people annually, Pittsburgh was forced to reformulate its identity. Relying less heavily on manufacturing, the city partnered with its universities and healthcare companies to diversify employment prospects and attract citizens and capital.

Investments in education and infrastructure were key to Pittsburgh's transformation. Carnegie Mellon and the University of Pittsburgh played enormous roles in the city's revitalization: the University of Pittsburgh Medical Center (a healthcare provider valued at more than $8 billion) became Pittsburgh's biggest employer. The city also collaborated with tech firms, and made important investments in public spaces (including a new convention center) and inexpensive housing. Pittsburgh's burgeoning health services industry, cutting-edge robotics research, and economic resilience have earned it commendations. In 2014, *The Economist* deemed Pittsburgh the most livable city in the continental United States.

The United States economy has benefited from many historic advantages. Our large immigrant community has been a constant source of entrepreneurship and innovation. Our steady increases in educational attainment over the period of 1890 to 1970 helped develop a highly-skilled workforce suited to the demands of the time. Our institutions of higher education, together with our public investments in basic science, generated the innovation and ingenuity that kept our industries at the world's frontier of knowledge. Our investments in infrastructure, from the interstate highway system to the internet, paid large dividends. Our inclusive political institutions provided for a strong, stable democracy. And our leadership in world affairs gave the United States an advantage in setting up a global trading and financial system that privileged the US dollar, that made US assets a highly desirable store of wealth, and that generally benefitted US workers and companies.

Many of these advantages are still intact, but there are also reasons for concern. Educational achievement has failed to keep pace with technological change, and our investments in public infrastructure have fallen short of our needs. Our politics have become increasingly polarized, and policy-makers increasingly suggest harmful solutions to our economic problems, such as restricting immigration and trade. We need to counter these harmful trends to keep American workers competitive in the world economy.

Foremost, we need to do no harm, avoiding policy "solutions" that are more akin to shooting oneself in the foot. But we also need to fortify traditional sources of American strength. Three fundamentals that particularly need strengthening are education, research, and infrastructure.

Our education system needs vast improvements and increased funding. As discussed in Chapter 4, our K–12 educational achievement is lagging, and we need greater investments in people from early childhood onward. Investments in early childhood reap large rewards. An influential study of two preschool experiments by Nobel laureate James Heckman reveals that comprehensive birth-to-five programs had a 13 percent return on investment; these returns far exceed the average return on stocks.[8]

Free community college would help workers build new skills and also provide students who do not plan to invest in a four-year college education with education and training resources. Keeping our higher education system strong will require continued funding as well as openness to the talent of the world, including foreign-born students who want to study in the United States. Welcoming these students to stay and work afterwards would compound these advantages.

Increasing funding for basic science and research would pay large dividends, and investments in education and basic research funding work well together. Workers will be better prepared for competing in the world economy, and for using technological change to their advantage, if they have the skills to make computers their assistants rather than their rivals. American companies will provide good job opportunities for workers if they are on the frontier of innovation and progress. Of late, federal R&D spending has been declining relative to the size of the economy. That trend should be reversed.[9] There are also ample opportunities for new investments in green energy technology. Given the large challenge of climate change, these investments are overdue.

Good public infrastructure is an important ingredient for making US workers productive. Well-functioning roads, bridges, ports, airports, and computing and internet access help ensure the smooth transport of goods, services, and ideas. Public investments are likely to pay large dividends, especially given our recent underinvestment in these areas.

The NIH and the NSF

The National Institutes of Health (NIH) and National Science Foundation (NSF) are responsible for giving America's researchers, students, and scientists the resources they need to go from hypotheses to revolutions. Across these organizations' histories, 223 NSF researchers, and 148 NIH researchers, have been awarded Nobel Prizes. The $7.5 billion under the direction of the NSF is an essential source of scientific, engineering, computer science, and mathematics funding, contributing to our innovation-driven economy. Many of the country's most successful businesses were helped by strong research spending; even the student researchers who founded Google were supported by an NSF grant.

The NIH provides more money to biomedical research than any other public institution on the planet. Each year, the NIH invests over $30 billion in medical research. Recipients of NIH funds are responsible for the first FDA-approved treatment for the most common type of stroke, the first human liver transplantation, and recent innovations in Zika, Ebola, and Marburg treatments. NIH research results in the introduction of life-saving drugs and vaccinations, providing investment returns many times larger than the long-term average return on stocks. These investments are essential to America's highly successful biotechnology sector, a sector responsible for about seven million jobs.[1]

---

1. See National Institutes of Health, "Our Society," https://www.nih.gov/about-nih/what-we-do/impact-nih-research/our-society.

Past investments in the nation's infrastructure have paid off. For example, the Federal-Aid Highway Act of 1956 created our system of interstate highways, now covering 46,876 miles of highways. The Interstate System supported and transformed a booming American economy. Researchers have found that highway investments resulted in many benefits; about thirty percent of the productivity growth in the late 1950s could be attributed to road infrastructure.[10]

However, in 2017, the American Society of Civil Engineers gave the country's infrastructure a grade of D+, and estimated that raising that grade one level would require a total investment between now and 2025 of $4.5 trillion. Given current budget proposals, it's unlikely that even America's fifty-six thousand "structurally deficient" bridges will be repaired. At present, the vast majority of infrastructure funding comes from local and state governments; only 25 percent of spending in 2014 came from federal sources.

In contrast, China has made enormous investments in infrastructure. The government's contributions to infrastructure constitute 9 percent of its economy. (The figure for the United States is 2.5 percent.) Chinese infrastructure efforts will soon link eight Asian nations under the auspices of the $1 trillion One Belt, One Road project. While some of these enterprises are highly indebted, Chinese infrastructure investments have also yielded impressive results.[11]

Education, research, and infrastructure are all areas where government funding could be usefully increased. And there are other fundamental factors that are inexpensive, yet essential. Sound macroeconomic policy can help steer the country clear of the harmful effects of recessions or unsustainable booms. The central bank plays a vital role here, but so does the

US Congress (and the president), by avoiding deficits and debt in good times, so that deficit expansion is more feasible when recessions arrive.[12] Adequate financial regulation is important to avoid systemic vulnerabilities and risk. And our legal and political institutions should be carefully looked after, with the enduring goal of assuring that they serve all Americans and not just elite groups.

The importance of solid fundamentals is difficult to overstate. People often argue that the mobility of international capital makes it difficult for high-wage countries to attract jobs and economic activity when they are competing with lower-wage countries. But the data tell a different story. For example, when US multinational firms send jobs offshore, a third of them go to high-wage countries in Europe, and many more in Canada, Japan, Australia and other rich countries.[13]

Why do US multinational firms send jobs to other high-wage, high-standard countries, when there are so many low-wage choices out there? In short, high-wage countries have high wages for a reason. Rich countries are home to productive workers, large consumer markets, stable institutions, and well-functioning infrastructure. If we keep these advantages, we need not fear losing the high-paying jobs that go with them.

Living in a modern, technologically sophisticated, global economy presents challenges. This chapter shows how to preserve the strengths that have made our economy so vibrant and successful. It is important to engage our trading partners and work toward improved trade agreements. But even more important, we need to give American workers tools to succeed in the global economy, we need to invest in our communities, and we need to nurture our fundamental strengths.

We also need to set rules of the game that are suited to a modern economy. The next chapter turns to one crucial aspect of these rules: the tax code.

Ten

A Grand Bargain for Better Tax Policy

Tax reform is long overdue. It has been more than thirty years since the last major US tax reform, and there is ample room for improvement. Our tax code is rife with inefficiencies and loopholes, it is not responsive to changes in the world economy, and it does not generate the revenue that we will need in the coming years.

The recent Tax Cuts and Jobs Act (TCJA), signed into law in the waning days of 2017, does not address these deficiencies.[1] Despite being marketed as a tax reform, the TCJA was focused on tax cuts rather than reform. Because of the TCJA, deficit forecasts are larger, the tax system is less progressive, and in many respects the tax base is narrower, with more distortions and loopholes. The final section of this chapter will discuss this legislation in detail. In short, the need for tax reform is even larger after the TCJA.

It may seem puzzling to devote a chapter to taxation in a book about the global economy. Yet the tax system is a crucial tool for responding to the dramatic changes that have affected the American middle class in recent decades. Many forces have buffeted American workers, but diminishing those forces directly is often undesirable or infeasible. For example, both technological change and international trade come with large benefits for the middle class; restricting international trade, or discarding innovation, would more likely harm than help American workers. Also, countering market power, or changing social norms, would undoubtedly be a slow process.

The Budget Pressures of Our Aging Population

Prior to the TCJA, the Congressional Budget Office forecast that deficits will increase substantially over the next decade, from about 3 percent of GDP to over 5 percent of GDP, increasing debt to GDP ratios from 77 percent in 2017 to 91 percent in 2027.[1] Such high debt levels raise the prospect of negative consequences in terms of worsening foreign accounts imbalances, higher interest rates, and reduced investment.

The upcoming increases in government budget deficits are attributable to greater outlays for Social Security and Medicare, due to demographic changes that have increased the ratio of retired citizens to workers. Spending on each program rises by more than 1 percent of GDP over the next decade.

The TCJA has worsened these budget pressures. The bill adds $1.5 trillion to deficits over the coming decade, as well as an additional $300 billion in debt service. As a result, the Congressional Budget Office forecasts that the debt-to-GDP ratio will rise to 98 percent in 2027.[2]

---

1. Congressional Budget Office, *Update to the Budget and Economic Outlook,* Report, June, 2017.

2. Congressional Budget Office, "Estimated Deficits and Debt under the Conference Agreement of H.R. 1," January 2, 2018, https://www.cbo.gov/publication/53437.

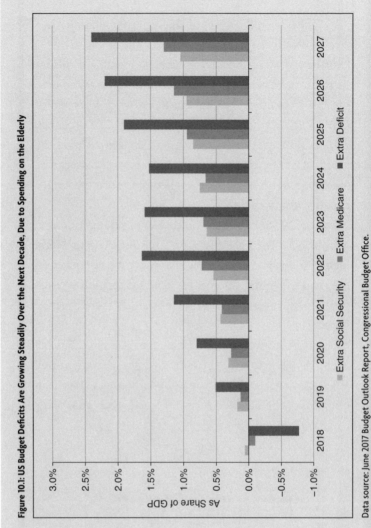

Figure 10.1: US Budget Deficits Are Growing Steadily Over the Next Decade, Due to Spending on the Elderly

As Share of GDP

3.0%
2.5%
2.0%
1.5%
1.0%
0.5%
0.0%
-0.5%
-1.0%

2018 2019 2020 2021 2022 2023 2024 2025 2026 2027

■ Extra Social Security   ■ Extra Medicare   ■ Extra Deficit

Data source: June 2017 Budget Outlook Report, Congressional Budget Office.

The tax system is a large, consequential tool that affects the after-tax incomes of all Americans; it also shapes the economic incentives motivating all businesses and individuals. The tax system therefore provides a powerful means to respond to those in economic pain. Further, an improved tax system will lessen the distortions caused by our present tax system, making it easier to raise the revenue that is needed for the urgent investment priorities discussed in Chapter 9.

In this chapter, I describe a possible tax reform grand bargain that achieves several goals simultaneously. First, it helps Americans consistently benefit from the economic challenges of technological change and the global economy, ensuring that after-tax incomes rise for most Americans as GDP increases. Second, it reduces the distortions in the current tax system by taxing all types of income received by the same taxpayers in the same way. This reduces the gimmicks and shenanigans that litter our present tax system, raising revenue, reducing waste, and curtailing international profit shifting. Third, it includes a carbon tax; this key feature of the bargain will simultaneously respond to revenue needs, keep other tax rates low, and help save the planet. These three pillars will ensure a US tax system that is ready for the twenty-first century, and that is fair, efficient, and competitive.

Responding to the Challenges of the World Economy and Technological Change

As Chapter 2 described, US workers have not sufficiently benefited from the economic growth of the past thirty-five years. While GDP per person has increased by 60 percent, typical household income has increased by only 16 percent over the same period. This increase has fallen short of long-held American expectations about improving standards of living. While 90 percent of children born in the 1940s outearned their parents, only half of those born in the 1980s do.[2]

There are several ways in which the tax system can respond to these economic challenges. The federal income tax, unlike the payroll tax and most state sales taxes, is strongly progressive. But more could be done through the tax system for low-earning workers. At present, low-wage taxpayers qualify for the earned income tax credit (EITC), which is fairly generous if one has children; for example, a single taxpayer with two children qualifies for a maximum tax credit of about $5,600. However, earners without children get much smaller tax credits.

The earned income tax credit has strong political support from thinkers and policy-makers on both the right and left; for low-wage workers, it increases the incentive to work, and for firms, it provides a stronger inducement to hire such workers. At low incomes, the credit provides additional rewards for working, as a worker with two children receives forty cents for every dollar earned. Past a certain income level, however, the credit is phased out. A parent of two children earning income between $18,340 and $45,007 loses about 21 cents of their prior EITC for each dollar earned.

As the figure shows, the EITC is far more generous for earners with children than for childless workers. This additional generosity may be justified by the higher costs of raising children and the higher poverty rates for children than for the population as a whole. The EITC has been effective at reducing poverty for families—as has the child tax credit, which allows most tax filers to reduce their tax bills for every child they claim as a dependent.

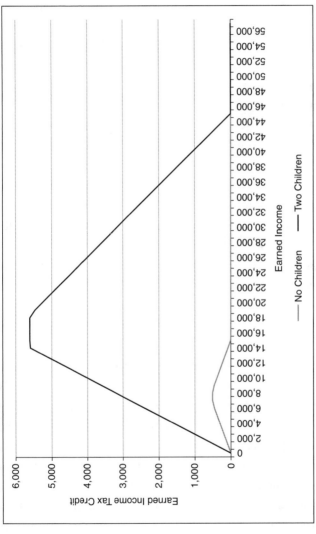

Figure 10.2: The Earned Income Tax Credit is Far More Generous for Parents

Earned Income Tax Credit

Earned Income

—— No Children   —— Two Children

Data source: 2017 EITC parameters, Tax Policy Center.

Still, the earned income tax credit could assist more workers living in poverty if it were more generous toward the childless. The earned income tax credit could usefully be expanded in several ways: by increasing the credit percentage for workers without children, by increasing the thresholds up to which the earned income tax credit can be earned for all taxpayers, and by limiting the phase-out of the tax credit, helping middle-class taxpayers who are higher in the earnings distribution.

These changes would make the tax system more suited to our modern global economy. On its own, our economy has not ensured that all groups benefit from economic growth. Over the past thirty-five years, gains in GDP have mostly accrued to those in the top 10 percent of the income distribution, while those in the bottom half have faced wage stagnation and unfulfilled expectations. We have tax policy tools that are capable of countering these increases in inequality. A more progressive tax system can help society share the prosperity associated with economic growth.

No Gimmicks, No Shenanigans

Our present tax system presents many tempting opportunities for tax avoidance, particularly for high earners and businesses. Some types of income are taxed more lightly than others, and this creates both inefficiencies and avenues for tax avoidance, eroding the tax base and raising the relative burden on other taxpayers. Indeed, the famous investor and third richest man in the world, Warren Buffett, has drawn attention to this problem, lamenting the fact that his secretary pays a higher tax rate than he does (see box on p. 249).

Innovative Ways to Help American Workers through the Tax System

Some have suggested other innovative ways to help the tax system adjust to changes in the world economy. For instance, Burman, Shiller, Leiserson, and Rohaly have suggested a "rising-tide" tax system, where the tax brackets of the income tax would automatically adjust in response to changes in the nationwide income distribution, to counter increases in income inequality.[1]

Leonard Burman has also suggested a reform that would couple a negative income tax, at a rate of 100 percent on the first $14,000 of earnings, with a new revenue source in the form of a value-added tax (VAT). This would be a strongly progressive change for those in the lower parts of the income distribution. Over time, the proposal indexes the amount of income subject to the tax benefit (the $14,000) to GDP increases. This ensures that economic growth automatically increases the tax benefit, sharing the benefits of growth more widely.[2]

---

1. Leonard E. Burman, Robert J. Shiller, Gregory Leiserson, and Jeffery Rohaly, "The Rising Tide Tax System: Indexing the Tax System for Changes in Inequality," Tax Policy Center, 2006.
2. Leonard E. Burman, "A Tax Credit to Give Middle-Class Workers a Raise," *Tax Policy Center*, August 2, 2017.

Here I suggest a simple tax reform that would tax all income of top taxpayers at the same rate, regardless of source. Importantly, labor income and capital income would face the same top tax rate, so there would be no distortion favoring capital income over labor income. There would also be no incentive to mischaracterize labor income as capital income to reduce tax burdens, so the wastefulness of our tax planning industry would be curtailed.

At present, capital gains (the difference between the selling price of a capital asset and its original cost) and dividends (issued by corporations to shareholders) receive generous tax preferences relative to labor income, with top capital gains and dividend tax rates of 20 percent (or 23.8 percent including the net investment income tax). These tax rates are about half the top rate on labor income, 39.6 percent. (The TCJA temporarily lowers the top rate to 37 percent from 2018 to 2025.)

Several tax preferences make capital gains tax burdens even lower than these tax rates reflect. Income from capital gains has the benefit of tax-free deferral; you do not pay tax on capital gains until the asset is sold, and gains grow tax-free in the meantime. Second, some capital gains escape taxation entirely, since the capital gain is zeroed out when a capital asset is inherited at death. (This is referred to as a step-up in basis. The new "cost" of the asset becomes its market value when the asset is transferred.) Third, capital income held in tax-free retirement accounts is untaxed, as is capital income in tax-free college savings accounts. Finally, capital gains in the form of real estate appreciation often go untaxed as well, since the first $250,000 or $500,000 of home sales capital gains are excluded from tax, depending on filing status.

Warren Buffett on Tax Policy

Warren Buffett is known for his brilliant investing, his philanthropy, and a tax policy idea that bears his name. The Buffett Rule is simple: raise effective tax rates on households making more than one million, raise them even higher for households making ten million or more, and cut employee contributions to the payroll tax. In 2012, the US Senate considered a bill inspired by these principles; it would have required taxpayers earning over a million dollars to pay income taxes of at least 30 percent. Buffett himself faced a rate of only 17.4 percent in 2010.

Tax rates on the wealthy are often low because investment is a much higher proportion of top incomes, and capital income is taxed at highly favorable rates. (Payroll taxes also do not apply above a certain cap.) Yet moves to increase tax rates on investment income are frequently met by claims that higher rates will discourage investment. Buffett's response is a verbal eye-roll: "I have worked with investors for 60 years and have yet to see anyone . . . shy away from a sensible investment because of the tax rate on the potential gain."[1] The plan is popular with the American public. A CNN survey about the Buffett-inspired legislation found 72 percent of respondents in favor of its adoption.

---

1. Warren E. Buffett, "Stop Coddling the Super-Rich," *New York Times*, August 14, 2011.

Following the Tax Reform Act of 1986, capital and labor income were taxed uniformly, at the same top rate. Lighter taxation of capital income is difficult to justify. For example, capital income is much more concentrated in the hands of the rich than labor income; the top 5 percent of taxpayers earn 37 percent of all income (including both labor and capital), but a whopping 68 percent of dividend income and 87 percent of long-term capital gains income.[3]

Also, there is little efficiency rationale for lighter tax burdens on capital income. Modern economic theory suggests that the optimal burden on capital income is likely at least as high as that on labor income, especially if we account for the fact that much of capital income may be "excess" profits due to monopoly power.[4]

Business income should be also be taxed similarly regardless of what form it takes. For example, corporate and noncorporate businesses should be treated similarly for tax purposes.[5] The treatment of debt-financed and equity-financed investments should also be harmonized.[6]

Business taxes also need updating for today's global economy, to help governments tax business incomes despite the increasing mobility of the business tax base. Business income should be treated the same regardless of where it is booked.[7] At present, we have a large profit shifting problem, as multinational corporations move their profits to tax havens, sometimes creating "stateless income" that goes untaxed by any jurisdiction. In recent years, this problem has cost the US federal government more than $100 billion a year, and tax revenues lost due to profit shifting have increased substantially over the previous two decades.[8]

Our corporate tax system can be modernized to better suit the reality of the world economy. There are simple reforms that would be highly effective at curtailing profit shifting. In the spirit of taxing all income at the same rate, I suggest simply taxing foreign income currently at the same rate as domestic income, allowing a foreign tax credit to avoid double-taxation when such income is taxed abroad. While some worry that this reform would encourage corporations to incorporate abroad, or undertake corporate inversions, there are easy legislative solutions to this concern.[9] In Chapter 7, I also discuss some other, more fundamental corporate tax reform options that would address this problem.[10]

At what tax rate should high-income taxpayers and businesses be taxed? Of course, this depends on the revenue needs of the country. But, by taxing all forms of income at the same rate, there will be greater revenue at any choice of top tax rates, since revenue will not leak out as taxpayers shift their income

Just How Special Are Tax Havens?

By almost any plausible metric, the affiliates of multinational firms book too much income in tax havens, relative to the true economic activity that occurs there. In 2010, affiliates of US multinational firms reported profits in Bermuda that were sixteen times the size of the entire Bermuda economy, and reported profits in the Cayman Islands that were twenty times the size of that economy.[1] US multina-

1. Even these figures underestimate the size of the problem, since tax haven GDPs are also distorted upwards by artificial profit shifting.

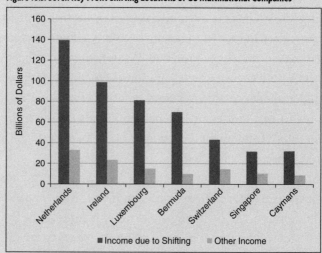

Figure 10.3: Seven Key Profit Shifting Locations of US Multinational Companies

Note: Figure shows results of data analysis of the underlying BEA data from Kimberly Clausing, "The Effect of Profit Shifting on the Corporate Tax Base in the United States and Beyond," National Tax Journal 69:4 (2016), 905–934. Data source: US Bureau of Economic Analysis.

tional firms have accumulated over $2.6 trillion in permanently reinvested earnings in low-tax locations, over $1 trillion of which is held in cash. Seven tax havens are responsible for over half the foreign profits of US multinational firms, and these seven havens have a combined population that is less than that of California. I estimate that most of the income booked in these tax havens is there artificially; absent profit shifting, reported profits would be much lower in tax havens and much higher in non-havens.[2]

---

2. Clausing, "The Effect of Profit Shifting."

Taxing Death or Taxing Patrimonial Capitalism? The Estate Tax

Prior to the TCJA, the federal estate tax applied to the portion of estates that are in excess of about $5.5 million; any estate worth less than the threshold amount is untaxed. The TCJA temporarily increases that threshold to $11 million for the period 2018 to 2025.

The federal estate tax generates significant tax revenue, but 99.8 percent of estates were tax exempt. (Even more estates will be tax exempt from 2018 to 2025.) There is little risk to family businesses from the tax; of the 5,200 estates taxed in 2017, estimates show that only about fifty include small farms and businesses, and they typically owe less than 6 percent of their value.[1]

The estate tax's top rate is 40 percent, but effective rates are often significantly lower due to loopholes and exemptions. Furthermore, capital gains (on assets like real estate or stock) go untaxed upon death. Any increase in the value of a capital gain over the course of its owner's life is ignored when capital assets are given to descendants. These unrealized capital gains are 56 percent of the value of estates over $10 million. Many have suggested reforming estate taxation to eliminate this "step-up" in basis at death, preventing capital gains from escaping taxation.

---

1. Center on Budget and Policy Priorities, "Policy Basics: The Estate Tax," Report, August 14, 2017.

Opponents of the estate tax argue that it is unfair to tax death, and the estate tax deters the incentive to save to leave bequests. It is important to note, however, that receiving an inheritance, or anticipating an inheritance, can also deter savings and work by heirs. More important, an estate tax can limit the passing of inherited wealth across generations, reducing the economic power of dynastic families living solely off the work effort of prior generations and investment returns. A robust estate tax helps counter the worries of *patrimonial capitalism* raised in Thomas Piketty's best-selling book, *Capital in the Twenty-First Century.* The masterful data collection efforts of this book documented worrisome trends in the role of capital in the economy.[2] Left unchecked, high capital-to-income ratios risk creating societies where wealth and political power are too concentrated.

---

2. Thomas Piketty, *Capital in the Twenty-First Century* (Cambridge, MA: Belknap Press of Harvard University Press, 2014).

into tax-favored forms. This should keep top tax rates lower than they would be in the counterfactual.

Saving the Planet: An Essential Part of the Grand Bargain

Economic inequality and middle-class stagnation are the essential economic problems of our time. But a larger concern, beyond economics, is the problem of climate change, which threatens the future of humanity if left unchecked. Even if climate change is slowed, the world will suffer from substantial costs associated with damage and mitigation efforts.[11]

Without government intervention, the market provides little incentive to solve this problem, as individuals and businesses have no reason (aside from public-spiritedness) to consider the spillover effects of their actions on the planet as a whole. For most people, decisions about where to fly, what car to buy, and where and how to live are usually made on the basis of other factors.

A carbon tax is perhaps the most wonderful economic policy of them all. Economists of all political stripes offer full-throated endorsements of carbon taxation for three reasons. First, a carbon tax helps save the planet. By making the use of carbon more expensive, it creates an incentive for people to conserve on their carbon use. Everyday decisions about how warm to heat the house, whether to drive or walk to the store, and whether to fly to see a cousin's wedding are profoundly influenced by prices; the more expensive it is to generate carbon dioxide emissions, the less people will chose to generate them.

More expensive carbon also encourages businesses to reduce the carbon footprint of their products, since doing so reduces carbon-tax inclusive energy costs. There is a built-in incentive to make products more energy-efficient. As a consequence, cumbersome regulations like the corporate average fuel economy (CAFE) standards would be unnecessary; both automakers and consumers would already have strong economic incentives to choose fuel-efficient cars. Tax credits for green appliances would be similarly unnecessary. Further, the pace of energy innovation and reform would accelerate, as there would be an ever-present reason to reduce carbon emissions.

Inefficiency at the CAFE

The Corporate Average Fuel Economy (CAFE) program was established in 1975 as part of an effort to reduce dependence on foreign oil. It seeks to raise the average miles per gallon (MPG) of the cars on America's roads by setting minimum standards for the fuel efficiency of companies' fleets, fining companies that fall short. CAFE can boast some success: the average MPG rose from 18 to 27.5 after its implementation, and estimates suggest that Americans would consume 2.8 million more barrels of oil each day without these CAFE standards. Standards were frozen between 1985 and 2007, but President Obama increased the required MPG of new cars to 54.5 in 2012 (to be realized by 2025).

While CAFE standards encourage the development of more fuel-efficient vehicles, the scheme itself is inefficient. Setting a single value for a manufacturer's entire fleet can incentivize the over-production of less-desirable, fuel-friendly vehicles, to compensate for the popularity of gas-guzzling favorites in the company fleet calculations. It would likely be far simpler to simply rely on a carbon tax, which would align consumer and company interests in more fuel-efficient cars.

The CAFE standards may not weather the current political climate. President Trump deemed CAFE an "assault on the American auto industry" and promised to work to eliminate them. Still, thanks to global markets, strict standards in Europe and Asia (and in large US states such as California) will keep car manufacturers focused on fuel efficiency.

Second, a carbon tax would generate government revenue in a highly efficient manner. A carbon tax of $25 per metric ton is estimated by the Congressional Budget Office to generate about a trillion dollars in revenue over ten years.[12] And, unlike most sources of revenue, a carbon tax makes the economy more efficient by discouraging something that the market, left to its own devices, overproduces. In contrast, most other taxes discourage things we would rather encourage, like labor effort, savings, and entrepreneurial effort.

Third, a carbon tax is an essential part of a tax policy grand bargain, since revenue raised from the carbon tax will help pay for the needs of government without resorting to higher tax rates on individuals or businesses.[13] While individuals and businesses will, of course, pay the carbon tax implicitly in the form of higher prices on energy consumption, that tax will not be as salient as the tax that is removed from a worker's paycheck. And a carbon tax rewards virtues (conserving on carbon emissions), whereas most taxes discourage virtues, such as working or savings.

The Politics of the Grand Bargain

There are several aspects of these proposed changes in tax policy that should bring people together to make a better tax system. First, there are big carrots for both those on the left and the right of the political spectrum. Most on the left wish for a more progressive tax system and more urgent responses to environmental challenges. The increased negative tax rates for low-wage workers and the tax relief for middle-class workers help ensure that tax burdens are lower for Americans who have not benefited from changes in the economy. And the carbon tax is a highly effective response to climate change.

On the right, the inefficiency and distortions of the tax code (and the high tax rates on some types of economic activity) are constant sources of frustration. The tax changes above will require global "winners" to pay their fair share, but tax rates will be reasonable. The top corporate rate and the top personal income tax rate will be the same, and slightly lower than they were prior to the TCJA. All income will be treated similarly, so the tax code with generate less frustration and distortion. The revenue raised from the carbon tax will reduce the need for higher top marginal rates. People will pay their fair share, but the tax code will not unduly hinder entrepreneurial drive or distort investment decisions.

These tax policy changes are grounded in the art of the possible, not abstract notions of optimal tax theory. They aspire to "rough justice" and to rules of thumb that people can easily understand. A progressive tax system has widespread political support, as does the notion that the tax system should be simple and non-distortionary.

The tax system can do a better job raising the revenue needs of the country if it is relatively modest in its aims. While it is tempting to pursue all sorts of social policy goals through the tax system (providing additional tax credits for savings, health care expenses, education, and so forth), the tax system can be both fairer and more effective if these temptations are resisted. Every time we try to encourage something "good" through the tax system, we raise less revenue—putting us in a position of having to increase tax rates on other activities or cut government spending. (A third option would be for the government to issue more debt, but that simply shifts tax burdens onto

What Do Taxpayers Really Want?

Polling data suggest that the tax code is ripe for reform, with a majority of Americans backing a total overhaul of the system. Overall, taxpayer opinions are aligned with the spirit of the reforms in this chapter.[1]

- Over 60 percent of people feel that corporations and wealthy people are not paying enough tax; just 20 percent feel that poor people don't pay their fair share.
- Fully 53 percent of Americans think they pay about the "right" amount in taxes, 4 percent too little, and 40 percent too much.
- 71 percent of Americans think it is morally problematic to underreport income to evade taxes, with 19 percent reporting that it is not a moral issue; only 6 percent deem underreporting morally acceptable.
- Nine out of 10 respondents think that income from investments should be taxed *at least* as much as wages. 57 percent of respondents think wages and investment income should be taxed the same, and 33 percent think investment income should have a higher tax rate.

.1. For polling data, see Seth Motel, "5 Facts on How Americans View Taxes," *Pew Research Center*, April 10, 2015; John S. Kiernan, "2016 WalletHub Tax Fairness Survey," *WalletHub*, September 1, 2016; Gallup, "Taxes," http://www.gallup.com/poll/1714/taxes.aspx; and Carbon Tax Center, "August 2018: Yale Maps of Public Opinion on Climate Change and Policy, https://www.carbontax.org/polls/.

- More than three-quarters of respondents find the tax code either 'complex' or 'extremely complex'; only one in twenty respondents find it either "simple" or "very simple."
- Consistently since the 1980s, a large majority of respondents call for a more even distribution of money and wealth in the country.
- People are warming to carbon taxes. The majority of Americans find climate change 'extremely' or 'very' important, and 50 percent of American's now support (strongly or somewhat) carbon taxes, a number that has been increasing steadily over the previous several years.

future generations.) A simple and fair tax code should be progressive at its root, taxing a lower percentage of the income of the poor than of the rich, but it should also tax all forms of income similarly for particular people or businesses. This principle keeps the tax code simple, efficiently raising the revenue that we need for the goals of civilized society.

The Tax Cuts and Jobs Act: A Big Step in the Wrong Direction

In late 2017, the Tax Cuts and Jobs Act (TCJA) was signed into law, after a rushed and chaotic process of tax policy-making. No hearings were held on the legislation, and revenue estimators scrambled to calculate its effects on deficits and distribution prior to hurried votes. In the end, the bill passed the House and the Senate without a single vote from the minority Democrats; it was signed into law by President Trump on December 22.

Republicans have long had a common zeal to cut taxes, and that goal was paramount in the legislation. However, while some tax cuts were permanent, others were temporary (covering the period 2018 to 2025), since budget rules meant that exceeding $1.5 trillion in new deficits would require sixty votes in the Senate, and thus the support of some Democratic senators. The main provisions of the legislation are as follows.

- Individual tax rates are cut for the period 2018 to 2025.
- On a temporary basis, the standard deduction is increased, personal exemptions are repealed, and the state and local tax deduction is limited to $10,000.
- The threshold for the estate tax is doubled, to $11 million, temporarily.
- On a temporary basis, 20 percent of pass-through business income is no longer taxable for some pass-through businesses.
- The corporate tax rate is cut permanently, from 35 to 21 percent.
- Foreign income of corporations is permanently exempt from taxation. Previously, foreign income was taxed at the domestic tax rate (35 percent) upon repatriation, with foreign tax credits for tax paid abroad.
- There is a one-time tax on prior unrepatriated foreign earnings of US corporations. These earnings

are taxed at a rate of either 8 or 15.5 percent, less foreign tax credits.

- For future foreign earnings, there is a minimum tax on foreign income earned by US multinationals of half the US tax rate. This tax is payable only on returns (relative to physical assets) that exceed 10 percent. The minimum tax is assessed on a global basis, so foreign tax credits from tax paid in higher-tax countries can offset the minimum tax due from operations in low-tax countries. This makes US income less desirable than either tax-haven income (which is taxed at half the US rate, after some threshold) or higher-tax foreign income (that helps reduce minimum tax burdens on low-tax income).

Overall, the tax law is a huge step away from the principles of tax reform suggested by this chapter. In particular, the legislation has at least four essential flaws: It increases deficits, worsening our budget pressures. It increases income inequality, widening the gulf between those who have prospered in recent decades and those who have not. It makes our tax code more complex, opening new opportunities for gimmicks and shenanigans. And it fails to tackle our large problem of international profit shifting.

First, deficits are increased by $1.5 trillion dollars.[14] These large deficits are dangerous, since they reduce our ability to respond to the next recession, and recessions always do arrive. Large deficits also reduce our ability to fund urgently needed priorities such as education, infrastructure, basic research funding, and healthcare.

Second, distributional analyses of the legislation show that the vast majority of the $1.5 trillion in tax cuts under the legislation go to those at the top of the income distribution, worsening income inequality. In 2018, the percent gain in after-tax income for those in the top five percent of the distribution (4 percent) is five times the gain of those in the bottom two quintiles (0.8 percent). In 2018, those in the bottom 80 percent of the income distribution have an average tax cut of a bit less than $800, whereas the top one percent have an average tax cut of over $50,000.[15]

By the time the law is fully phased in, the bottom 80 percent of the population will (on average) pay $15 more in tax, while the top one percent will have a tax cut of over $20,000. Individual tax cuts expire, and the inflation indexing of the tax system is also changed, resulting in stealth tax increases for individuals, since inflation pushes them into higher tax brackets.

This legislation clearly makes our tax system less progressive. It is also important to remember that deficits are not free; they translate into tax obligations for future taxpayers. Once the dust settles, it is quite likely that the legislation will make most middle-class taxpayers worse off.

Third, the legislation creates many new sources of complexity. While raising the standard deduction will reduce one source of complexity (since fewer taxpayers will itemize), the legislation adds far more complexity than it removes. New tax breaks for business income (both pass-through and corporate) will lead to large incentives for taxpayers with discretion (typically those at the top of the income distribution) to distort their compensation in favor of business or capital income. The legislation leads to a great divide between the relatively light taxation of capital income and the relatively heavy taxation of labor income.[16]

Finally, the legislation continues to tilt the playing field in favor of foreign income. The United States already has a very large profit shifting problem, and this legislation makes that problem slightly worse; all things considered, the international business provisions of the tax law lose revenue.[17] This implies that our corporate tax base erosion problem will actually be somewhat worse under the new law, a difficult feat given how large the problem was under prior law.[18]

But the most disheartening feature of the legislation is that it makes future tax reforms more difficult. By giving businesses such large permanent tax cuts, it creates less incentive for the business community to come to the table in support of true tax reform. While budget pressures will undoubtedly require future tax legislation in upcoming years, and higher tax payments from some taxpayers, the TCJA provides a more difficult starting point for the grand bargain suggested in this chapter. But we must choose to persevere.[19]

Achieving True Tax Reform

True tax reform would look very different from the TCJA, but it is needed now more than ever. That said, moving a true tax reform through the halls of Congress will be difficult. Still, there is some precedent for comprehensive tax reform in the Tax Reform Act of 1986. The passage of this reform was a feat so amazing that it was chronicled in a gripping book: *Showdown at Gucci Gulch*.[20] Within, there are lessons for today in terms of framing, agenda setting,

Gucci Gulch

The passage of the Tax Reform Act of 1986 was a golden moment in the history of American taxation. The hard-won victories of the legislation, chronicled in the *Showdown at Gucci Gulch*, were shocking, unlikely, and all-too-impermanent . . . rather like the fleeting joy of a perfectly completed return.

The Tax Reform Act of 1986 derived its battle name from the pricey ensembles sported by the crowds of lob-byists that lined the halls outside the committee hearing room. The high costs of their suits and shoes were minis-cule in comparison with the amount of money under the scope of the legislation: the Tax Reform Act cut the top individual tax rate from 50 percent to 28 percent, closed loopholes valued at $100 billion, subjected labor and cap-ital to the same tax rates, and slashed the tax burdens of the poorest Americans, all during the presidency of the famously tax-hating Ronald Reagan.

Importantly, the Tax Reform Act of 1986 was intended to be revenue-neutral (not reducing tax revenues), distributionally-neutral (not shifting tax burdens among groups in the income distribution) and non-partisan. In the end, the bill cleared the Senate Committee on Finance unanimously, and it passed the Senate 97-3! This marks a stark contrast with the TCJA legislation, which increased deficits, increased after-tax income inequality, and re-ceived strictly party-line support from both the Senate Committee on Finance and the Senate.

and the importance of persistent leadership, as discussed in the related text box.

A grand bargain on tax reform is long overdue. Reforming the tax code is an essential step in modernizing economic policy to suit our global, technologically-sophisticated economy. Tax reform can achieve three critical goals.

First, it can help lower- and middle-class workers whose economic fortunes have not kept pace with our country's economic growth, making sure that economic prosperity is more widely shared. Progressive changes in the tax system help ensure that disruptive changes, whatever their source, benefit the vast majority of society.

Second, tax reform can remove inefficiencies that generate distortions and waste. Bright young minds should spend their time developing the next great products, furthering science, and engaging in creative endeavors, not exploiting arcane tax loopholes to divert tax revenue from the Treasury. By countering loopholes, including international profit shifting, the tax system can raise more revenue without resorting to higher tax rates.

Third, adding a carbon tax to this grand bargain is a crucial step toward a healthier planet and a healthier tax system. The carbon tax provides a new source of revenue that can be used to pay for lower tax rates, while at the same time preserving the planet for ourselves and for future generations. These three pillars of tax reform will ensure a US tax system that is ready for the twenty-first century, and that is fair, efficient, and competitive.

This tax reform will create a steady, predictable environment for business activity. While some businesses will end up paying more tax, overall the tax code will be simpler and more efficient. Tax rates will be set at reasonable levels, with the expectation that all businesses pay tax on their profits at those reasonable rates. But there is more to a partnership with the business community than taxes; Chapter 11 discusses other components of a better partnership.

Eleven

A Better Partnership with the Business Community

It is tempting in today's discourse to blame villains for our economic problems. This simplifies the story while making it more dramatic, often generating the pleasing side effect of simple, clear-cut policy solutions. Some blame foreigners and immigrants for depressing American wages. Some blame government for hindering entrepreneurship with burdensome taxes and regulations. Some blame the greed and self-interest of corporations, as they send business activities offshore to cut costs and boost profits. Where there is someone to blame, there is typically a quick and easy policy fix: withdraw from trade agreements and build walls, cut taxes and regulations, or crack down on corporate greed through government intervention.

Is such blaming useful? Presumably there are elements of truth in all of these stories. There are distributional effects associated with trade and immigration, some taxes and regulations are quite distortionary, and corporations have moved profits offshore with impunity, more to the benefit of their shareholders than their communities. But in no case is blame constructive. Chapters 5 and 8 showed that reducing trade and immigration will generate more harm than help, and Chapter 7 discussed why tax and regulatory burdens are not our chief problem.

This chapter argues that we need a new partnership with the business community. Yet blaming corporations and their

Is New Zealand the Best Place to do Business?

According to the World Bank, New Zealand is the best place to start a business, and the easiest place to run one.[1] But if you are unprepared to move across the world, don't despair: the United States does well by many measures. The United States ranked sixth for ease of doing business, and the World Economic Forum determined that the United States is the world's second most competitive economy.[2] The US rank is buttressed by highly sophisticated businesses, a huge market, innovation, and strong institutions of higher education, overcoming the negative effects of relatively poor infrastructure and primary education.

---

1. The full set of rankings can be found at its website: http://www.doingbusiness.org/rankings.
2. World Economic Forum, *The Global Competitiveness Report 2017–2018*, September 26, 2017.

shareholders is as unproductive as blaming foreigners or government. Most business leaders take pride in what they do: creating jobs, making good products, generating innovation and progress. What is good for society and what is good for business often overlap. A healthy business community generates good job opportunities, a steady stream of innovation, and a dizzying array of affordable consumer options. A healthy, prosperous society helps business, providing thriving customer markets, a well-educated labor force, and the stable, inclusive institutions and policies that make for a good business climate.

To create the conditions necessary for a more equitable globalization, we need a better partnership with the business community. To create a strong, prosperous, open economy where a rising tide lifts all boats, the government and the business community need to come together in support of large, smart policy changes. Five key pillars support this partnership:

- An embrace of the global economy
- Simple, fair regulations
- A simple, fair tax code and more transparency on taxes
- More transparency on pay structure and labor inclusion
- More robust antitrust laws

Several of these agenda items will be embraced by the business community, whereas some may meet with resistance. Companies will benefit from open markets, and from simple, fair taxes and regulations. Some companies, however, will end up paying more in tax, seeing their market dominance threatened by antitrust laws, or resenting the intrusiveness of greater transparency on tax and pay structure.

Still, all of these pillars work together to form a good partnership between the business community and society at large. Keeping the world safe for capitalism and democracy requires responding to economic challenges when they arise, not ignoring them and hoping for the best. We are in a time of economic discontent. A bold, yet balanced, response is the best way forward.

The business community has its part to play in responding to these challenges. Yet the suggestions of this chapter do not

Figure 11.1: Balancing a Better Business Partnership

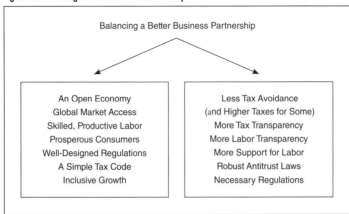

rely on the public-spiritedness of voluntary corporate actors, working like a thousand points of light to brighten a dark room. Government must work to legislate and implement responses to our economic challenges. This will require tough compromises with the business community, but it need not be an antagonistic struggle. Cooperation can be built around the notion that tough problems require everyone at the table, building a modern foundation for a more inclusive and prosperous economy.[1]

Pillar 1: An Embrace of the Global Economy

In general, the business community has much to gain from access to an open global economy. Many companies rely on global supply chains; they have production processes that are spread throughout the globe. Imported intermediate goods are an essential part of many American businesses, and the ability to sell products in foreign markets is also essential. International capital markets provide key sources of finance for American investment. Immigration is also vital to American business success. Not only are immigrants disproportionately entrepreneurial, but immigrants also provide labor skills that are in short supply, helping American firms stay competitive.

I was recently at a forum with Oregon business leaders, and all of them spoke clearly and passionately about international trade as a factor in their business success. A railcar manufacturer sells rail cars throughout the world, but they can only do so efficiently since some of the production occurs in Mexico; otherwise, they could never compete with their foreign competitors. Local winemakers note that their wine barrels, glass bottles, and yeast are all imported, and that exports provide key market opportunities for them. Columbia Sportswear and Nike are successful companies that provide large numbers of design and marketing jobs in the United States, selling their goods throughout the world, and manufacturing their clothing and footwear abroad. A knife manufacturer sources parts locally but sells throughout the world. All of these companies have a vital interest in maintaining the free flow of international commerce. (And companies grumble about the trade restrictions already in place. Both Columbia Sportswear and Nike pay large tariffs on imported goods; this raises prices for American consumers.)

American businesses often emphasize the importance of a "level" playing field, and international agreements such as those reached under the auspices of the World Trade Organization can help make sure that businesses are not disadvantaged by unfair sources of foreign competition; for example, there are many rules that are designed to restrict governments from pursuing "beggar thy neighbor" trade policies in the form of export subsidies or unfair trade barriers. Continued negotiations with trading partners in the World Trade Organization and in smaller regional forums can help governments avoid harmful policy competition while giving companies access to the global marketplace. Chapters 5 and 9 discuss how our trade agreements can be modernized, but fundamentally, the United States should stay open and engaged with the world economy.

Pillar 2: Fair Regulations

Without doubt, regulations are needed to address health and safety issues that the market would not handle well on its own. Food and drug safety, workplace safety, environmental regulations, and building regulations are all necessary for a safe and productive economy. That does not mean that regulations should not be continuously reviewed and streamlined to be as efficient as possible. We can learn from previous successes in such efforts, such as *Reinventing Government.*

When possible, reliance on price-based mechanisms should be increased in lieu of regulation. By taxing environmental harms, for example, revenue can be raised to help fund civilized society, while at the same time making the environment cleaner and safer. This provides a powerful and efficient way to address environmental costs in a non-intrusive manner that businesses can easily understand and adjust to.

Reinventing Government

In 1993, the Clinton administration launched an interagency task force to streamline the workings of the federal government. The National Partnership for Reinventing Government, or ReGo, was active during both of Clinton's terms and overseen by Vice President Al Gore. ReGo was a serious reform: it saw the shrinking of the federal workforce by 426,000 employees between 1993 and 2000, the cutting of about 640,000 pages of internal agency rules, and the elimination of 2,000 field offices and 250 programs and agencies. Legislation required agencies to articulate strategic plans, and to create new performance plans each year describing their progress. This process drew on insights from government workers; the best ideas earned "hammer awards" (so named for over-priced Pentagon hammers).

ReGo consisted of more than simple cost reduction. A focus on performance, customer satisfaction, and innovation began a process of modernization that was continued by future administrations. The Bush Administration introduced the Program Assessment Rating Tool (PART), which was used to evaluate more than a thousand programs. Agencies were compelled to conduct surveys on service quality and satisfaction. A 2011 executive order signed by President Obama called on agencies to reformulate their customer service plans, in part by incorporating technology. In the end, ReGo showed that trimming government excess can be both popular and pragmatic.

British Columbia's Carbon Tax

The success of British Columbia's carbon tax is a model of what can be achieved with price-based environmental regulations. The carbon tax, introduced to the province in 2008 by Canada's right-leaning Liberal Party, increased from C$10 to C$30 ($8 to $23 in US dollars) per metric ton from 2008 to 2012, without negative effects on the province's economy. Within five years of its introduction, British Columbia's per-capita emission rate fell by 12.9 percent, more than three times as quickly as the rest of Canada's reduction, while the province's GDP growth outpaced the growth of other provinces. Citizens are warming to the tax. Despite its increasing rate, they support the idea in higher percentages now than at the time of its adoption. Next, Canada intends to begin a national carbon tax in 2018, starting at C$10 per metric ton, and increasing to C$50 per metric ton by 2022.

Pillar 3: A Simple, Fair Tax Code and More Tax Transparency

Relative to 2017 and prior law, for some businesses, the tax policy changes suggested in Chapter 10 would raise their effective tax rates; for others, effective tax rates would go down. Still, an ideal tax reform would tax all forms of business income alike. Such a system would dramatically reduce the resources devoted to tax planning, reducing tax compliance costs and tax administration costs. In parallel, it would reduce the opportunities for tax avoidance, buttressing the tax base. Relative to prior law, such changes would allow room for revenue-neutral tax rate reductions, or some combination of increased revenues and lower rates.

Unfortunately, the tax law changes passed in late 2017 make these compromises more difficult. The Tax Cuts and Jobs Act (TCJA) cut business taxes so dramatically that the winners and losers of Chapter 10's tax reform are no longer likely to be balanced. While these recent changes in the law make tax reform more difficult, budgetary pressures will still provide a powerful impetus for future tax reform.[2]

Beyond tax law changes, I also suggest that every US resident company be required to submit to the public an annual *"sunshine tax report"* on their global operations, listing every country in which they operate, simple aggregate data on the scale of their operations (sales, employment, and physical assets), and importantly, their tax payments and income earned in each country. They should also include detailed data on US state operations and US state tax payments.

Companies will argue that such a report would give away too many of their business secrets, but such arguments are self-serving and implausible. *If* there is really something so special about a company's Irish or Cayman operations, such that revealing income booked in such jurisdictions (and the associated low tax payments!) is revealing a company secret, then perhaps that itself is a problem. In short, firms should stand by their global operations and their financial reporting. If it is embarrassing to report 90 percent of global profits in island jurisdictions, then don't.[3]

Under the tax proposals of Chapters 7 and 10, there would be far less of an incentive to move profits offshore artificially.

However, even if such reforms are desirable, they may not come to pass. In the meantime, shining sunlight on companies' global operations can provide valuable benefits through several mechanisms.

First, corporate social responsibility motives will be important. Companies care about their reputations, in part because both customers and investors care about company behavior. The sunshine tax report will incentivize companies to avoid taking particularly aggressive tax positions, better aligning their economic interests with those of the societies in which they operate.

GE, Dodgeball Champion

The closest playground equivalent to corporate taxation is dodgeball, and its savvy champion is General Electric. The industrial behemoth deftly avoided all United States income taxes between 2008 and 2015, according to the Institute on Taxation and Economic Policy, relying on tax havens to achieve an effective tax rate of negative 3.4 percent. By shifting profits to havens, US-based GE booked large foreign profits while keeping the company's multibillion dollar earnings away from the reach of the United States Treasury.

While GE might be playing by the rules, its behavior hasn't escaped the notice of the public. The Reputation Institute, a firm that studies corporations' reputations, gave GE a middling ranking of 199 on its annual RepTrak list, and the bad publicity surrounding GE's tax avoidance was a key factor in the score. Tax avoidance also factors into others' assessments of corporate responsibility. MSCI, an investment company that offers index funds of screened, responsible corporations, has indicated that a corporation's tax practices will soon affect its decisions about which companies to include.

Second, country by country reporting (see box) helps governments resolve cross-border tax disputes, avoid the pressures of harmful tax competition, and enforce the tax laws that are on the books.

Finally, more tax transparency can be useful in changing social norms regarding taxation among the corporate community. While companies have an understandable focus on the bottom line, not all cultures celebrate tax avoidance as a good thing. Taxpayer morale, and societal attitudes about tax compliance and tax avoidance, vary a great deal across countries.[4] While culture can be difficult to change, a sunshine tax report is a useful step that would encourage companies to value paying tax in their home jurisdictions.

Pillar 4: More Transparency and Support for Labor

Much like the annual "sunshine tax report," I also recommend an annual "sunshine labor report." Within the report, firms would be required to release data on a set of benchmarks on pay structure and labor inclusion. This could include data on top management salaries, data on median worker salaries, and

Show Us the Money

The OECD and G20 countries (the largest economies of the world) have been collaborating on the BEPS (Base Erosion and Profit Shifting) project. The BEPS project combats the tax-avoidance strategies of multinational corporations that artificially shift corporate profits toward tax havens. One key recommendation of the BEPS action plan is "country-by-country reporting." With country-by-country reporting, companies are required to annually disclose to national tax authorities where their income is booked, and where their taxes are paid, on a per-country basis. Absent this reporting, companies frequently obfuscate their financial arrangements in stupefying layers of complexity, often resulting in dramatically reduced tax payments.

Country-by-country reporting provides tax authorities with a complete view of the financial operations of their multinational company taxpayers, allowing for cooperation on enforcement and clarity in tax administration. Governments could also require that a simplified version of these reports be made public, providing much needed transparency to the debate over corporate tax policy. While companies would resist the scrutiny that such disclosure would generate, tax transparency is a big step toward a more honest tax culture.

some broad information on the distribution of pay throughout the company. Companies could also report indicators of worker inclusion, such as worker-shareholders, indicators of labor representation in corporate decision making, and measures of worker satisfaction.

Companies should also bear some reporting responsibility for their outsourcing decisions, both domestically and offshore. As companies have focused on their core competencies, more and more business activities have been outsourced or subcontracted to other companies: activities like janitorial services, payroll processing, accounting, and human resources services. These outsourced labor markets are typically fiercely competitive, and this "fissuring" of the workplace makes sellers of products less responsible for the workers involved in bringing goods to market. Still, companies have the ability to monitor and enforce quality standards with their subcontractors, and it is feasible for them to also monitor the labor practices of their suppliers.[5] Thus, transparency on labor practices might usefully go beyond the company's employees to consider the suppliers of business services.

The aim of these measures is to encourage companies to treat the empowerment and satisfaction of their workers as another objective of their business. This is only a reporting requirement, not a regulation that would, for example, limit CEO pay or require particular changes in labor representation. The aim is to harness a company's own profit motive to guide it toward valuable social ends. Since customers, investors, potential new hires, and the media would pay attention, these annual "sunshine" reports would create an incentive for companies to consider these factors in their management decisions.

Costco's Success and Sanity

Costco and Walmart have similar businesses, but they provide a stark contrast in modern labor practices. In 2014, the average Costco employee made $21 an hour; these wages are about 75 percent higher than typical Walmart wages ($12). Around 82 percent of Costco employees are covered by health insurance (and they pay only 8 percent of their premiums), while less than half of Walmart workers have coverage. Yet better pay and benefits haven't hindered Costco's profits: Costco's stock price has soared by 150 percent over the previous ten years, while Walmart's stock price has increased 78 percent over the same period.

How do profits stay high despite generous labor policies? An average Costco employee nets far more revenue than their Walmart counterpart, and low turnover keeps Costco's "employee churn" costs low. While part of Costco's success is likely due to other factors, its market dominance also depends on the well-paid workers that sell its bulk provisions.

These proposals are far less intrusive than regulations that would require companies to limit executive pay, or regulations that might prevent companies from laying off workers. Companies should make such decisions based on economic factors. At the same time, company labor practices should still be exposed to the sunshine of public scrutiny. Such scrutiny gives managers "cover" from shareholders when they want to raise worker wages or provide a more balanced work life for their employees. There would be a natural incentive to put a higher weight on reputational factors when making such decisions, since reputation affects consumer marketing, share prices, and employee recruitment.

While the press often provides sensational stories about particular companies, momentarily riveting the public's attention on the instances in the spotlight, these sunshine reports will provide more even, timely, and systematic information about the entire corporate community, easily available online to any interested consumer, advocate, worker, or investor.

These tax and labor sunshine reports are a market-friendly nudge toward rethinking social norms. With more information, people can use their power as citizens, consumers, employees and investors to help build a more inclusive economy, moving capital and customers toward companies that are responsible corporate citizens. Workers looking for jobs will have information at their fingertips regarding companies' labor practices and pay structure, helping inclusive companies attract talented workers. While the effectiveness of these measures should not be oversold, they are an important step toward changing social norms. And social norms help to determine labor outcomes. For example, in Germany, excellent labor market outcomes are often attributed to the fact that labor stakeholders are more involved in business decision-making.[6]

Finally, there are several useful ways to modernize labor laws for today's economy that warrant consideration. As one example, labor laws likely need updating to account for the fact that many workers work independently in the "gig economy" (for example, for online intermediaries like Lyft or Uber).[7]

Flying the Friendly Skies?

Recently, American Airlines announced a plan for pay raises for their pilots and flight attendants, in part due to competitive pressures associated with higher wages at Delta and United. In response, stock market analysts wrote disapproving commentary about how shareholders would be harmed by this undue generosity toward labor, and American Airlines' stock price fell 5 percent in one day. Other airline stocks also declined on the news, presumably due to fears of higher wages in the industry as a whole. A J.P. Morgan analyst wrote that he was "troubled by AAL's wealth transfer of nearly $1 billion to its labor groups."[1] Investors provide pressure on managers to hold down costs and raise profits, due to fears of lower stock prices. Yet arguably these pressures reduce wages and consumer spending in the economy as a whole, holding down the profits of other companies. As Chapter 2 discussed, social norms and bargaining power are important causal factors behind the declining labor share of income.

---

1. Associated Press, "American Airlines Announces Pay Raises, and Investors Balk," *Los Angeles Times*, April 27, 2017. For an incisive analysis, see Matthew Yglesias, "American Airlines Gave Its Workers a Raise. Wall Street Freaked Out," *Vox*, April 29, 2017.

Pillar 5: More Robust Antitrust Laws

As Chapter 7 demonstrates, the world's largest companies are becoming both more powerful and more profitable. Corporate profits and the capital share of income are rising, and the top 10 percent of the world's public companies earn 80 percent of the profits.[8] These large, profitable firms do amazing things. Many of us have benefitted immensely from the creativity and innovation of Apple, Google (Alphabet), Amazon, Starbucks, and other global giants.

Yet, in this increasingly concentrated global environment, it is important that modern antitrust laws are used to preserve competition. As recognized since Adam Smith, market competition is vital for ensuring that market outcomes are consistent with the public interest. When companies become too large or powerful, this can hurt both consumers and the future path of innovation.

Government regulation of monopoly power can be tricky, and there are legitimate disagreements about the threat monopolies pose to consumers. Some famous monopolies, such as AT&T, have been leaders in innovation; Bell Laboratories (the associated research company) was responsible for important innovations such as the laser and the transistor, and *eight* Nobel prizes have been awarded for work at Bell Labs. Yet too much power in the hands of too few firms can harm consumers and competition. And supersized companies exert undue influence on the political process.

Comcast and Downcast

A Google search of Comcast is testament to the immense creativity engendered by rage, an emotion stoked by Comcast's monopoly power in many markets. Comcast customers create webpages solely to rant about their disgruntlement. Comcast has consistently received lower customer satisfaction ratings than its top "competitors" (and almost all other providers) in television, internet, and telephone services. In 2007, it had the lowest customer satisfaction ratings of any US company or government agency, and in 2013, its approval rating was 28 percentage points lower than that of the Internal Revenue Service. Yet Comcast remains a top provider in the United States, with millions of customers, because it is often the only option. In France, comparable internet services (with better service) cost about a quarter of what Americans pay; in Zurich, that figure drops to a fifth, and in Seoul, a tenth.[1] Comcast may not officially be recognized as a monopoly, but it sure acts like one.

1. John Cassidy, "We Need Real Competition, Not a Cable-Internet Monopoly," *New Yorker*, February 13, 2014.

Playing Monopoly with AT&T

As it turned 140 years old in 2017, AT&T had a lot to celebrate: enormous revenues ($160 billion), a number two spot in the United States' wireless carrier market, a planned acquisition of entertainment juggernaut Time Warner, and the evasion of antitrust authorities. The United States government has closely monitored AT&T's activities almost since its founding as the Bell Telephone Company, in 1877, by Scottish inventor Alexander Graham Bell. In 1913, AT&T settled the first regulator-led antitrust suit by permitting local phone providers to make use of its extensive network. A second suit in 1949 petered out by 1956, when the company agreed to exclude the computer business from its sphere of operations. The Justice Department sued AT&T for a third time in 1974, an action that led to its fragmentation into seven regionally-focused phone companies (the "Baby Bells") in 1984. Like their human counterparts, however, the Baby Bells grew up—and they also grew together. Two (Bell Atlantic and Nynex) became Verizon, another (US West) is now CenturyLink, and the remaining four are today's AT&T Inc., after Southwestern Bell purchased its previous parent (Ma Bell), in a move that would make Zeus jealous. AT&T is currently facing off against the US Justice Department, hoping to resolve lingering legal issues surrounding its deal with Time Warner. If the firm's history is any indicator, such obstacles may ultimately prove weaker than the magnetism of monopoly power.

The Way Forward

This chapter, and the two previous chapters, propose an agenda for change. We need to respond to the challenges of global markets, and the speed of technological change, with bold and serious policies that address the downsides of the modern economy. We live at a time when astounding economic progress has been made, and where technology has transformed our lives, typically for the better. But there are also serious downsides. Foremost, the benefits of the global economy and technological change have reached too few in the United States.

Technological change and global markets do not lead to one uniform destiny; countries can respond to these challenges in a variety of ways. And, as Chapter 2 described, there is more than technology and trade at the root of our problems: market power, winner-take-all markets, tax policy, social norms, and reductions in labor bargaining power all play important roles. The suggestions of Chapters 9 to 11 respond to middle-class economic concerns in ways that go directly to the problems at hand, modernizing economic policy to make it compatible with a twenty-first century economy.

Foremost, we need to avoid damaging policies that hurt the very people we are trying to help. An agenda of trade barriers, immigration barriers, tax cuts for high-income Americans, greater insecurity in health care access, financial market deregulation, and weak anti-trust laws are the polar opposite of the best way forward. We can do better than that.

Twelve

A More Equitable Globalization

The previous three chapters have proposed bold policies to create a more equitable globalization: better policies to equip workers for the modern economy, better tax policies, and a better partnership with the business community. Yet these beneficial steps require politics, an area in which economists can be naive. In my policy recommendations, I've identified areas where agreements can be forged between reasonable people on both sides of the political spectrum, and I've focused on simple ideas that are pragmatic and easily understood. But that does not mean that these ideas are politically feasible, particularly in today's polarized political climate.

Alas, I do not have a magic solution to the problem of political polarization. But I do offer several principles to move the conversation forward:

- *Positivity*: It is important to offer an agenda that provides positive steps forward regarding jobs, growth, and opportunity. This agenda should be built around a common sense of purpose, without blaming villains. Demonizing others is not productive.
- *Boldness*: We live in a time of great economic challenges. These challenges require bold, smart solutions. Timid incremental reforms are not sufficient given the magnitude of the challenges.

- *Openness*: We share a common humanity on our planet. Ideal economic policies should not pit countries against each other in an imagined zero-sum battle. Instead, economic policies can promote common interests. An open world economy is the best path forward for humanity, both at home and abroad.
- *Pragmatism*: Policies need to be efficient, easily understood, easy to administer, and simple.

Countering polarization is no simple task, and it is beyond the scope of this book to suggest precisely how to do that. But a few preliminary steps would be helpful. First, reform of Congressional districts is long overdue. Congressional districts should be drawn by a computer algorithm, not by statehouses with an interest in gerrymandering districts to their electoral advantage. Gerrymandered districts have less competitive elections, leading to more polarized members of congress, less voter engagement, and a less functional democracy.

Second, we need to take every step possible to engage the public with the policy-making process. This includes efforts to encourage voter participation as well as public debate. While voter fraud should always be guarded against, there is absolutely no reason for people to have to wait in long lines on a workday to participate in democracy. Elections should be held on weekends, and mail-in ballots and automatic voter registration would both be promising steps forward.

Third, we need to create a common foundation of facts on which to build a lively public debate, generating better policy decisions. Due to the Internet, our news and information systems have changed dramatically in recent years. This offers the

Protecting Democracy, One Oregonian at a Time

Oregon is at the forefront of a trend less frothy than artisanal coffee or microbrews. It was the first state in the nation to adopt a vote-by-mail system (in 1998), and the first to transition to automatic voter registration (in 2015). Washington and Colorado switched to mail-based systems in 2011 and 2014, respectively, and thirteen other states and the District of Columbia have passed automatic voter registration bills. Twenty-eight more statehouses are entertaining similar proposals this year.[1] Oregon's automatic voter registration requires eligible citizens to fill out a form to opt out of registration if they wish (rather than opt in). The change generates large administrative savings, and large increases in registered voters. In 2016, over 280,000 Oregonians were automatically registered, and voter expansion reached groups that were otherwise less likely to vote.[2] The Brennan Center for Justice estimates that a nationwide enactment of this policy would swell the country's voter rolls by fifty million.[3]

If Oregon's turnout rates are anything to go by, these changes will result in greater participation. Oregon turnout in the November 2016 general election beat the national

---

1. For data on state adaptation, see https://www.brennancenter.org/analysis/automatic-voter-registration.

2. See data from the Oregon Secretary of State's office, http://sos.oregon.gov/elections/Documents/OMV/OMV_MonthlyReport_All_December2016.pdf; and Rob Griffen, Paul Gronke, Tova Wang, and Liz Kennedy, "Who Votes with Automatic Registration?" Center for American Progress, 2017.

3. See Brennan Center for Justice, *The Case for Automatic Voter Registration*, July 2016.

average by over eight points. And there is no evidence of increased fraud. Oregon's election authorities found only two potential cases of noncitizens voting in the state's 2016 elections, a rate on par with the rest of the country. Following Oregon's lead would make our national politics more inclusive.

advantage of easier access to a wealth of information from around the globe. Yet there are also serious downsides. The personal tailoring of news information and the spread of misinformation (also known as "fake news") have caused large groups of the public to live in widely disparate realities.[1]

Back when I was a child, there were four news stations on our television (CBS, NBC, ABC, and PBS), and whichever one we turned the dial to, the same basic facts about the world spilled out. There was no way to get one's television to report only news that was left-leaning or right-leaning, and it was far more difficult for rogue actors to reach large groups of people with "fake news" aimed at manipulating public sentiment.

We need a common set of facts, even if we disagree about the proper policy response to these facts. This will require more education about how to use the Internet and greater outreach to provide the public with information about reputable sources of information that are less prone to bias (or fiction). We need more public conversations about these issues so that people can respond by considering their media choices carefully.[2]

The tech industry, a key source of these troubles, can also play a role in addressing them.[3] For example, Facebook is working to counter "fake news" through several initiatives, including efforts to expand its fact-checking program and to reduce the prominence of disputed content on newsfeeds. Wikipedia has developed Wikitribune, a service that pairs journalists with volunteers to cultivate a fact-checked, proofread, constantly updated article database. Nonprofits are also working to slow the spread of falsehoods across the Internet.

Fourth, campaign finance reform would help make our political process more responsive to people and less responsive to economic power. The populist sense that the system is rigged in favor of the interests of our richest citizens and businesses is fueled by the disproportionate political power of those at the top. Our economic policies and our social norms reflect this disproportionate political power. While campaign finance is one of the most difficult areas to reform, it is also one of the most important.

Finally, just as negative economic outcomes create polarizing political movements, economic successes can generate a virtuous circle. When jobs and opportunities are plentiful, there is a greater sense of common public interest. Moderate, incremental policies are then more attractive to move society forward. Good economic policies pay political dividends.

There are reasons for optimism about the American people. While polling data show that pockets of Americans have fearful attitudes toward foreigners and immigrants, most Americans support an open attitude toward international trade and believe that immigrants strengthen our economy. Most Americans also support the types of policy ideas that are in this book, agreeing that we should have a progressive tax system, that we should invest in education and infrastructure, and that we should expect businesses to do their fair share.

We need leaders that can appeal to the best instincts of Americans, showing a way forward that is positive, bold, open, and pragmatic.

More Equitable Globalization

This book has argued that global markets generate far more good than harm. Global trade makes countries richer, raises living standards, benefits consumers, and brings nations together. When countries borrow or lend, international capital markets can make them better off, and trade deficits are not a pressing problem for the United States. International business fosters efficiency and innovation. Immigration has been an enormous blessing for the United States historically, and immigrants bring essential benefits today. Immigrants boost economic growth, innovation, and entrepreneurship, and they help relieve the demographic pressures of an aging population.

American workers have large and important worries. After several decades of middle-class wage stagnation, economic insecurity is a large problem. Income inequality has divided society, and the role of labor in the economy has changed in unsettling ways. These trends have resulted in skepticism about a "rigged" system and unresponsive, ineffective politicians. Contemplating today's modern economy, people are concerned that the benefits of globalization are not worth their costs.

Foreign trade, and foreign workers, provide quick and easy targets for frustrated Americans. Yet, closing borders and erecting walls is not the right answer to these pressing societal problems. Such restrictions are more likely to harm workers than help them. Such restrictive policies come with unintended consequences, large collateral damage, and disruption.

And, importantly, such policies only respond to a small fraction of the influences that have caused labor market disruption in recent decades. For example, one important factor is technological change—particularly the rise of automation, computerization, and the Internet. These changes in our economy make it impossible to go back to the labor market of the 1960s and 1970s. And many more factors are at work in shaping labor outcomes, including evolving social norms, changes in tax policy, a larger role of companies with market power, and the role of "superstars" in winner-take-all markets.

This book puts forward a positive policy agenda for responding to the economic stagnation of the middle class and the recent dramatic increases in income inequality. These are not small problems; they require big responses. The agenda outlined in Chapters 9, 10, and 11 is not Democratic or Republican, but brings together pragmatic ideas that are pro-growth, pro-jobs, and pro–middle class. These ideas acknowledge both what works about the global economy and what doesn't.

This agenda for change is grouped into three big categories, all focused on moving toward a more equitable globalization. They can be broadly described as calling for better policies to equip workers for a modern global economy, better tax policy, and a better partnership with the business community.

Steps toward a More Equitable Globalization

Step One: Better Policies to Equip Workers for a Modern Economy

- Make better use of trade agreements to counter policy competition, keeping an open world economy
- Help workers meet the demands of the world economy through the earned income tax credit, wage insurance, free community college, and greater economic security
- Support community adjustment to trade and technology shocks
- Solidify economic fundamentals to compete in the world economy, especially education, research and development funding, and infrastructure

Step Two: Tax Policy Suited to Our Modern Global Economy

- Strengthen the earned income tax credit for lower income workers, helping those at the bottom prosper
- Retain and strengthen progressive tax system, to ensure that all benefit from the modern global economy
- Tax all types of income earned by the same person or business at the same rate, regardless of form or location; close loopholes, including international tax avoidance

- Address climate change and keep tax rates lower with a carbon tax
- Bring together stakeholders in a grand bargain to reform the tax system

Step Three: A Better Partnership with Business

- An embrace of the global economy
- Simple, fair regulations
- A simple, fair tax code; more transparency on taxes
- More transparency on pay structure and labor inclusion
- More robust antitrust laws

First, Do No Harm: Peace, Prosperity, and Openness

The above policy ideas go straight to the problems of middle-class economic stagnation and income inequality. But even if these policies prove slow to implement, a starting point is simply to do no harm. We should avoid policies that move in the opposite direction, making workers less economically secure and making the tax system less fair. This may seem obvious, but after thirty-five years in which economic growth has benefited only the top parts of the income distribution, the ideal policy response is not more tax cuts for the top parts of the income distribution. Cutting social safety nets and making health care less accessible is similarly wrongheaded and will only exacerbate the economic insecurity of the middle class.

Moreover, the substantial challenges facing workers do not require a retreat from globalization. Such a retreat would be wrongheaded, simplistic, and dangerous. Blaming foreign trade and immigrants for our economic woes risks hurting the very workers that have suffered slow economic progress in recent decades.

If the United States erects trade barriers, workers in export industries will be harmed by a less open trading system and by the retaliation of trading partners. Higher costs of imported intermediate goods will make US manufacturing less productive, lowering the market share of US firms in the world economy. Consumers will find shopping trips more expensive, and real wages will fall due to the higher costs of imported consumption (and the higher prices of domestic products that compete with imports).

If the United States reduces immigration flows, we will have fewer engineers in Silicon Valley, fewer entrepreneurs opening their first small businesses in New York City, fewer workers to pick fruit and to do eldercare, fewer inventors, and fewer Nobel Prize–winning scientists. We will also have fewer patriotic, hardworking new Americans grateful for their improved living standards. And the demographic pressures of our aging population will weigh more heavily as birthrates and population growth slow.

A retreat from globalization also risks pitting nations against each other, making it more difficult to solve the problems that face humanity, such as climate change, refugees, world poverty, and international security. After World War II, world leaders worked to learn the lessons of two world wars and the Great Depression. They fostered international institutions like the IMF, the World Bank, and an International Trade Organization to bring the world together, working toward peace and prosperity.[4] These institutions set up an international trading system, an international financial system, and an international funding source for reconstruction and development. In Europe, the European Union worked toward similar aims, encouraging peace through closer integration.[5] These institutions were largely successful in bringing nations together and fostering peace. The last seventy years in European history were the most peaceful time in recorded history, and while there are many tragic exceptions, worldwide deaths due to violent conflict have been declining steadily in recent decades.[6]

The policy threats to this era of peace and prosperity are real. In addition to the threats to global trade and migration made by the Trump Administration, many other nations are experiencing similar backlashes against globalization. Britain has recently invoked Article 50 to leave the European Union, a victory for those opposing immigration and free labor mobility in Britain and a clear turn inward. Parties on the far right and far left have been ascendant throughout Europe, leading to a hollowing out of the middle ground, and even threatening democratic institutions in countries like Poland and Hungary.

Of course, there are encouraging exceptions, such as the victory of En Marche and Emmanuel Macron in France. And there are other supporters of an open trading system. Xi Jinping has articulately defended an open trading system, and China has fostered international trade through large public investments in the One Belt, One Road initiative.[7] India, the world's largest democracy, has pursued more open economic policies in recent decades.

Still, it is deeply problematic to have the United States step back from this role. Of late, our position on the global stage has moved from leader to laughingstock and, at times, villain. The United States is now the only country not to support the Paris Agreement on Climate Change, having withdrawn its support early in the Trump administration. And when representatives from over seventy countries gathered in June 2017 to sign a convention on tax treaties that would help prevent corporate tax base erosion, the United States was also conspicuously absent. The United States is stepping back from global economic leadership.

At this important moment in our history, it is essential to make the case for globalization well, and to place this argument within a context that recognizes the very real struggles of the middle class. The strain of several decades of poor economic outcomes has frustrated voters. Political polarization is deep, as each side of the political spectrum considers the disappointing economic results to be a vindication of their particular view. Elites are reevaluating the best way to respond to the frustrations of voters. Are there quick and easy solutions that would be preferable to the slow, grinding work of building up a country's potential? Should America continue to look outward, or turn inward? How do we build economic and political institutions that are inclusive and that lead to shared prosperity?

The world has made tremendous progress since World War II. While many troubling situations exist all around us, things could be a lot worse. The world is more peaceful, and less poor, than at any time in history. Learning the lessons of the past, and of economics, will keep us from repeating the policy mistakes of the 1920s and 1930s, or turning to new variations of those old mistakes. While bad policy choices can be politically appealing, they are also destructive to prosperity and humankind. We can do better. With kind hearts and tough minds, we should move forward—toward a more equitable globalization.[8]

Notes
Acknowledgments
Index

Notes

1. Making the Global Economy Work for Everyone

1. Recent work by Raj Chetty and collaborators shows that the percentage of American children that can expect to exceed the living standards of their parents has fallen steadily in recent decades. Children born in 1940 had a greater than 90 percent chance of earning more than their parents, whereas those born in 1980 had only a 50 percent chance of earning more than their parents. See the Equality of Opportunity Project's website (http://www.equality-of-opportunity.org/) for more on this line of research.

2. Corporate profits data are from Federal Reserve Economic Data at https://research.stlouisfed.org/fred2. Data on the declining labor share are discussed in Margaret M. Jacobson and Filippo Occhino, "Labor's Declining Share of Income and Rising Inequality," Working Paper 2012-13, Economic Commentary, Federal Reserve Bank of Cleveland, 2012; ILO and OECD, "The Labour Share in G20 Economies," Report, International Labour Organization and Organisation for Economic Co-operation and Development, 2015; Loukas Karabarbounis and Brent Neiman, "The Global Decline of the Labor Share," *Quarterly Journal of Economics* 129:1 (2013), 61–103; and Loukas Karabarbounis and Brent Neiman, "Capital Depreciation and Labor Shares around the World: Measurement and Implications," Working Paper 20606, NBER Working Papers, National Bureau of Economic Research, 2014.

3. I suspect those that assume American negotiators are not acting "toughly" in our national interest know very little about US trade negotiations.

4. For more on polarization, see Marina Azzimonti, "The Political Polarization Index," Working Paper 13-41, FRB of Philadelphia Working Papers, Federal Reserve Bank of Philadelphia, 2013. For evidence linking income inequality and political polarization, see Adam Bonica, Nolan McCarty, Keith T, Poole, and Howard Rosenthal, "Why Hasn't Democracy Slowed Rising Inequality?" *Journal of Economic Perspectives* 27:3 (2013), 103–123.

5. The eight wealthiest men have $426 billion; the assets of the bottom half of the world's income distribution total $409 billion. The fact that many people in the bottom half of the wealth distribution have negative wealth,

however, may cloud such comparisons. See "Are Eight Men as Wealthy as Half the World's Population?" *Economist*, January 19, 2017; Gerry Mullany, "World's 8 Richest Have as Much Wealth as Bottom Half, Oxfam Says," *New York Times*, January 16, 2017.

2. Middle-Class Stagnation and Economic Inequality

1. See Raj Chetty, David Grusky, Maximilian Hell, Nathaniel Hendren, Robert Manduca, and Jimmy Narang, "The Fading American Dream: Trends in Absolute Income Mobility since 1940." *Science* 356:6336 (April 2017), 398–406.

2. Some of these ideas are discussed in greater detail within Kimberly Clausing, "Labor and Capital in The Global Economy," *Democracy: A Journal of Ideas*, 43:1 (2017).

3. See Loukas Karabarbounis and Brent Neiman, "The Global Decline of the Labor Share," *Quarterly Journal of Economics* 129:1 (2013), 61–103.

4. For capital income data, see https://www.irs.gov/uac/soi-tax-stats-individual-statistical-tables-by-tax-rate-and-income-percentile for all income, and http://www.taxpolicycenter.org/model-estimates/distribution-capital-gains-and-qualified-dividends/distribution-long-term-capital-2. The US Treasury also reports data on the top four hundred taxpayers. This particularly small group of taxpayers reports 1.48 percent of total income in 2012, but 0.16 percent of total wage and salary income, 8.3 percent of total dividend income, and 12.3 percent of total capital gains income. This group of taxpayers is a tiny fraction of an American population totaling about 325 million people. See https://www.irs.gov/pub/irs-soi/13intop400.pdf.

5. See ILO and OECD, "The Labour Share in G20 Economies," Report, International Labour Organization and Organisation for Economic Co-operation and Development, 2015; Margaret M. Jacobson and Filippo Occhino, "Labor's Declining Share of Income and Rising Inequality," Working Paper 2012-13, Economic Commentary, Federal Reserve Bank of Cleveland; Loukas Karabarbounis and Brent Neiman, "The Global Decline of the Labor Share," *Quarterly Journal of Economics* 129:1 (2013), 61–103; Loukas Karabarbounis and Brent Neiman, "Capital Depreciation and Labor Shares Around the World: Measurement and Implications," Working Paper 20606, NBER Working Papers, National Bureau of Economic Research, 2014; Michael W. L. Elsby, Bart Hobijn, and Ayşegül Şahin, "The Decline of the US Labor Share," *Brookings Papers on Economic Activity*, 2013, no. 2 (2013): 1-63. https://muse.jhu.edu/.

6. The graph focuses on major countries included in the Group of 20; these are the largest economies in the world.

7. Some argue that the capital share of income is also declining, and that it is the profit share (excess profits above the "normal" return to capital) that is driving down the other two shares. These trends may result from the increasing market power of large companies. See Simcha Barkai, "Declining Labor and Capital Shares," Working Paper No. 2, New Working Paper Series, University of Chicago Booth School of Business, November 2016. And see David Autor, David Dorn, Lawrence F. Katz, Christina Patterson, and John Van Reenen, "Concentrating on the Fall of the Labor Share," Working Paper 23108, NBER Working Papers, National Bureau of Economic Research, 2017.

8. A diminished labor share of income, an increased dispersion of labor incomes, and an increased dispersion of capital incomes *all* contributed to rising income inequality. Increased dispersion of capital incomes occurs when those at the top have higher returns to their investments than those at the bottom. Most data confirm that pattern.

9. These data are frequently omitted from surveys.

10. China's income share of the bottom half of the population has shrunk, and it is now similar to that in the United States. But income for US workers in the bottom half has stagnated, while income for Chinese workers in the bottom half of the population has increased fivefold over its 1978 level, See "The Great Divide of China," *Economist,* February 16, 2017.

11. For example, see Bruce Sacerdote, "Fifty Years of Growth in American Consumption, Income, and Wages," Working Paper 23292, NBER Working Papers, National Bureau of Economic Research, 2017.

12. Sarah Sattelmeyer and Sheida Elmi, "Policymakers Should Focus on Economic Security in 2017," *The PEW Charitable Trusts,* March 1, 2017.

13. For example, survey results in multiple countries show that respondents without growing income view both trade and immigration much more negatively than others. See Laura Tyson and Anu Madgavkar, "The Great Income Stagnation," *Project Syndicate,* September 7, 2016.

14. For more on polarization, see Marina Azzimonti, "The Political Polarization Index," Working Paper 13-41, FRB of Philadelphia Working Papers, Federal Reserve Bank of Philadelphia, 2013. For evidence linking income inequality and political polarization, see Adam Bonica, Nolan McCarty, Keith T. Poole, and Howard Rosenthal, "Why Hasn't Democracy Slowed Rising Inequality?" *Journal of Economic Perspectives* 27:3 (2013), 103–123.

15. See Bonica et al., "Why Hasn't Democracy," for evidence on political contributions and income concentration as well as the increasing

importance of the top 0.01 percent and large donors in driving political campaign funding.

16. See Robert J. Gordon, *The Rise and Fall of American Growth: The US Standard of Living since the Civil War* (Princeton: Princeton University Press, 2016), 624–625.

17. See Anya Kamenetz and Cory Turner, "The High School Graduation Rate Reaches a Record High—Again," *NPR Oregon Public Broadcasting*, October 17, 2016.

18. National Center for Education Statistics, "International Educational Attainment," May 2016.

19. Angel Gurría, "PISA 2015 Results in Focus," *PISA in Focus: Paris* 67 (2016), 1–14.

20. The WTO website lists the history of membership for each country. WTO, "Members and Observers," wto.org, https://www.wto.org/english /thewto_e/whatis_e/tif_e/org6_e.htm. Officially, members did not belong to the WTO until it became an organization in 1995; prior to that, members were merely "contracting parties" under the General Agreement on Tariffs and Trade (GATT).

21. Foreign countries are not typically more open to international trade in terms of their policy choices.

22. For an extensive discussion of these indicators of the importance of multinational companies, see Chapter 7.

23. For example, see World Bank Group, *Taking on Inequality*, 2016, 10–12.

24. It could also be the case that international trade raises demand for skill and capital across all countries. In poor countries, for example, jobs sewing shirts could require *more* skill than the average job, whereas that would not be the case in the United States, where sewing shirts would be a job for unskilled workers. Thus, when the United States trades software or soybeans with a poor country in exchange for shirts, that increases demand for capital (for tractors and computers) and skilled labor the United States, but it may also increase demand for capital (for sewing machines and factories) and skilled labor in poor countries. While this is not a standard result of trade theory, it is possible. Traditional Heckscher-Ohlin trade theory requires international trade to reduce income inequality in poor countries, since demand for unskilled labor must increase in the unskilled-labor-abundant country. However, other models of trade (for example, those based on the disintegration of the production process) can allow for the demand for skilled workers to increase in both rich and poor countries.

25. See Marie Connolly and Alan B. Krueger, "Rockonomics: The Economics of Popular Music," in *Handbook of the Economics of Art and Culture* 1, eds. Victor A. Ginsburgh and David Throsby (Amsterdam: Elesevier, 2006), 667–719.

26. See David Autor et al., "Concentrating"; and David Autor, David Dorn, Lawrence F. Katz, Christina Patterson, and John Van Reenen, "The Fall of the Labor Share and the Rise of Superstar Firms," Discussion Paper 1482, CEP Discussion Papers, Centre for Economic Performance, 2017.

27. In the United States, corporate profits in recent years are higher as a share of GDP than they have been at any point in the last fifty years, in both before-tax and after-tax terms, as shown by Federal Reserve data. Since 1980, after-tax corporate profits have increased several percentage points, from about 6 percent of GDP to over 9 percent. See Chapter 7 for more data on these trends.

28. See Figure 1 in Loukas Karabarbounis and Brent Neiman, "Declining Labor Shares and the Global Rise of Corporate Saving," Working Paper 18154, NBER Working Papers, National Bureau of Economic Research, 2012.

29. Interested readers are referred to Larry Summers's excellent pieces on these concerns. Lawrence H. Summers, "The Age of Secular Stagnation," *Larry Summers Blog*, February 15, 2016. And Lawrence H. Summers, "Secular Stagnation and Monetary Policy," *Federal Reserve Bank of St. Louis* 98:2 (2016), 93–110.

30. Treasury economists calculate that the fraction of the corporate tax base that consists of excess profits averaged 60 percent from 1992 to 2002, but has since increased to about 75 percent over the period 2003–2013. See Laura Power and Austin Frerick, "Have Excess Returns to Corporations Been Increasing Over Time?" *National Tax Journal* 69:4 (2016): 831–846.

31. See McKinsey Global Institute, *Playing to Win: The New Global Competition for Corporate Profits*, Report, September 2015.

32. See David Autor et al., "Concentrating," and see David Autor et al., "The Fall of the Labor Share."

33. US data are from the US Bureau of Labor Statistics. Data from other OECD countries are from https://stats.oecd.org/Index.aspx?DataSetCode =UN_DEN#. Other aspects of labor bargaining power, aside from the unionization rate, are also important. For example, while the unionization rate in Germany has fallen, observers note that labor has more power in Germany due to greater representation in corporate decision making, a greater cultural emphasis on including labor "stakeholders," a greater sense

of trust between management and workers, and a strong social commitment to providing a safety net. For a good news story on this issue, see Stephen J. Dubner, "What are the Secrets of the German Economy, and Should We Steal Them?" *Freakonomics Radio,* October 11, 2017.

34. See Brantly Callaway and William J. Collins, "Unions, Workers, and Wages at the Peak of the American Labor Movement," *Explorations in Economic History,* August 2017.

35. Right-to-work laws prevent agreements between businesses and workers that require employees to belong to a union or pay union dues.

36. This example is discussed further in Chapter 9.

37. See Lawrence Mishel and Alyssa Davis, "Top CEOs Make 300 Times More than Typical Workers," Issue Brief 399, Economic Policy Institute, June 2015. Opinions differ within the profession regarding whether high CEO pay is merely a reflection of very high productivity. For a review of studies that argue in both directions, see James Kwak, *Economism: Bad Economics and the Rise of Inequality* (New York: Pantheon Books, 2017), 80.

38. This is also true in several other countries, including Australia, Canada, and the United Kingdom. Other countries such as Japan, Germany, France, and Sweden have seen a different pattern, where the top share fell in the first half of the century, but did not rise in the second half of the century. See Facundo Alvaredo, Anthony B. Atkinson, Thomas Piketty, and Emmanuel Saez, "The Top 1 Percent in International and Historical Perspective," *Journal of Economic Perspectives* 27:3 (2013), 3–20.

39. Additional evidence on this mechanism is provided within Enrico Rubolino and Daniel Waldenström, "Tax Progressivity and Top Incomes: Evidence from Tax Reforms," IZA Discussion Paper No. 10666, IZA Institute of Labor Economics, March 2017.

40. These are long-term capital gains tax rates. Data are available at http://www.taxpolicycenter.org/statistics/historical-capital-gains-and-taxes.

41. While statutory corporate tax rates remained relatively high until 2018 (at 35 percent), the effective tax rates paid by businesses have fallen steadily in the same time period, due to tax avoidance through both international profit shifting and changes in the organizational form of business. This issue is covered more extensively in Chapter 7.

42. See Alvaredo et al. "The Top 1 Percent," and Thomas Piketty, Emmanuel Saez, and Stefanie Stantcheva, "Optimal Taxation of Top Labor Incomes: A Tale of Three Elasticities," Working Paper 17616, NBER Working Papers, National Bureau of Economic Research, 2011.

43. Poorer countries also often experience increasing inequality, but in some important cases, it occurs amidst much stronger growth. In China, economic growth has raised standards of living for even the poorest workers, even as economic inequality has increased. See "The Great Divide," *Economist*, February 16, 2017.

44. After climate change—if that is classified as an "economic" problem. Many refer to climate change as an environmental problem, though economic questions surely have an essential role to play in understanding the causes, consequences, and policy responses to climate change.

3. The Case for International Trade

1. For a discussion, see Yuval Noah Harari and Derek Perkins, *Sapiens: A Brief History of Humankind* (New York: Harper, 2015), 34–36; and "Homo Economicus?" *Economist*, April 7, 2005.

2. John Mueller and Karl Mueller, "Sanctions of Mass Destruction," *Foreign Affairs* 78:3 (May 1999), 43–53.

3. During recessions, there may be a lot of "slack" in the economy, and it will be comparatively easy to raise employment.

4. For a discussion of recent trends in labor force participation, see Stephanie Aaronson, Tomaz Cajner, Bruce Fallick, Felix Galbis-Reig, Christopher Smith, and William Wascher, "Labor Force Participation: Recent Developments and Future Prospects," *Brookings Papers on Economic Activity*, Fall 2014, 197–275.

5. For detailed data, see Council of Economic Advisers, *Economic Report of the President*, (Washington, DC: United States Government Printing Office, 2015), 291, 307. For more background, see Council of Economic Advisers, *The Economic Benefits of US Trade*, Report, May 2015.

6. This share could be as large as 40 percent. See Robert Koopman, William Powers, Zhi Wang, and Shang-Jin Wei, "Give Credit Where Credit Is Due: Tracing Value Added in Global Production Chains," Working Paper 16426, NBER Working Papers, National Bureau of Economic Research, 2010, Table A3. A more recent analysis suggests a share of 27 percent. See Alonso de Gortari, "Disentangling Global Value Chains," Harvard University Working Paper, November 26, 2017.

7. Andrew B. Bernard, J. Bradford Jensen, Stephen J. Redding, and Peter K. Schott, "Global Firms," Working Paper 22727, NBER Working Papers, National Bureau of Economic Research, 2016.

8. See Kenneth L. Kraemer, Greg Linden, and Jason Dedrick, "Capturing Value in Global Networks: Apple's iPad and iPhone," University of California,

Irvine, University of California, Berkeley, and Syracuse University Working Paper, 2011.

9. Jeffrey Hall, *Jobs Supported by State Exports, 2016*, Report, Office of Trade and Economic Analysis, International Trade Administration, December, 2017.

10. Joseph Parilla and Mark Muro, "US Metros Most Exposed to a Trump Trade Shock," Brookings Institution, January 30, 2017.

11. Examples of such factors include whether the economy is in a recession or not, the actions of the Central Bank that determine the liquidity of the economy (monetary policy), and government decisions regarding the budget balance (fiscal policy).

12. Paul Krugman, "The China Shock and the Trump Shock," Blog, *Opinion: The New York Times*, December 25, 2016. Krugman used the joke to argue that "a protectionist turn, reversing the trade growth that has already happened, would be the same kind of shock [as prior trade shocks] given where we are now."

13. See David Dollar and Aart Kraay, "Trade, Growth, and Poverty," *The Economic Journal* 114:493 (2004), F22–F49. Findings are updated here using more current World Bank data and the same methodology. "Rich countries" are OECD members (omitting Chile, Hungary, Mexico, and Poland) and Hong Kong, Singapore, Malta, Lithuania, and San Marino, while "globalizers" are the top twenty-four non-advanced economies in terms of trade-to-GDP ratio growth between 1975–1979 and 2000–2007. "Non-globalizers" are the remaining economies for which data are available. The seventy-four "non-advanced" economies were classified by comparing their trade-to-GDP ratio growth between these two periods. Dollar and Kraay applied this same method, but compared data from 1975–1979 and 1995–1997. Average GDP per capita growth and average unemployment rate were both population-weighted, using data from the final year of each period of observation.

14. One intriguing study uses geographic variation across countries to identify the exogenous effects of trade on growth, finding that trade has helpful effects on economic growth. See Jeffrey A. Frankel and David Romer, "Does Trade Cause Growth?" *The American Economic Review*, 89:3 (1999): 379–399.

15. These figures are from the World Bank's World Development Indicators database; all dollar figures are in 2011 international dollars.

16. As one example, say there are ten hours in each workday and Karen makes four units of *H* per hour of hunting and four units of *G* per hour of gathering; Peter makes one unit of *H* per hour or hunting and two units of *G* per hour of gathering. If they each spend seven hours of the day hunting and

three hours of the day gathering, they will end up with thirty-five units of H ((7 hours *4)+(7 hours *1)) and 18 units of G ((3 hours *4)+(3 hours *2)). However, if they specialize by having Karen focus solely on the hunting at which she is relatively better, and Peter on the other good, the household will make forty (10 hours *4) units of *H* and twenty (10 hours *2) units of *G*, so they can have more of both goods. More generally, we can show that production of both goods can increase if each person specializes in the good that they are *relatively* better at producing. In this case, Karen is relatively better at hunting than gathering, and Peter is relatively better at gathering, in that his relative disadvantage in this activity is lower.

17. Robert L. Heilbroner, *Teachings from the Worldly Philosophy* (New York: WW Norton, 1997), 24–28.

18. This is true in general, but when the labor share of income (GDP) falls, this need not always be the case. While countries with higher productivity reliably have higher wages, many countries have also recently experienced declining shares of labor income, as discussed in Chapter 2. This implies that capitalists are receiving disproportionate amounts of the productivity gains. However, unless the declining share of labor income is more severe for some countries than others, countries with higher productivity gains should generally experience higher wage growth.

4. Winners and Losers from International Trade

1. The US government also subsidizes many farm products, including cotton, corn, soybeans, and others. Nonetheless, even absent subsidies, the high productivity of US agriculture would likely generate substantial US exports.

2. Here I follow the professional convention of referring to less-educated workers as *less-skilled*. Of course, less-educated workers often have substantial practical skills. But since the term has been used so extensively in the economics literature, I continue to use it here.

3. For an important study that documented stylized facts on the labor market outcomes of trade-displaced workers, see Lori G. Kletzer, "Trade-related Job Loss and Wage Insurance: A Synthetic Review," *Review of International Economics* 12:5 (2004), 724–748.

4. See David Autor, David Dorn, and Gordon H. Hanson, "The China Shock: Learning from Labor-Market Adjustment to Large Changes in Trade," *Annual Review of Economics* 8:1 (2016), 205–240.

5. See Daron Acemoglu, David Autor, David Dorn, Gordon H. Hanson, and Brendan Price, 2015, "Import Competition and the Great US Employment Sag of the 2000s," *Journal of Labor Economics* 34 (S1): S141–S198.

6. See David Autor, David Dorn, Gordon Hanson, and Kaveh Majlesi, 2016, "Importing Political Polarization? The Electoral Consequences of Rising Trade Exposure," Working Paper 22637, NBER Working Papers, National Bureau of Economic Research.

7. The numbers have since rebounded somewhat, as trade has become a less noticeable issues in the early days of the Trump Presidency. In April 2017, the numbers were 52 percent good and 40 percent bad. See: http://assets .pewresearch.org/wp-content/uploads/sites/12/2017/04/24163506/Trade _agreements_topline_for_release.pdf.

8. This section's subtitle was inspired by the title of another study: Edward E. Leamer, Lawrence Mishel and T. N. Srinivasan, "Foreigners and Robots: Assistants of Some, Competitors of Others," in *Social Dimensions of US Trade Policies* Alan V. Deardorff and Robert M. Stern, eds. (Ann Arbor: University of Michigan Press, 2000), 19–52.

9. Jon Sheesley, "The 80's Supercomputer That's Sitting in Your Lap," *TechRepublic*, October 13, 2008; "A Modern Smartphone or a Vintage Supercomputer: Which Is More Powerful?" *Phone Arena*, June, 2014.

10. Michael J. Hicks and Srikant Devaraj, "The Myth and Reality of Manufacturing in America," Ball State University, Center for Business and Economic Research, 2015.

11. Brett Smith, quoted in Danielle Paquette, "The Real Reason Ford Abandoned Its Plant in Mexico Has Little to Do with Trump," Washingtonpost .com, Wonkblog, January 4, 2017.

12. Stanley Lebergott, "Labor Force and Employment, 1800-1960," in *Output, Employment, and Productivity in the United States after 1800* (New York: National Bureau of Economic Research, 1966), 117–204. Also see "Farm Demographics: US Farmers by Gender, Age, Race, Ethnicity, and More," *USDA Census of Agriculture*, May, 2014.

13. J. Bradford DeLong, "NAFTA and Other Trade Deals Have Not Gutted American Manufacturing—Period," *Vox*, January 24, 2017.

14. See, for example, Xuejun Liu, Albert Park, and Yaohui Zhao, "Explaining Rising Returns to Education in Urban China in the 1990s," IZA Discussion Paper No. 4872, IZA Institute of Labor Economics, 2010.

15. Note that while inequality is increasing in many countries throughout the world, between-country inequality is falling, as incomes are rising in poorer countries relative to incomes in richer countries, particularly when one considers the large populations in the fastest-growing poor countries.

16. Increasing company concentration is documented across all major industries. See David Autor, David Dorn, Lawrence F. Katz, Christina

Patterson, and John Van Reenen, "Concentrating on the Fall of the Labor Share," Working Paper 23108, NBER Working Papers, National Bureau of Economic Research, 2017. There is also evidence that conventional measures of market concentration may understate the problem due to common ownership patterns of large firms, as large institutional investors hold large shares of competitor companies. For a discussion of the implications of this problem, see Jose Azar, Martin C. Schmalz, and Isabel Tecu, "Anti-Competitive Effects of Common Ownership," *Journal of Finance*, 2017; Jose Azar, Sahil Raina, and Martin C, Schmalz, "Ultimate Ownership and Bank Competition," CEPR Working Paper, July, 2016.

17. For a discussion of these trends, see Jason Furman and Peter Orszag, "A Firm-Level Perspective on the Role of Rents in the Rise in Inequality," presented at the "A Just Society" Centennial Event in Honor of Joseph Stiglitz, Columbia University, October 16, 2015. More evidence is found in Erling Barth, Alex Bryson, James C. Davis, and Richard Freeman, "It's Where You Work: Increases in the Dispersion of Earnings across Establishments and Individuals in the United States," *Journal of Labor Economics* 34:S2 (2016), S67–S97; and Jae Song, David J. Price, Fatih Guvenen, Nicholas Bloom, and Till von Wachter, "Firming Up Inequality," NBER Working Paper no, 21199, National Bureau of Economic Research, 2015.

18. Over the previous thirty years, corporate savings have increased their share of total global savings by about twenty percentage points. See Chapter 2. Also see Loukas Karabarbounis and Brent Neiman, "Declining Labor Shares and the Global Rise of Corporate Saving," Working Paper 18154, NBER Working Papers, National Bureau of Economic Research, 2012.

19. In the United States, corporate profits in recent years are higher as a share of GDP than they have been at any point in the last fifty years, in either before-tax or after-tax terms. Since 1980, after-tax corporate profits have increased more than 50 percent as a share of GDP, from about 6 percent of GDP to over 9 percent of GDP.

20. Treasury economists calculate that the fraction of the corporate tax base that is excess returns averaged 60 percent from 1992 to 2002, but has since increased to about 75 percent over the period 2003–2013. See Laura Power and Austin Frerick, "Have Excess Returns to Corporations Been Increasing Over Time?" *National Tax Journal* 69:4 (2016), 831–846.

21. For a discussion of the evidence, see David Autor, David Dorn, Lawrence F. Katz, Christina Patterson, and John Van Reenen, "Concentrating on the Fall of the Labor Share," *American Economic Review: Papers & Proceedings 2017*, 107:5, 180–185.

5. Trade Politics and Trade Policy

1. See Christian Broda and David E. Weinstein, "Globalization and the Gains from Variety," *Quarterly Journal of Economics* 121:2 (2006), 541–585; Shalah M. Mostashari, "Expanding Variety of Goods Underscores Battle for Comparative Advantage," *Economic Letter, Federal Reserve Bank of Dallas,* 5:15 (2010).

2. Gary Clyde Hufbauer, Diane T. Berliner, and Kimberly Ann Elliott, *Trade Protection in the United States: 31 Case Studies*, Washington: Peterson Institute for International Economics, 1986.

3. See Gary Clyde Hufbauer and Sean Lowry, "US Tire Tariffs: Saving Few Jobs at High Cost," Policy Brief PB 12-9, Peterson Institute for International Economics, 2012.

4. See Edward Gresser, "Toughest on the Poor: America's Flawed Tariff System Comment," *Foreign Affairs* 81:6 (2002): 9–14.

5. See Pablo D. Fajgelbaum and Amit K. Khandelwal, "Measuring the Unequal Gains from Trade," *The Quarterly Journal of Economics* 131:3 (2016): 1113–1180.

6. See Jason Furman, Katheryn Russ, and Jay Shambaugh, "US Tariffs Are an Arbitrary and Regressive Tax," *VoxEU.org.* January 12, 2017.

7. See J. Bradford DeLong, "NAFTA and Other Trade Deals Have Not Gutted American Manufacturing—Period," *Vox*, January 24, 2017.

8. See M. Angeles Villarreal and Ian F. Fergusson, "The North American Free Trade Agreement (NAFTA)," R42965, Congressional Research Service, April 16, 2015; Gary Clyde Hufbauer, Cathleen Cimino, and Tyler Moran, "NAFTA at 20: Misleading Charges and Positive Achievements," PB 14-13, Peterson Institute for International Economics, 2014.

9. For one example, see Andrew K. Rose, "Do We Really Know That the WTO Increases Trade?," *The American Economic Review* 94:1 (2004): 98–114.

10. Andrew Rose, the author of the WTO study, notes that countries' desire to join the "club" may affect trade in prior years in a manner akin to how the author's child gained access to an airport lounge based on good behavior ahead of time. Once they are in, there is no longer any incentive to behave well; it is prior to joining that behavior improves.

11. The European Union is integrated in many ways that go further and deeper than a mere customs union. For instance, there are agreements establishing a single market, allowing free labor mobility, and adopting a common currency. The adoption of the Euro is considered by many economists to have been a step too far in terms of economic integration, since it is

unclear that Euro member countries were well suited to share one monetary policy. For a review of some of the related troubles, see Joseph E. Stiglitz, *The Euro: How a Common Currency Threatens the Future of Europe* (New York: W. W. Norton & Company, 2016).

12. Under a free trade agreement (FTA), members are free to determine their own trade policies on other (non-member) nations independently. This necessitates rules of origin—that is, agreed criteria to assign nationality to products, since goods are often transshipped from a country outside the FTA to a member country through another member country.

13. WTO members generally agree to treat other members as "most favored nations," so they are not allowed to single out particular members for more or less advantageous trade treatment. There are, however, various exceptions, including provisions that allow free trade agreements so long as all trade among members of such agreements is completely liberalized.

6. Who's Afraid of the Trade Deficit?

1. Figure 6.1 shows the current account balance, which is a broader measure than the simple balance of traded goods and services. It also includes investment income, which can be loosely thought of as trade in the services of financial capital, and net international transfers such as foreign aid.

2. Such tariffs sometimes result from "antidumping" disputes, for example, which accuse foreign exporters of selling goods abroad at prices lower than what their domestic customers pay. These disputes are often protectionist moves in disguise, as dumping rulings typically have little to do with whether the foreign firm engaged in predatory pricing practices. See Douglas A. Irwin, *Free Trade under Fire: Fourth Edition.* (Princeton: Princeton University Press, 2015), 164–194.

3. See, as one example, the meta-analysis by Ross Levine and David Renelt. "A Sensitivity Analysis of Cross-Country Growth Regressions," *American Economic Review* 82:4 (1992): 942–963.

4. See "China and Currency Manipulation," *Economist.* March 2, 2017; and Eduardo Porter, "Trump Isn't Wrong on China Currency Manipulation, Just Late," *New York Times*, April 11, 2017.

5. 529 plans are so called because they are authorized by Section 529 of the Internal Revenue Code; likewise, 401K plans are named for the subsection that describes them.

6. Governments, like individuals, would be wiser to finance investments with their borrowings than to spend on greater consumption. A person who takes out a student loan, for example, may spend more than he or she earns while in school, but the investment in education typically yields greater

income in the years that follow. The person who goes into debt throwing lavish parties, by contrast, does not typically benefit from financial returns later.

7. Multinational Corporations

1. Indeed, if one goes back to the East India Company (1600–1874) or the Hudson Bay Company (1670–), one finds two companies with extraordinary market power and control over international trade. In the *Inquiry into the Nature and Causes of the Wealth of Nations*, Adam Smith persistently critiques the market power of large businesses, and expresses dismay at the role of the state in sponsoring and facilitating their market power. For example, Smith argues: "To widen the market and to narrow the competition, is always the interest of the dealers . . . . The proposal of any new law or regulation of commerce which comes from this order, ought always to be listened to with great precaution, and ought never to be adopted till after having been long and carefully examined, not only with the most scrupulous, but with the most suspicious attention. It comes from an order of men, whose interest is never exactly the same with that of the public, who have generally an interest to deceive and even oppress the public, and who accordingly have, upon many occasions, both deceived and oppressed it."

2. All data on multinational operations are from the US Bureau of Economic Analysis. As in Figure 7.1, GDP numbers are provided to give an indication of scale, not to imply that sales of different parties would add up to GDP. GDP is a value-added concept, whereas sales are not.

3. While multinational companies perform the vast majority of trade by volume, about 97 percent of the companies that export are small companies with fewer than five hundred employees. However, the 3 percent of companies that export that are large are doing the vast majority of trade. For more discussion of the role of small companies in trade, see Patrick Delehanty, "Small Businesses Key Players in International Trade," Office of Advocacy Issue Brief No. 11, Small Business Administration, December 1, 2015, https://www.sba.gov/sites/default/files/advocacy/Issue-Brief-11-Small-Biz-Key-Players-International-Trade.pdf

4. See studies and data cited within Andrew B. Bernard, J. Bradford Jensen, Stephen J. Redding, and Peter K. Schott, "Global Firms," Working Paper 22727, NBER Working Papers, National Bureau of Economic Research, 2016.

5. Mihir A. Desai, "The Decentering of the Global Firm," *World Economy* 32:9 (2009): 1271–1290.

6. "How Much of Your Car Is Made in America," *Consumer Reports News*, June 15, 2011, https://www.consumerreports.org/cro/news/2011/06/how-much-of-your-car-is-made-in-america/index.htm.

7. "Trade in Value Added," TiVA Indicators database, Organisation for Economic Co-operation and Development (OECD), http://www.oecd.org/industry/ind/measuringtradeinvalue-addedanoecd-wtojointinitiative.htm.

8. Richard Dobbs, Tim Koller, Sree Ramaswamy, Jonathan Woetzel, James Manyika, Rohit Krishnan, and Andreula Nicolo, "The New Global Competition for Corporate Profits," *McKinsey Global Institute*, September 2015. Beyond these measures, the problem may be even larger due to the common ownership patterns of large firms. For discussions of the implications of common ownership, see Jose Azar, Martin C. Schmalz, and Isabel Tecu, "Anticompetitive Effects of Common Ownership," *Journal of Finance*, 73:4 (2018); Jose Azar, Sahil Raina, and Martin C. Schmalz, "Ultimate Ownership and Bank Competition," CEPR Working Paper, July 2016.

9. For an overview of the data describing these trends and a discussion of their implications, see Jason Furman and Peter Orszag, "A Firm-Level Perspective on the Role of Rents in the Rise in Inequality," presented at "A Just Society" Centennial Event in Honor of Joseph Stiglitz, Columbia University, October 16, 2015.

10. US Treasury Department economists calculate that the fraction of the corporate tax base that is excess returns averaged 60 percent from 1992 to 2002, but has since increased to about 75 percent over the period 2003–2013. Laura Power and Austin Frerick, "Have Excess Returns to Corporations Been Increasing Over Time?" *National Tax Journal* 69:4 (2016): 831–846.

11. David Autor, David Dorn, Lawrence F, Katz, Christina Patterson, and John Van Reenen, "Concentrating on the Fall of the Labor Share," Working Paper 23108, NBER Working Papers, National Bureau of Economic Research, 2017; David Autor, David Dorn, Lawrence F. Katz, Christina Patterson, and John Van Reenen, "The Fall of the Labor Share and the Rise of Superstar Firms," Discussion Paper 1482, CEP Discussion Papers, Centre for Economic Performance, 2017.

12. Over the previous thirty years, corporate savings have increased their share of total global savings by about twenty percentage points. See Loukas Karabarbounis and Brent Neiman, "Declining Labor Shares and the Global Rise of Corporate Saving," Working Paper 18154, NBER Working Papers, National Bureau of Economic Research, 2012.

13. Yet, the typical firm is not more profitable; the highly successful companies at the top of the distribution drive these trends.

14. See Germán Gutiérrez and Thomas Philippon, "Investment-Less Growth: An Empirical Investigation," Working Paper 22897, NBER Working Papers, National Bureau of Economic Research, 2016.

15. On the savings glut, see: Ben S. Bernanke, "Why Are Interest Rates so Low, Part 3: The Global Savings Glut," *Brookings*, April 1, 2015, https://www.brookings.edu/blog/ben-bernanke/2015/04/01/why-are-interest-rates-so-low-part-3-the-global-savings-glut/. On secular stagnation, see Lawrence H. Summers, "Secular Stagnation and Monetary Policy," *Federal Reserve Bank of St. Louis* 98:2 (2016), 93–110.

16. See David Weil, *The Fissured Workplace: Why Work Became So Bad for So Many and What Can Be Done to Improve It* (Cambridge, MA: Harvard University Press, 2014).

17. Furman and Orszag, "A Firm-Level Perspective." Firms with market power do not generate optimal outcomes for pricing, capital allocation, or labor mobility, unlike their perfectly competitive counterparts.

18. Furman and Orszag, "A Firm-Level Perspective."

19. US Treasury data indicate that the top 5 percent of taxpayers receive 65 percent of dividends and 80 percent of long-term capital gains. See Tax Policy Center, "Distribution of Long-Term Capital Gains and Qualified Dividends by Cash Income Percentile, 2017," Tax Policy Center T17-0082, March 21, 2017.

20. Opinions differ within the profession regarding whether high CEO pay is merely a reflection of very high productivity. For a review of studies that argue in both directions, see James Kwak, *Economism: Bad Economics and the Rise of Inequality* (New York: Pantheon Books, 2017), 80.

21. Thomas Akabzaa, "African Mining Codes, a Race to the Bottom," *African Agenda* 7:3 (2004): 62–63; Enrico Carisch, "Conflict Gold to Criminal Gold," Open Society Initiative of Southern Africa (OSISA), November 13, 2012; Mark Olalde, "The Haunting Legacy of South Africa's Gold Mines," *Yale Environment 360*, November 12, 2015.

22. For a thorough discussion of this example, see Elizabeth R. DeSombre, *Flagging Standards* (Cambridge, MA: MIT Press, 2006).

23. A rigorous empirical investigation confirms that employment and other real measures of multinational activity are less negatively correlated with tax rates across countries, when controlling for other variables, than are profits or financial measures. See Kimberly Clausing, "The Nature and Practice of Capital Tax Competition" *Global Tax Governance* (Colchester, UK: ECPR Press, 2016), 27–54.

24. This is the share of total net income earned by foreign US multinational firm affiliates that was booked in Bermuda. Data are from the US Bureau of Economic Analysis surveys of US multinational companies. For data on the

Ohio State study body, see "Ohio State University Statistical Summary," https://www.osu.edu/osutoday/stuinfo.php.

25. Indeed, this comparison understates the likely magnitude of the problem, since the measurement of GDP in Bermuda is likely distorted by tax avoidance and the huge amounts of "paper profits" that are booked in Bermuda. In 2014, Bermudan GDP was $5.9 billion, implying an implausibly high GDP per capita of about $91,500.

26. While law requires companies to price such transactions as if they were occurring at "arm's length" with unrelated entities, in practice these laws are difficult to enforce, as there is often substantial ambiguity regarding the true arm's-length price. Evidence of tax-motivated transfer pricing is substantial; see Kimberly Clausing, "Tax-Motivated Transfer Pricing and US Intrafirm Trade Prices," *Journal of Public Economics* 87:9 (2003), 2207–2223; Kimberly Clausing, "International Tax Avoidance US International Trade," *National Tax Journal* 59:2 (2006), 269–287.

27. For examples of press coverage, see articles on tax avoidance by Jesse Drucker, including "Google 2.4% Rate Shows How $60 Billion Is Lost to Tax Loopholes," Bloomberg, October 21, 2010, https://www.bloomberg.com /news/articles/2010-10-21/google-2-4-rate-shows-how-60-billion-u-s -revenue-lost-to-tax-loopholes. For a seminal treatment of the larger problem, see Edward D. Kleinbard, "The Lessons of Stateless Income," *Tax Law Review* 65:1 (2011), 99–171.

28. See Kimberly Clausing, "The Effect of Profit Shifting on the Corporate Tax Base in the United States and Beyond," *National Tax Journal* 69:4 (2016): 905–934. The numbers in the text reflect some extrapolation to the present year from estimates for 2012, which were $77 to $111 billion in revenue loss for the United States, and about $280 billion in revenue loss for non-haven countries, including the United States.

29. Related issues will be discussed in greater detail in Chapter 9.

30. Office of the US Trade Representative, "Transatlantic Trade and Investment Partnership (T-TIP)," September 28, 2017.

31. The agreement was reached in October 2016; it must still be approved by parliaments before implementation. For details regarding the agreement, see "CETA Chapter by Chapter," *Trade—European Commission*, September 28, 2017, http://ec.europa.eu/trade/policy/in-focus/ceta/ceta-chapter -by-chapter/.

32. Environmental issues present a classic example of market failure. Without government intervention, the market will produce too much of goods that cause environmental harms, since neither the producer nor consumer of

harmful products bear the full social cost of their production. This means governments must intervene to discourage the production of goods that generate environmental harms, either by taxing the harm directly (for example, a tax on pollutant emissions) or by implementing regulatory policies that seek the same aim.

33. See Eric V. Edmonds and Nina Pavcnik, "International Trade and Child Labor: Cross-Country Evidence," *Journal of International Economics* 68:1 (2006), 115–140; ILO, "The End of Child Labour: Within Reach," Report, International Labour Organization, 2006.

34. PPP numbers adjust for price differences across countries. Such data make the United States a smaller share of the world economy since price levels are lower in most developing countries. For example, India's economy is much larger in terms of PPP than in terms of USD, since a dollar of income can buy more goods and services in India than in the United States.

35. For example, the Pfizer-Allergan inversion deal was scuttled due to the Treasury inversion regulations, although there is talk of possible revival given the changing regulatory climate in the Trump Administration.

36. Kimberly Clausing, "Corporate Inversions," Tax Policy Center; Urban Institute and Brookings Institution, August 20, 2014.

37. The official title of the law is Public Law 115-97.

38. The US tax base is notoriously narrow and there is a preference in the US tax code for noncorporate business structures. There are also important distortions within the corporate tax code. For example, debt-financed investments are tax-favored relative to equity-financed investments. By providing an incentive to increase leverage, this creates financial vulnerability for the US economy. For more, see Kimberly A. Clausing, "Strengthening the Indispensable US Corporate Tax," Working Paper, Washington Center for Equitable Growth, September 12, 2016.

39. Only about 30 percent of US equity income is taxable at the individual level by the US government, in part due to tax-free treatment for most income earned in retirement accounts, pensions, college savings accounts, and non-profits. Also, the corporate tax is a "backstop" for the individual tax; without a corporate tax, the corporate form becomes a tax shelter. See Leonard E. Burman, Kimberly A. Clausing, and Lydia Austin, "Is US Corporate Income Double-Taxed?" *National Tax Journal* 70:3 (2017): 675–706.

40. For a thorough treatment of the burden of the corporate tax, see Kimberly A. Clausing, "In Search of Corporate Tax Incidence," *Tax Law Review* 65:3 (2012), 433–472.

41. Double taxation is avoided by providing foreign tax credits for taxes paid to foreign governments. Still, foreign tax credits will be very small for income earned in tax havens since so little foreign tax is paid.

42. A per-country minimum tax especially reduces the incentive to earn income in tax havens. A global minimum tax may perversely encourage foreign income in both high- and low- tax (haven) foreign countries relative to income earned in the United States, since high-tax foreign income can offset minimum tax due on haven income.

43. An astounding 82 percent of profit shifting occurs with respect to seven havens with effective tax rates lower than 5 percent. See Clausing, "The Effect of Profit Shifting."

44. Corporate inversions occur when companies are driven by tax considerations to rearrange their organizational structure to move their headquarters overseas on paper. An exit tax would require such corporations to pay their tax due before expatriating. For more on inversions, see Kimberly Clausing, "Corporate Inversions," Tax Policy Center; Urban Institute and Brookings Institution, August 20, 2014.

45. It would also necessitate rules to help establish corporate residence. The anti-inversion laws suggested in Clausing, "Corporate Inversions," would be a useful step in that direction.

46. Multinational companies exist because they earn more working together as one commonly-owned global company than they would if they were separate domestic companies operating at arms' length. Yet, where should this extra income be booked? In some respects, it has no true national source, since it is the global integration of business activity that generates the additional income.

47. A thorough discussion of such proposals is provided in Reuven S. Avi-Yonah and Kimberly A. Clausing, "Reforming Corporate Taxation in a Global Economy: A Proposal To Adopt Formulary Apportionment" in *Path to Prosperity: Hamilton Project Ideas on Income Security, Education, and Taxes* (Washington: Brookings Institution Press, 2008), 319–344; Reuven S. Avi-Yonah, Kimberly A. Clausing, and Michael C. Durst, "Allocating Business Profits for Tax Purposes: A Proposal to Adopt a Formulary Profit Split," *Florida Tax Review* 9:5 (2009), 497–553.

48. See Kimberly A. Clausing, "The US State Experience under Formulary Apportionment: Are There Lessons for International Reform?" *National Tax Journal* 69:2 (2016), 353–385. For more on implementation details, see Michael C. Durst, *A Formulary System for Dividing Income among Taxing Jurisdictions*, Bloomberg BNA Tax Management Portfolio No. 6938 (2015), https://www.bna.com/formulary-system-dividing-p73014475964/.

49. For a more detailed treatment of these issues, see Clausing, "Strengthening the Indispensable US Corporate Tax."

8. Immigrants, We Get the Job Done!

1. At a key point in the musical, as Alexander Hamilton fights the Revolutionary War alongside Marquis de Lafayette, they turn to each other and exclaim, "Immigrants, we get the job done!" This line forms the basis of an excellent song on *The Hamilton Mixtape*, an album released in December 2016 by the brilliant creator of the Hamilton musical, Lin-Manuel Miranda.

2. In recent decades, much evidence indicates that American economic mobility is no greater than that of other countries. The narrative of the American dream, however, lives on.

3. This figure includes both legal and undocumented migrants.

4. For an example from Germany, see "Startup-Kultur: Immigrants Are Bringing Entrepreneurial Flair to Germany," *Economist*, February 4, 2017.

5. The Partnership for a New American Economy and the Partnership for New York City, "Not Coming to America," May 22, 2012. Together, immigrants and their children are nearly one in four Americans. See Francine Blau and Christopher Mackie, eds. *The Economic and Fiscal Consequences of Immigration*. National Academy of Sciences, Engineering and Medicine Panel Report. September 2016.

6. Information is for the 87 U.S. startup companies valued at over $1 billion (as of January 1, 2016) that are not yet publicly traded and that are tracked by The Wall Street Journal and Dow Jones VentureSource. See Stuart Anderson "Immigrants and Billion Dollar Startups," Policy Brief, National Foundation for American Policy, 2016.

7. Stuart Anderson, *American Made 2.0: How Immigrant Entrepreneurs Continue to Contribute to the US Economy*, National Venture Capital Association, July 2013.

8. Rachel Massaro, "2016 Silicon Valley Index," Institute for Regional Studies, 2016.

9. Ethan Lewis and Giovanni Peri, "Immigration and the Economy of Cities and Regions," In *Handbook of Regional and Urban Economics Volume 5* (New York: Elsevier, 2015), 625–685.

10. For evidence on higher patent rates, see Jennifer Hunt and Marjolaine Gauthier-Loiselle, "How Much Does Immigration Boost Innovation?" *American Economic Journal: Macroeconomics*. 2:2 (2010), 31–56. For evidence on greater innovation in communities with immigrants, see William R. Kerr

and William F. Lincoln, "The Supply Side of Innovation: H-1B Visa Reforms and US Ethnic Invention," *Journal of Labor Economics* 28:3 (2010), 473–508. For resulting positive effects on native workers, see Asadul Islam, Faridul Islam, and Chau Nguyen, "Skilled Immigration, Innovation, and the Wages of Native-Born Americans," *Industrial Relations: A Journal of Economy and Society* 56:3 (2017): 459–488.

11. The number for economics is 58 percent. For data, see "Table 21: Graduate students in science, engineering, and health in all institutions, by detailed field, citizenship, ethnicity, and race: 2015," National Science Foundation. "Survey of Graduate Students and Postdoctorates in Science and Engineering, Fall 2015," https://ncsesdata.nsf.gov/datatables/gradpostdoc/2015/html/GSS2015_DST_21.html.

12. Giovanni Peri, Kevin Shih, and Chad Sparber, "STEM Workers, H-1B Visas, and Productivity in US Cities," *Journal of Labor Economics* 33:S1 (2015): S225–S255.

13. Seth Stephens-Davidowitz, *Everybody Lies: Big Data, New Data, and What the Internet Can Tell Us About Who We Really Are.* (New York: HarperCollins, 2017), 184–185.

14. Sari Pekkala Kerr, William Kerr, Çağlar Özden, and Christopher Parsons, "Global Talent Flows," *Journal of Economic Perspectives* 30:4 (2016), 83–106: 87.

15. These trends also hold for immigrants in other rich countries. See "Six Degrees and Separation: Immigrants to America Are Better Educated than Ever Before," *Economist*, June 8, 2017; and Jeanne Batalova and Michael Fix, "New Brain Gain: Rising Human Capital among Recent Immigrants to the United States," Fact Sheet. Migration Policy Institute, 2017.

16. Blau and Mackie, *The Economic and Fiscal Consequences*, 243.

17. There is substantial evidence that immigrant diversity enhances measures of economic prosperity. Alberto Alesina, Johann Harnoss, and Hillel Rapoport, "Birthplace Diversity and Economic Prosperity," *Journal of Economic Growth* 21:2 (2016): 101–138.

18. Lewis and Peri. "Immigration."

19. For a review of studies and evidence on these points, see Blau and Mackie, *The Economic and Fiscal Consequences*, chapter 6.

20. Gustavo López and Kristen Bialik, "Key Findings about US Immigrants," *Pew Research Center*, May 3, 2017.

21. In 2015, this excluded natives of the following countries: Bangladesh, Brazil, Canada, China (mainland-born, excluding Hong Kong SAR and Taiwan), Columbia, Dominican Republic, Ecuador, El Salvador, Haiti,

India, Jamaica, Mexico, Nigeria, Pakistan, Peru, The Philippines, South Korea, United Kingdom (except Northern Ireland) and its dependent territories, and Vietnam. See "Diversity Visa Lottery Results," USA Diversity Lottery, http://www.usadiversitylottery.com/diversity-visa-lottery-results/dv2015-result.php.

22. Michael A. Clemens, Claudio E. Montenegro, and Lant Pritchett, "The Place Premium: Wage Differences for Identical Workers Across the US Border," SDT Working Paper Series 321, Universidad de Chile, 2010.

23. Dani Rodrik, "Is Global Equality the Enemy of National Equality?" SSRN Scholarly Paper, Social Science Research Network, 2017, 7.

24. Michael A. Clemens, "Economics and Emigration: Trillion-Dollar Bills on the Sidewalk?" *Journal of Economic Perspectives* 25:3 (2011), 83–106. See also John Kennan, "Open Borders," *Review of Economic Dynamics* 16:2 (2013), L1–L13.

25. Peri, "Immigrants, Productivity"; Blau and Mackie, *The Economic and Fiscal Consequences.*

26. For examples of studies with this conclusion, see George J. Borjas, Jeffrey Grogger, and Gordon H. Hanson, "Immigration and the Economic Status of African-American Men," *Economica* 77:306 (2010), 255–282; and George J. Borjas, Jeffrey Grogger, and Gordon H. Hanson, "Substitution Between Immigrants, Natives, and Skill Groups," Working Paper 17461. NBER Working Papers. National Bureau of Economic Research, 2011.

27. See Giovanni Peri, "Immigrants, Productivity, and Labor Markets," *Journal of Economic Perspectives* 30:4 (2016), 3–30; and Blau and Mackie, *The Economic and Fiscal Consequences*, for overviews of studies that consider the labor market effects of immigrants on wages and employment. Employment effects are generally small, and where they are negative, the adverse consequences are confined to hours worked (rather than employment rates) of native teens and employment of prior immigrants.

28. As one example, see Islam, Islam, and Nguyen, "Skilled Immigration."

29. Immigrants were even more concentrated in the top five cities in 1990–2000, with about half of all migrants in New York, Miami, Los Angeles, Chicago, and San Francisco. See William H. Frey, "Where Immigrant Growth Matters Most," *Brookings*, May, 2017.

30. Lisa Christensen Gee, Matthew Gardner, and Meg Wiehe, "Undocumented Immigrants' State & Local Tax Contributions," The Institute on Taxation & Economic Policy, 2016.

31. For an overview of the evidence on this question, see Blau and Mackie, *The Economic and Fiscal Consequences.*

32. Data are from the US Census.

33. Data are from the US Census.

34. Yet fears of terrorism by refugee immigrants border on the absurd; over the period 1975 to 2015, "the annual chance of an American being killed in a terrorist attack committed on U.S. soil by a refugee was one in 3.6 billion." See Nowrasteh, Alex. 2017. "Syrian Refugees and the Precautionary Principle." *Cato Institute.* January 28.

35. J. R. Clark, Robert Lawson, Alex Nowrasteh, Benjamin Powell, and Ryan Murphy, "Does Immigration Impact Institutions?" *Public Choice* 163:3-4 (2015): 321–335.

36. Muzaffar Chrishti and Michelle Mittelstadt, "Unauthorized Immigrants with Criminal Convictions: Who Might Be a Priority for Removal?" *Migrationpolicy.org.* November 2016; Vivian Yee, "Here's the Reality about Illegal Immigrants in the United States," *New York Times*, March 6, 2017.

37. National Academies of Sciences, Engineering, and Medicine, Division of Behavioral and Social Sciences and Education, Committee on Population, *The Integration of Immigrants into American Society.* National Academies Press, 2016.

38. Keith Head and John Ries, "Immigration and Trade Creation: Econometric Evidence from Canada," *The Canadian Journal of Economics / Revue Canadienne d'Economique* 31:1 (1998), 47–62; Sourafel Girma and Zhihao Yu, "The Link between Immigration and Trade: Evidence from the United Kingdom," *Weltwirtschaftliches Archiv* 138:1 (2002): 115–130.

39. Kerr et al., "Global Talent Flows," 95.

40. Facts for India are from the US Census and the World Bank. Facts for Mexico are from The Pew Research Center, Global Attitudes and Trends, and the World Bank.

41. Michael A. Clemens, "Do Visas Kill? Health Effects of African Health Professional Emigration," Working Paper 114, Center for Global Development, 2007.

42. John Gibson and David McKenzie, "Eight Questions about Brain Drain," *Journal of Economic Perspectives* 25:3 (2011), 107–128: 135.

43. There is a possible two-year extension for STEM (science, technology, engineering, and mathematics) students.

44. A 2015 survey found that 48 percent of international doctoral STEM (science, technology, engineering, and mathematics) students want to stay in the United States after graduation, with 40.5 percent undecided and 12 percent wanting to leave. Those who planned to return home cited family

as an important motivator. See Xueying Han and Richard P. Appelbaum, "Will They Stay or Will They Go?: International STEM Students Are Up for Grabs," Ewing Marion Kauffman Foundation, 2016.

45. For a discussion of recent aspects of this problem, see Deanne Fitzmaurice and Katie Benner, "Meet the Foreign Tech Workers Left in Limbo by Trump," *New York Times*, April 19, 2017.

46. Moni Basu, "Why the Highly Coveted Visa That Changed My Life Is Now Reviled in America," *CNN.com*. June 4, 2017.

47. William A. Kandel, "US Family-Based Immigration Policy," R43145, Congressional Research Service, February 9, 2018.

48. Presently, the largest sources of refugee migrants to the United States are the Democratic Republic of Congo, Syria, Burma, and Iraq. Gustavo Lopez and Kristin Bialik, "Key Findings about US Immigrants," Pew Research Center. May 3, 2017.

49. There is no single number that would be ideal here. Thirty percent is an increase that could be handled without creating undue stress to our infrastructure or to state and local budgets. Completely open borders are not realistic, or even desirable, but there is certainly a strong case for more immigration.

50. William N. Evans and Daniel Fitzgerald, "The Economic and Social Outcomes of Refugees in the United States: Evidence from the ACS," NBER Working Paper 23498, June 2017.

51. Lopez and Bialik, "Key Findings."

52. While tough enforcement may have contributed to these trends, the dominant reason that migrants have returned home is family reunification. Rising standards of living in Mexico may have also played a role. See Ana Gonzalez-Barrera, "More Mexicans Leaving than Coming to the US," *Pew Research Center's Hispanic Trends Project*. November 19, 2015.

53. An electronic employment verification system could be effective. For statistics on the relative size of border-control spending, see Council of Economic Advisers, *Economic Report of the President* (Washington DC: United States Government Printing Office, 2013), 152.

54. See Robert Warren and Donald Kerwin, "The 2,000 Mile Wall in Search of a Purpose: Since 2007 Visa Overstays have Outnumbered Undocumented Border Crossers by a Half Million," *Journal on Migration and Human Security* 5:1 (2017), 124-136.

55. Congressional Budget Office, *Senate Amendment 1150 to S. 1348, the Comprehensive Immigration Reform Act of 2007*, June 4, 2007.

9. Equipping Workers for a Modern Global Economy

1. Of course, countries often have different preferences about the optimal tax rate or level of regulation, and cooperation need not involve harmonization. Cooperation can, however, help countries avoid some of the harmful aspects of tax and regulatory competition.

2. Milton Friedman argued for a negative income tax similar to the Earned Income Tax Credit (EITC), and such proposals are also popular with thinkers on the left. Both House GOP Speaker Paul Ryan and President Barack Obama have supported expanding the EITC. While design issues are important, the EITC is a deservedly popular tool for fighting poverty.

3. In theory, a net positive inducement to work requires that the work-encouraging effect of the tax credit (the substitution effect) prevail over the desire to work less due to higher incomes (the income effect). For workers in this economic group, this is likely. There are also possible adverse effects due to the phase-out of the tax credit at higher incomes.

4. Trade adjustment programs include various types of assistance, including training benefits, job search allowances, relocation allowances, and health tax credits.

5. The Congressional Budget Office has estimated that the repeal of the individual mandate will mean that 13 million fewer Americans will be insured by 2027. Insurance premiums are likely to rise for others, since healthy individuals are more likely to opt out of buying insurance. The repeal was enacted as part of tax legislation, known as the Tax Cuts and Jobs Act (TCJA), to save $314 billion (over ten years) that would otherwise have gone to subsidize the premiums of people legally required by the Affordable Care Act (ACA) to have insurance but unable to afford it. This weakens the entire structure of the ACA. See Congressional Budget Office, *Repealing the Individual Health Insurance Mandate: An Updated Estimate*, November 8, 2017.

6. The 2008 financial crisis was caused in part by insufficient financial regulation, leading to hazardous lending practices and large systemic risks that endangered the economy. In response, Congress passed the Dodd-Frank Wall Street Reform and Consumer Protection Act in 2010. Among other things, this legislation established the Consumer Financial Protection Bureau (CFPB), the first financial agency specifically tasked with looking out for consumers' interests. The CFPB's straightforward mandate—to give consumers the tools they need to achieve financial success and stability—has kept its staff busy. For example, in January 2017, the CFPB found that two of the three major credit-reporting agencies, Equifax and Transunion, engaged in deceptive marketing practices, and demanded that Equifax and

Transunion pay more than $23 million to their victims. Yet the goals of the CFPB are in danger. Congress has recently revisited many key components of Dodd-Frank, including the requirement that compels retirement advisers to value their clients' interests above their own.

7. See James Feyrer and Bruce Sacerdote, "How Much Would US Style Fiscal Integration Buffer European Unemployment and Income Shocks? (A Comparative Empirical Analysis)," *The American Economic Review* 103:3 (2013), 125–28; and Xavier Sala-i-Martin and Jeffrey Sachs, "Fiscal Federalism and Optimum Currency Areas: Evidence for Europe from the United States," Working Paper 3855, NBER Working Papers, National Bureau of Economic Research, 1991.

8. About 43 percent of American children live in low-income households; providing these children with care and resources can counteract some of poverty's negative health and life outcomes. Education and adult-income outcomes are substantially better for people who were enrolled in high-quality care as children than for those who received lower-quality care or stayed at home. See https://heckmanequation.org/resource/13-roi-toolbox /for an overview of this research area. Also see Jorge Luis García, James J. Heckman, Duncan Ermini Leaf, and María José Prados, "Quantifying the Life-Cycle Benefits of a Prototypical Early Childhood Program," Working Paper 23479, NBER Working Papers, National Bureau of Economic Research, 2017.

9. In 1980, federal civilian R&D spending was about 1.2 percent of GDP. In 2015, it was only 0.8 percent of GDP. For a discussion, see Jeffrey D. Sachs, *Building the New American Economy: Smart, Fair, and Sustainable* (New York: Columbia University Press, 2017), Chapter 2.

10. M. Ishaq Nadiri and Theofanis P. Mamuneas, "The Effects of Public Infrastructure and R&D Capital on the Cost Structure and Performance of US Manufacturing Industries," *The Review of Economics and Statistics* 76:1 (1994), 22–37.

11. Chris Buckley, "China's New Bridges: Rising High, But Buried in Debt," *New York Times,* June 10, 2017.

12. Unfortunately, recent tax legislation—known the Tax Cuts and Jobs Act—violates this principle. TCJA will increase deficits by about $1.5 trillion over the coming ten-year period, at a time when the economy is already at, or perhaps beyond, full employment. As the legislation was passed in December 2017, the unemployment rate was 4.1 percent.

13. These facts are based on 2014 data from the US Bureau of Economic Analysis survey of US multinational companies and their affiliates abroad.

10. A Grand Bargain for Better Tax Policy

1. The official title of the law is Public Law 115-97.

2. Raj Chetty, David Grusky, Maximilian Hell, Nathaniel Hendren, Robert Manduca, and Jimmy Narang, "The Fading American Dream: Trends in Absolute Income Mobility since 1940," *Science* 356 (6336) (2017), 398–406.

3. Data are from 2012. Sources can be found at https://www.irs.gov/uac/soi -tax-stats-individual-statistical-tables-by-tax-rate-and-income-percentile and http://www.taxpolicycenter.org/model-estimates/distribution-capital -gains-and-qualified-dividends/distribution-long-term-capital-2.

4. See Juan Carlos Conesa, Sagiri Kitao, and Dirk Krueger, "Taxing Capital? Not a Bad Idea after All!" *American Economic Review* 99:1 (2009), 25–48; Peter Diamond and Emmanuel Saez, "The Case for a Progressive Tax: From Basic Research to Policy Recommendations," *Journal of Economic Perspectives* 25:4 (2011), 165–190; Emmanuel Farhi, Christopher Sleet, Iván Werning, and Sevin Yeltekin, "Non-Linear Capital Taxation Without Commitment," *The Review of Economic Studies* 79:4 (2012), 1469–1493; Thomas Piketty and Emmanuel Saez, "A Theory of Optimal Capital Taxation," Working Paper 17989, NBER Working Papers, National Bureau of Economic Research, 2012; Thomas Piketty and Emmanuel Saez, "A Theory of Optimal Inheritance Taxation," *Econometrica* 81:5 (2013), 1851–1886.

5. In recent years, there was a large preference for pass-through income relative to corporate income for domestic companies. A key study shows that the US government likely loses substantial revenue due to the favorable treatment of noncorporate business income, which has increased the share of business income that is more lightly taxed. If the corporate share of business income had remained constant in recent years, the US government would have over $100 billion additional revenue from the taxation of business income. See Michael Cooper, John McClelland, James Pearce, Richard Prisinzano, Joseph Sullivan, Danny Yagan, Owen Zidar, and Eric Zwick, "Business in the United States: Who Owns It, and How Much Tax Do They Pay?" *Tax Policy and the Economy,* 30:1 (2016), 91–128. The TCJA may have changed that relative preference, since the statutory corporate tax rate was cut dramatically, from 35 percent to 21 percent. However, there are also new preferences for pass-through income, as many pass-through business owners are allowed to deduct 20 percent of their qualified business income.

6. In recent years, our business tax system subsidized debt-financed investments and may have taxed equity-financed investments twice. One option for reform is to exempt the "normal" return to capital at the business

level by allowing immediate expensing of investment purchases and removing the deductibility of interest expense; this would treat different types of investment the same. Since most of the corporate tax base is "excess" returns to capital, and the normal returns to capital would still be taxed at the individual level, this favorable treatment of the normal return to capital may have a smaller impact on the tax base than one might think. US Treasury Department economists calculate that the fraction of the corporate tax base that is excess returns was about 75 percent over the period 2003–2013. See Laura Power and Austin Frerick, "Have Excess Returns to Corporations Been Increasing Over Time?" *National Tax Journal* 69:4 (2016), 831–846. However, it is important to note that the vast majority of US equity income is not taxed at the individual level by the US government. See Leonard E. Burman, Kimberly A. Clausing, and Lydia Austin, 2017, "Is US Corporate Income Double-Taxed?" *National Tax Journal* 70 (3), 675–706. Thus, some taxation of the normal return to capital at the corporate level is likely justified. Also, rethinking some of the tax preferences that shelter capital income from tax at the individual level makes good sense. Options include mark-to-market taxation for high-income individuals, limits on the size of tax-exempt retirement accounts, interest charges for deferred capital gains, and reforms to estate taxation that would eliminate the nontaxation of capital gains due to step-up in basis at death.

7. A foreign tax credit for foreign taxes paid avoids double taxation.

8. Extrapolating to the present year generates larger estimates, but for 2012 estimates, see Kimberly Clausing, "The Effect of Profit Shifting on the Corporate Tax Base in the United States and Beyond," *National Tax Journal* 69:4 (2016), 905–934. For a discussion of stateless income tax planning, see Edward D. Kleinbard, "The Lessons of Stateless Income," *Tax Law Review* 65:1 (2012), 99–171. In many respects, this problem will be worse under the TCJA. The legislation exempts foreign income from taxation, making explicit, and permanent, the tax preference for foreign income. While a minimum tax is meant to reduce profit-shifting to low-tax havens, it still incentivizes income earned abroad relative to that earned in the United States. The first ten percent of return on assets in foreign countries is tax free, and the minimum tax rate is half the US rate. Also, since income earned in high-tax countries can generate foreign tax credits that offset the minimum tax due, the new system makes the United States the least desirable place to book income: both havens and high-tax countries are tax-preferred relative to the United States.

9. Kimberly Clausing, "Corporate Inversions," Tax Policy Center; Urban Institute and Brookings Institution, August 20, 2014.

10. A particularly promising long-term reform option is formulary apportionment of corporate income. Chapter 7 discusses this option further. See also Reuven S. Avi-Yonah and Kimberly A. Clausing, "Reforming Corporate Taxation in a Global Economy: A Proposal to Adopt Formulary Apportionment," In *Path to Prosperity: Hamilton Project Ideas on Income Security, Education, and Taxes* (Washington: Brookings Institution Press, 2008), 319–344. And for details on the US state experience with formulary apportionment, see Kimberly Clausing, "The US State Experience under Formulary Apportionment: Are There Lessons for International Reform?" *National Tax Journal* 69:2 (2016), 353–385.

11. According to the OECD, the cumulative effects of climate change will reduce global annual GDP between 1.0 and 3.3 percent by 2060. Estimates vary due to the impossibility of predetermining the planet's sensitivity to changes in the atmospheric concentration of greenhouse gases. Research done by the US Environmental Protection Agency suggests that efforts to reduce the temperature rise due to climate change could save the US economy hundreds of billions of dollars due to saved lives, and the avoidance of property damage, droughts, flooding, and other costs. See US Environmental Protection Agency, OAR, "Climate Change in the United States: Benefits of Global Action," Report, *US EPA*, April, 2015.

12. This tax rate is lower than many estimates of the tax rate that would cause market participants to find the ideal level of carbon dioxide emissions, but it would be a sizable step in the right direction, and the tax rate could be increased over time. Arguably, the rate should eventually be about twice as high.

13. One option would be to simply refund the revenue from the carbon tax to the population on an equal per-person basis. Although the poor spend a higher *share* of their income on carbon-intensive products than the rich, those with higher incomes pay higher carbon taxes in absolute terms. Thus, refunding the revenue evenly would make the majority of Americans better off, with particularly large benefits for those in the lower half of the income distribution.

14. This does not include the additional costs of servicing the debt. Some "dynamic" estimates suggest the deficit cost will be lower due to higher economic growth, but still greater than $1 trillion. Other dynamic estimates suggest that the growth drag of higher deficits will offset any positive growth effects, so that the overall effect will still be about $1.5 trillion in new deficits. There are also concerns that the new loopholes provided in the legislation will raise deficits beyond these forecasts. See, for example, Reuven Avi-Yonah et al. "The Games They Will Play: An Update on the Conference

Committee Bill," Social Science Research Network Working Paper, December 28, 2017.

15. The best source for information on the effects of this legislation is the nonpartisan Tax Policy Center. They estimate the effects on both deficits and distribution. See Tax Policy Center, *Distributional Analysis of the Conference Agreement for the Tax Cuts and Jobs Act*, Report, December 18, 2017; and Benjamin R. Page, Joseph Rosenberg, James R. Nunns, Jeffrey Rohaly, and Daniel Berger, *Macroeconomic Analysis of the Tax Cuts and Jobs Act*, Report, Tax Policy Center, December 20, 2017. Also, the Joint Committee on Taxation website provides the full breakdown of the forecast revenue costs of the bill's provisions. Additional distributional estimates are available from both the Joint Committee on Taxation and the Congressional Budget Office.

16. A nice study on the additional complexity generated by the legislation is provided by thirteen expert tax lawyers: Reuven Avi-Yonah et al. "The Games They Will Play: An Update on the Conference Committee Bill," Social Science Research Network Working Paper, December 28, 2017.

17. This observation is based on JCT revenue estimates of the bill's provisions. The comparison sets aside the revenues associated with the one-time tax on prior unrepatriated earnings. While that provision raises revenue, it represents a tax cut relative to prior law.

18. The overall influence of the legislation on profit shifting is confounded by several conflicting effects. The fact that foreign income is typically exempt from US taxation, even upon repatriation, will increase incentives for profit shifting, but there are also provisions in the legislation that combat profit shifting, including the colorful acronyms GILTI and BEAT. Overall, however, the JCT revenue estimates indicate that the international provisions in the bill lose revenue over ten-years, relative to prior law. (Again, this disregards the revenues from the tax on prior repatriated earnings.)

19. As Barack Obama put it, "The real test is not whether you avoid this failure, because you won't. It's whether you let it harden or shame you into inaction, or whether you learn from it; whether you choose to persevere." Barack Obama, "Our Past, Our Future, and Vision for America," Speech to the Campus Progress Annual Conference, July 12, 2006.

20. *Showdown at Gucci Gulch* is an excellent book on the passage of the Tax Reform Act of 1986, written by two *Wall Street Journal* journalists who covered this chapter in tax history. Alan Murray and Jeffrey Birnbaum, *Showdown at Gucci Gulch: Lawmakers, Lobbyists, and the Unlikely Triumph of Tax Reform* (New York: Vintage, 1988).

11. A Better Partnership with the Business Community

1. International organizations like the International Monetary Fund and the World Bank have long promoted inclusive growth. Inclusive growth has even become a marquee goal of the World Economic Forum, an organization best known for its annual meeting hosting the global elite each winter in Davos, Switzerland. Since 2015, the World Economic Forum has compiled and published an Inclusive Development Index. Despite being one of the richest countries in the world, the United States ranks twenty-third among advanced economies in the Inclusive Development Index in 2018.

2. The Tax Cuts and Jobs Act (TCJA) cut business (corporate and pass-through) tax revenues by over $900 billion over ten years, putting to one side the temporary revenue gains from the repatriation tax break. Thus, starting from the reduced revenues scheduled for 2018 and beyond, most true tax reforms would likely increase taxes on most businesses. It is also important to keep in mind that the TCJA is likely to expand the business tax base by causing artificial shifting of labor income into capital income, since capital income is now taxed far more lightly than labor income. This will act to buttress business tax revenues even as it drains individual income tax revenues. However, this effect is not due to additional business activity; instead, it results from a tax-motivated relabeling of existing economic activities.

3. Companies may argue that such reporting is burdensome, but this, too, is a red herring. Companies already have this information at their fingertips, and providing such simple breakdowns is far less administratively burdensome than most reporting requirements.

4. See Ahmed Riahi-Belkaoui, "Relationship between Tax Compliance Internationally and Selected Determinants of Tax Morale," *Journal of International Accounting, Auditing and Taxation* 13:2 (2004), 135–143; Grant Richardson, "Determinants of Tax Evasion: A Cross-Country Investigation," *Journal of International Accounting, Auditing and Taxation* 15:2 (2006), 150–169; Grant Richardson, "The Relationship between Culture and Tax Evasion across Countries: Additional Evidence and Extensions," *Journal of International Accounting, Auditing and Taxation* 17:2 (2008), 67–78; and Jason DeBacker, Bradley T. Heim, and Anh Tran, "Importing Corruption Culture from Overseas: Evidence from Corporate Tax Evasion in the United States," *Journal of Financial Economics* 117:1 (2015), 122–138.

5. David Weil, *The Fissured Workplace: Why Work Became So Bad for So Many and What Can Be Done to Improve It* (Cambridge, MA: Harvard University Press, 2014).

6. For detailed reporting on the German case, see Steven J. Dubner, "What Are the Secrets of the German Economy, and Should We Steal Them?" *Freakonomics Radio,* October 11, 2017.

7. For one set of proposals to modernize labor laws with this in mind, see Seth D. Harris and Alan B. Krueger, "A Proposal for Modernizing Labor Laws for Twenty-First-Century Work: The 'Independent Worker,'" Discussion Paper 2015-10, The Hamilton Project, 2015.

8. Also, conventional measures of market concentration may understate the problem due to common ownership patterns of large firms. There is evidence that common ownership can worsen competitive outcomes. See José Azar, Martin C. Schmalz, and Isabel Tecu, "Anticompetitive Effects of Common Ownership," *Journal of Finance*, 73:4 (May 2018); Jose Azar, Sahil Raina, and Martin C. Schmalz, "Ultimate Ownership and Bank Competition," CEPR Working Paper, July, 2016.

12. A More Equitable Globalization

1. Although, interestingly, research suggests that people are more likely to interact with people of disparate political views on the internet than in their personal lives. See Seth Stephens-Davidowitz, *Everybody Lies: Big Data, New Data, and What the Internet Can Tell Us about Who We Really Are* (New York: HarperCollins, 2017), 144.

2. One nice, short book makes this call to action clearly and persuasively: Bruce R. Bartlett, *The Truth Matters: A Citizen's Guide to Separating Facts from Lies and Stopping Fake News in Its Tracks* (New York: Crown, 2017).

3. Some have even called for antitrust solutions to address these problems. See, for example, Luther Lowe, "It's Time to Bust the Online Trusts," *Wall Street Journal*, October 31, 2017.

4. The International Trade Organization itself never came into being. Instead, the General Agreement on Tariffs and Trade (GATT) liberalized trade, and nations worked together as contracting parties to the agreement. Eventually, the GATT evolved into the World Trade Organization in 1995, after the Uruguay Round of trade liberalization.

5. This process began with the Treaty of Rome in 1957. Originally the European Economic Community, the European Union was established in 1993.

6. See Max Roser, "War and Peace," *Our World in Data*, 2016, https://ourworldindata.org/war-and-peace/.

7. At a recent World Economic Forum in Davos, Xi Jinping said: "Pursuing protectionism is like locking oneself in a dark room. Wind and rain may be kept outside, but so are light and air."

8. The phrasing of this last line evokes a book that I found inspirational early in my college education: Alan S. Blinder, *Hard Heads, Soft Hearts: Tough-Minded Economics for a Just Society* (Reading, MA: Basic Books, 1987).

Acknowledgments

This book contributes to the battle of ideas that surrounds us, hoping to improve the world in some small way. Whether or not it succeeds in this aim, it has been an immense pleasure to bring together knowledge I've accumulated in three decades of thinking about international economics. I'm deeply grateful for this opportunity, and for the unwavering support of colleagues, friends, and family.

I first conceived of writing this book in November 2016, and I am thankful for several sources of inspiration during that bleak time. Having belatedly discovered *Hamilton* the month before, the inimitable genius of Lin-Manuel Miranda provided optimism and reinforced my sense that writing could be important. I also thank Alan Blinder for his 1987 book *Hard Heads, Soft Hearts: Tough-Minded Economics for a Just Society*. This book played an important role in my earliest thoughts about how to be a good economist. Since then, I have often reflected on what that means in a world filled with practical limitations.

Now, I will thank people I actually know. In the middle of November 2016, a phone call with the tireless and brilliant Heather Boushey was crucial in strengthening my resolve to write this book. Heather's contributions were many. She provided ideas, enthusiasm, and support for the project, and she also put me in touch with Ian Malcolm, my editor at Harvard

University Press. Ian has been a joy to work with every step of the way, and I appreciate his steadfast enthusiasm, his skill, and his discovery of the *Open* title. I'm immensely thankful to Olivia Woods at the Press for her cheerful and industrious work on the project. My production editor, Julia Kirby, provided careful edits with both skill and understanding. Jill Breitbarth did beautiful work conveying openness in her cover design. I appreciate my readers. Kadee Russ provided extensive, timely, and enthusiastic comments on the manuscript. Michael Klein provided crucial feedback at a key point in the project.

In the conceptual phase of the project, Tamara Metz put me in touch with her former editor, Tim Sullivan, who provided essential advice about how to navigate the world of publishing; David Wessel also provided excellent advice on this front. Reuven Avi-Yonah, Eric Bernstein, Walter Frick, Alice Harra, Robert Kuttner, and Thomas Piketty all provided helpful advice.

My friends and colleagues were a constant source of support throughout the project. I am thankful to Steven Arkonovich for his laudable efforts in brainstorming titles, and for his steadfast bullishness about the project. Mark Burford generously offered his invaluable perspective on early sample chapters. Paul Silverstein was an enduring and stalwart supporter. Andrew Jalil was an enthusiastic early reader; I remain grateful for his relentless optimism. Paul Buchanan and Andrew Altschul provided key votes of confidence with a reading of the draft manuscript. I also received support and encouragement from Leonard Burman, Chris Koski, Amy Koski, Edward Kleinbard, Alan Taylor, Karen Perkins, Kelly Riordan, Jill Horwitz,

Ted Parson, Peter Andreas, Penny Serrurier, James Hines, Lorraine Arvin, Myles Buchanan, Shelly Buchanan, Kevin Myers, Dawn Teele, Josh Simon, Mariela Szwarcberg Daby, Walter Englert, Morgan Luker, Dipali Mukhopadhyay, Jay Mellies, Earl Blumenauer, and Ron Wyden.

My students have been an important part of the project. My teaching provides a constant reminder of the importance of translating the economics literature for the broader public. My students have cheered on the project at every opportunity. My former thesis students (and soon to be PhDs) Michael Kincaid and Ahyan Panjwani provided useful advice and feedback. My department colleagues Denise Hare and Jon Rork generously shared insights.

I am particularly grateful to the formidable team of four research assistants who helped with the project. Uma Ilavarasan is one of the most capable individuals I have met; her willingness to lead this team substantially impacted my enthusiasm for the project. I am so thankful to all four of them: Uma, Soha Ahmed, Carolyn Cole, and Oona Palmer. They were marvelously efficient, attentive to detail, and consistently enthusiastic. I also thank Florin Feier for his work formatting references, and Gabby Blackman for her animated interest in the project.

I am deeply grateful to the Washington Center for Equitable Growth for providing grant funding for this project and enthusiastically supporting my work. Their vote of confidence was immensely valuable. I am grateful to Reed College and the economics department for their support, and for indirectly enhancing the breadth of this book. At most other institutions, my teaching duties would not have fostered such a broad synthesis of important topics in economics.

Finally, I thank my parents, Arthur and Willa Clausing, for being truly wonderful and inspirational people. I deeply appreciate their unflagging support and their thorough reading of early drafts. And I thank my children, Ursula and Holden. You are the lights of my life.

Index